VIRGINIA SETTLERS IN MISSOURI

by

A. Maxim Coppage III

and

Dorothy Ford Wulfeck

SOUTHERN HISTORICAL PRESS, INC.

Book Publishers

Please direct all correspondence and orders to:

www.southernhistoricalpress.com
or
SOUTHERN HISTORICAL PRESS, Inc.
PO BOX 1267
375 West Broad Street
Greenville, SC   29601
southernhistoricalpress@gmail.com

Originally published: Naugatuck, CT. 1960
Reprinted by:
Southern Historical Press, Inc.
Greenville, SC
ISBN #0-89308-651-7
All rights Reserved.
Printed in the United States of America

CONTENTS

FOREWORD

This book has been published as an aid to one of the most difficult problems in Genealogy: To trace the migration from the native county in Virginia to the new home in Missouri for the hundreds of settlers who went West in the early 1800's.

Three searchers have combined their efforts to give facts available to them in their special fields.

Arthur Maxim Coppage III, born 18 June, 1915, son of Arthur M. Coppage of Carroll County, Missouri, and his wife, the late Pearl G. (Stephens) Coppage, daughter of William Joseph and Lois A. (Palmer) Stephens, also of Carroll County, Missouri, is married to the former Nora O'Dell Ormsbee, daughter of George Robert Ormsbee of Rolla, Missouri. Mr. Coppage has two sons, Christopher Moore Coppage, born 4 August, 1953, and Keith Peyton Coppage, born 22 August, 1957, Antioch, California.

During World War II, Mr. Coppage served overseas in the Pacific Theater, receiving six bronze stars and a silver star, numerous campaign ribbons. He compiled a dictionary of the Trobriand dialect and kept a diary of a forty day trip on the QUEEN MARY, which is in the Missouri Historical Society, Columbia, Missouri.

Much of the research for "Virginia Settlers in Missouri" was done while he was a student at the University of Missouri, from which he graduated in 1955. Mr. Coppage was an Archivist with the National Archives in Washington, D. C. His book, "The Coppage-Coppedge Family, 1542-1955," published at Radford, Virginia, 1955, was compiled in collaboration with his cousin, Dr. John E. Manahan, who was the first President of the Coppage-Coppedge Family, Association, Inc. The second President was A. Maxim Coppage, who presided at the three-day reunion in Lexington, Kentucky, in 1949. Mr. Coppage has completed a manuscript on the Stephens Family and Stephens College of Columbia, Missouri.

Ancestors of Mr. Coppage include many well-known Virginia families: Ball and Peyton appear in both his paternal and maternal lines, and the latter includes Burton, Stepp, and Crawley.

The next book to be published by Mr. Coppage and Mrs. Wulfeck provides Court Records and Family Lineages from Stafford County, Virginia.

Mr. Coppage served on the Bishop's Committee in St. Barnabas Church, Antioch, California, and has been elected recently to a three-year term for St. David's Episcopal Church, Pittsburg, California, where he lives at 4284 Hillview Drive.

Mrs. Ilene Yarnell, a 1942 Graduate of Southwest Baptist College, Bolivar, Missouri, was a 1946 Senior at Texas College of Arts and Industries, Kingsville, Texas. She is a charter Member of the Niangua Chapter of Daughters of the American Revolution, Camdenton, Missouri. Writing, preserving and compiling family history of the local area is the hobby of Mrs. Yarnell, who lives at 509 North Tweedie Street, Versailles, Morgan County, Missouri. Many early tombstone inscriptions have been copied to preserve them for future genealogists and researchers. On her field trips she is accompanied by her future assistants, "the Yarnell children.

Mrs. Dorothy Ford Wulfeck was born in Bowling Green, Kentucky, and married Dr. Wallace Howard Wulfeck, born in Cincinnati, Ohio, son of Wallace Edward and Elizabeth (Panter) Wulfeck; divorced.

Mrs. Wulfeck received A. B. degree from Brenau College, Gainesville, Georgia; B.C.S. degree from College of Commerce, Bowling Green, Kentucky; M. A. degree in Business Administration, Vanderbilt University; M. A. degree in Education, Yale University. She taught college for ten years and was Advertising Manager of department stores in Nashville, Tennessee, and Akron, Ohio. For 16 years she was Manager of the Veterans' Service Center, Naugatuck, Connecticut. She is a member of Alpha Delta Pi Sorority, American Association of University Women, Kentucky Historical Society, Naugatuck Historical Society, Boone Family Research Association, and the Daughters of the American Revolution. She has a son, Joseph Wallace Wulfeck, who lives with his wife and three sons in Santa Monica, California.

Mrs. Wulfeck has compiled and published the following books:
WILCOXSON AND ALLIED FAMILIES. Descendants of Daniel Boone's sister, Sarah Boone, and her husband, John Willcockson, and his two brothers, George and Isaac. 530 pp.
MARRIAGES OF SOME VIRGINIA RESIDENTS, 1607-1800. Vol. I. Surnames A and B, 262 pp. Vol. II. Surnames C, D and E, 377pp. Vol. III. Surnames F, G and H, 364 pp.
CARTER OF VIRGINIA. 59pp.
HAWKINS OF VIRGINIA, NORTH CAROLINA AND KENTUCKY. 86 pp.
MOSS OF VIRGINIA. 42 pp.
THE VIRGINIA GAZETTE: GENEALOGY PAGE - 1959. 100 pp.
HARDIN AND HARDING OF VIRGINIA AND KENTUCKY. 106 pp.

PART I

SETTLERS FROM VIRGINIA TO MISSOURI
FROM PATRONS' LISTS IN MISSOURI ATLASES.

compiled by

A. Maxim Coppage III

ABELL, William S.
   settled, 1859, Daviess Co.

ABINGTON, Henry
   settled, 1830, St. Charles Co.

ADAMS, G. F.
   settled, 1835, Chariton Co.

ADAMS, J. B.
   settled, 1839, Callaway Co.

ADAMS, James D.
   settled in Pettis Co.

ADAMS, Lynchburg
   settled, 1819, Cooper Co.

ADKINS, J. K.
   settled, 1842, Boone Co.

ADKINS, John Richard
   settled, 1857, Boone Co.

AGEE, P. C.
   settled, 1839, Lewis Co.

AGNEW, Felicia
   settled, 1857, Howard Co.

ALDERSON, John
   settled, 1837, Jefferson Co.

ALEXANDER, George W.
   settled in Caldwell Co.

ALEXANDER, John
   settled in Linn Co.

ALEXANDER, Thomas
   settled in Cooper Co.

ALLEGRE, William T.
   1850 Census, Franklin Co.

ALLEN, C. E.
   settled, 1852, Chariton Co.

ALLEN, Charles B.
   settled, 1851, Chariton Co.

ALLEN, Hugh
   settled in Pike Co.

ALLEN, Capt. J. W.
   settled, 1870, Chariton Co.

ALLEN, James F.
   settled, 1852, Chariton Co.

ALLEN, James T.
   settled, 1855, Daviess Co.

ALLEN, James W.
   settled, 1853, Callaway Co.

ALLEN, John B.
   settled, 1829, St. Charles Co.

ALLEN, John M.
   settled, 1858, Audrain Co.

ALLEN, John P.
   settled, 1853, Callaway Co.

ALLEN, (family)
   settled, 1853, Pike Co.

ALSOP, (family)
   settled in Howard Co.

ALTON, D. F.
   settled, 1866, Boone Co.

ALTON, J.
    settled, 1866, Boone Co.

ALSOP, (family)
    settled in Howard Co.

AMICK, Isaac
    settled, 1837, Marion Co.

ANCELL, F. W.
    settled, 1836, Randolph Co.

ANCELL, John S.
    settled, 1836, Randolph Co.

ANDERSON, B.
    settled, in Linn Co.

ANDERSON, Caleb
    settled, 1838, Montgomery Co.

ANDERSON, Edward
    settled, 1847, Clark Co.

ANDERSON, J. W.
    settled in Callaway Co.

ANDERSON, John
    1850 Census, Franklin Co.

ANDERSON, Robert S.
    settled in Vernon Co.

ANDERSON, W. T.
    settled, 1837, Lafayette Co.

ANDERSON, William

ANDERSON, William W.
    settled, 1853, Pike Co.

ANDERSON, Willis
    settled, 1873, Johnson Co.

APPLETON, John
    settled, 1871, Pike Co.

AREY, John
    settled, 1869, Jasper Co.

ARMENTROUT, James M.
    settled, 1857, Lafayette Co.

ARMSTRONG, James
    settled, 1820, Franklin Co.

ARMSTRONG, James H.
    settled, 1871, Newton Co.

ARMSTRONG, T. J.
    settled, 1850, Monroe Co.

ARMSTRONG, ____

ARNES, Dr. W. H.
    settled, 1868, Jefferson Co.

ARNOLD, George A.
    settled, 1836, Clark Co.

ARNOLD, O. F.
    settled, 1867, Cooper Co.

ARTHUR, M. H.
    settled, 1828, Pike Co.

ASHAR, Robert
    settled, 1849, Holt Co.

ASHBIRE, J. H.
    settled, 1858, Livingston Co.

ASBURY, Ai Edgar
    settled, 1856, Lafayette Co.

ASHBY, Daniel
    settled, 1818, Chariton Co.

ASHBY ? N. W.
    settled, 1851, Knox Co.

ASHWORTH, L. R.
    settled early in Cedar Co.

ATKINS, James H.
    settled, 1869, Holt Co.

ATTERMAN, Elijah
    settled, 1854, Daviess Co.

AUSTIN, P. E.
    settled, 1842, Carroll Co.

AUSTIN, R. A.
    settled, 1836, Carroll Co.

AYRES, Ritchie
    settled in Pike Co.

B

BABBIT, James T.
    settled, 1868, Pike Co.

BAGBY, Julian
    settled, 1856, Franklin Co.

BAGBY, Richard
    settled, 1850, Franklin Co.

BAILEY, J. P.
    settled, 1858, Mercer Co.

BAILEY, J. W.
    settled, 1838, Mercer Co.

BAILEY, Richard
    settled in Lafayette Co.

BAKER, P. P.
    settled in DeKalb Co.

BAKER, S. R.
    settled, 1857, Boone Co.

BAKER, Samuel T.
    settled, 1854, Franklin Co.

BALDWIN, Thomas H.
    settled in Henry Co.

BALES, E.
    settled, 1840, Cooper Co.

BALL, B. H.
    settled, 1835, St. Charles Co.

BALL, James
    settled, 1835, St. Louis Co.

BALL, James
    settled, 1867, Newton Co.

BALL, John B.
    settled, 1834?, Morgan Co.

BALL, Sheltial (Shelton?)
    settled, 1838, St. Charles Co.

BALL, Taliaferro
    settled, 1836, Lewis Co.

BALL, Smith
    settled, 1834, St. Charles Co.

BALL, W. S.
    settled, 1836, St. Charles Co.

BALL, (family)
    settled, 1832, Pike Co.

BALTHIS, W. H.
    settled, 1854(?), Chariton Co.

BALTHROPE, G. R.
    settled in Knox Co.

BANKHEAD, Archer
    settled, 1844, Pike Co.

BARGER, William G.
    settled, 1868, Marion Co.

BARLEY, S. H.
    settled in Pike Co.

BARLOW, J.
    settled, 1869, Harrison Co.

BARNES, Charles E.
    settled, 1866, Holt Co.

BARRETT, John C.
    settled in Greene Co.

BARRETT, Robert H.
    settled in Marion Co.

BARTLETT, S. S.
    settled, 1858, Carroll Co.

BARTLEY, George G.
    settled, 1829, Callaway Co.

BASHOR, (family)
    settled, 1859, Andrew Co.

BASHORE, John
    settled, 1849, Marion Co.

BASKERVILLE, William
    settled in Bates Co.

BASKETT, J. M.
    settled, 1865, Ralls Co.

BASKETT, Robert
    settled, 1839, Howard Co.

BASKETT, W. T.
    settled in Howard Co.

BASS, Albert
    settled, 1844, Howard Co.

BASS, Dabney
    settled, 1841, St. Charles Co.

BASSETT, Samuel S.
    settled, 1836, Monroe Co.

BASYE, Henry
    settled in Howard Co.

BASYE, Michael
    settled in Howard Co.

BATES, C. F.
    settled, 1837, Ray Co.

BATES, Lemuell
    settled, 1855, Franklin Co.

BATES, W. E.
    settled, 1866, Monroe Co.

BEALE, William
    settled, 1841, Clay Co.

BEAN, William
    settled, 1870, Greene Co.

BEARD, Samuel J.
    settled, 1865, Lafayette Co.

BEASLLY, Alfred
    1850 Census, Franklin Co.

BEASLY, James
    1850 Census, Franklin Co.

BEASLY, Noah
    settled, 1857, Boone Co.

BEASLY, William
    1850 Census, Franklin Co.

BEATY, Bird (col'd.)
    settled, 1834, Cooper Co.

BECKNER, Aaron
    settled, 1864, Greene Co.

BEDWELL, E. J.
    settled, 1855, Cooper Co.

BELL, C. W.
    settled, 1843, Chariton Co.

BELL, Giles
    settled, 1838, Callaway Co.

BELL, J. P.
    settled, 1858, Callaway Co.

BELL, Jacob
    settled, 1841, Macon Co.

BELL, James
    settled in Bates Co.

BELL, John W.
    settled in Howard Co.

BELL, W. J.
    settled, 1858, Callaway Co.

BELL, Wm. T.
    settled, 1870, Pike Co.

BELT, James
    settled, 1852, Lafayette Co.

BENNETT, J. H.
    settled, 1865, Pike Co.

BERFORD, ____
    settled, 1839, Lewis Co.

BERKS, A. L. C.
    settled, 1841, Pike Co.

BERNARD, W. R.
  settled in Jasper Co.

BERTON, T. J.
  settled, 1839, Ray Co.

BERY, Wm. R. (family)
  settled in Putnam Co.

BETTS, Wm. C. (family)
  settled in Jasper Co.

BEVAN, Mrs. Mary
  settled, 1847, Holt Co.

BIGGS, George
  settled, 1866, Greene Co.

BIGGS, (family)
  settled in Greene Co.

BILLINGSLY, S. W.
  settled in Cedar Co.

BILLUPS, Anne
  1850 Census, Franklin Co.

BIRD, N. J.
  settled, 1835, Lafayette Co.

BIRSTOE, Edward
  settled in Cedar Co.

BISHOP, Wm.
  settled, 1867, Jasper Co.

BISHOP, (family)
  settled in Holt Co.

BISWELL, Joseph
  settled in Chariton-Howard Co.

BLACK, Mrs. Blanche
  settled in Buchanan Co.

BLACK, Henry
  settled, 1841, Clark Co.

BLACK, J. W.
  settled in Ray Co.

BLACK, W. E.
  settled, 1867, Callaway Co.

BLACKBURN, C. J.
  settled, 1854, Harrison Co.

BLACKBURN, E. L.
  settled, 1875, Montgomery Co.

BLACKWELL, A. C.
  settled, 1838, Carroll Co.

BLACKWELL, ____
  settled in Greene Co.

BLACKWELL, ____
  settled in Henry Co.

BLAIR, J. M.
  settled, 1853, Greene Co.

BLAIR, Wm.
  settled, 1853, Greene Co.

BLAKEMORE, George E.
  settled in Henry Co.

BLAKENBAKER, ____
  settled, 1838, Chariton-Howard Co.

BLAKLEY, F.
  settled, 1865, Chariton Co.

BLAKLEY, M. D.
  settled, 1845, Monroe Co.

BLAND, Daniel
  settled in Cedar Co.

BLANKHEAD, Archer
  settled in Pike Co.

BLANKS, Joel
  settled in Linn Co.

BLANTON, J. P.
  settled in Adair Co.

BLANTON, J. P.
  settled in Linn Co.

BLEDSOE, (family)
   settled in Jefferson Co.

BLOSSOM, Elizabeth
   settled in Barton Co.

BOARD, J. J.
   settled, 1857, Lafayette Co.

BOERING, ____
   settled in Bates Co.

BOHANAN, A.
   settled, 1864, Macon Co.

BON DURANT, ____
   settled, 1871, Warren Co.

BOOKER, E. D.
   settled in Ralls Co.

BOOKER, E. D.
   settled, 1873, Sullivan Co.

BOOKER, Wm.
   settled in Sullivan Co.

BOOKER, Wm.
   settled, 1859, Ralls Co.

BOON, N. T.
   settled in Chariton Co.

BOOTH, R. T.
   settled, 1853, Boone Co.

BOOTHE, J. P.
   settled, 1870, Callaway Co.

BOSSERMAN, H. B.
   settled, 1879, Newton Co.

BOSWELL, P. M.
   settled in Boone Co.

BOULWARE, W. F.
   settled, 1836, Cooper Co.

BOULWARE, ____
   settled in Bates Co.

BOURQUENAT, ____
   settled, 1876, Greene Co.

BOWEN, James A.
   settled, 1857, Livingston Co.

BOWEN, John M.
   settled, 1857, Livingston Co.

BOWEN, ____
   settled, 1844, Knox Co.

BOWMAN, D. B.
   settled, 1851, Ray Co.

BOWRN, Morton
   1850 Census, Morton Co.

BOYD, M. A.
   settled, 1871, Howard Co.

BOYD, Wm.
   settled in Greene Co.

BRADFIELD, Lee
   settled, 1834, Jefferson Co.

BRADLEY, A. H.
   settled, 1850, Callaway Co.

BRADLEY, George W.
   settled, 1852, Howard Co.

BRADLEY, R. L.
   settled, 1874, Cooper Co.

BRAGG, S. I.
   settled, 1840, Shelby Co.

BRAGG, Thomas S.
   settled, 1845, Holt Co.

BRAME, John Baker
   settled in Henry Co.

BRAMELL, Nancy
   1850 Census, Franklin Co.

BRANAMON, J. A.
   settled, 1856, Adair Co.

BRANCH, C. A.
  settled, 1872, Greene Co.

BRAR, John P.
  settled, 1844, Lafayette Co.

BRATTEN, J. B.
  settled in Boone Co.

BREEDEN, ___
  settled, 1839, Barton Co.

BRENERMAN, Samuel S.
  settled, 1868, Jasper Co.

BRIDGEMON, J. W.
  settled, 1849, Holt Co.

BRIDGES, Andrew Watson
  settled in Chariton-Howard Co.

BRIDGES, Jerome
  settled, 1846, Schuyler Co.

BRINSON, Frank M.
  settled in Buchanan Co.

BRISTOW, R. B.
  settled, 1870, Monroe Co.

BRISTOW, Sue A.
  settled, 1853, Carroll Co.

BRITON, John R.
  settled, 1841, Lincoln Co.

BRITT, C. E.
  settled, 1855, Pike Co.

BRITTON, James H.
  settled in Lincoln Co.

BRITTS, Dr. George
  settled in Henry Co.

BROCK, Adam
  settled, 1870, Carroll Co.

BROCK, William
  settled, 1835, Jefferson Co.

BROGAN, Wm.
  settled, 1838, Randolph Co.

BRONAUGH, ___
  settled in Henry Co.

BRONAUGH, J.
  settled, 1842, Clay Co.

BROOKS, J. W.
  settled, 1857, Andrew Co.

BROOKS, O.
  settled, 1874, Harrison Co.

BROOKS, P. D.
  settled, 1834, Callaway Co.

BROOKS, Wm. A.
  settled, 1834, Callaway Co.

BROWN, A. F.
  settled, 1874, Ralls Co.

BROWN, A. H.
  settled, 1837, Newton Co.

BROWN, Allen W.
  1850 Census, Franklin Co.

BROWN, B. A.
  settled in Harrison Co.

BROWN, B. D.
  settled, 1853, Callaway Co.

BROWN, Daniel
  settled in Howard Co.

BROWN, E. R.
  settled in Pike Co.

BROWN, E. R.
  settled, 1856, Montgomery Co.

BROWN, Elizabeth
  settled in Howard Co.

BROWN, Hugh
  settled, 1853, Knox Co.

BROWN, J. A.
    settled, 1868, Marion Co.

BROWN, J. H.
    settled, 1868, Marion Co.

BROWN, J. P.
    settled, 1860, Adair Co.

BROWN, James B.
    1850 Census, Franklin Co.

BROWN, John
    settled in Johnson Co.

BROWN, John O.
    settled in Franklin Co.

BROWN, John R.
    settled in Franklin Co.

BROWN, Julia
    settled in Howard Co.

BROWN, Louden
    settled in Caldwell Co.

BROWN, Samuel
    settled, 1843(?), Pike Co.

BROWN, Susan
    settled in Caldwell Co.

BROWN, Walker P.
    1850 Census, Franklin Co.

BROWN, Wm.
    settled, 1843, Linn Co.

BROWN, Wm. G.
    settled, 1835, Howard Co.

BROWN, Wm. J.
    1850 Census, Franklin Co.

BROWNFIELD, Jonathan
    settled, 1836, Cooper Co.

BROWNING, A. J.
    settled, 1841, Sullivan Co.

BROWNING, F. A.
    settled in Linn Co.

BROYLES, Wm. E.
    settled, 1857, Howard Co.

BRUBAKER, D. R.
    settled, 1873, Cooper Co.

BRUBAKER, Noah
    settled in Jefferson Co.

BRUCE, C. H.
    settled, 1853, Audrain Co.

BRUCE, T. D.
    settled, 1853, Audrain Co.

BRUCE, Wm. B.
    settled, 1844, Chariton Co.

BRUMFIELD, _____
    settled in Barry Co.

BRUNK, G. E.
    settled in Cedar Co.

BRYANT, D. D.
    settled, 1880, Newton Co.

BUCHANAN, A. S.
    settled, 1837, Lincoln Co.

BUCHANAN, James W.
    settled in Adair Co.

BUCK, S. S.
    settled, 1866, Henry Co.

BUCKNER, R. R.
    settled, 1844, Callaway Co.

BUCKNER, Thomas
    1850 Census, Franklin Co.

BUFFORD, Preston W.
    settled in Cedar Co.

BUFFORD, W.
    settled, 1844, Knox Co.

BULL, S.
  settled, 1852, Harrison Co.

BULLARD, O. M.
  settled, 1847, Lafayette Co.

BULLOCK, A. L.
  settled, 1836, Bates Co.

BULLOCK, D. C. (family)
  settled in Jasper Co.

BUNSON, H.
  settled in Newton Co.

BURBAKER, Noah
  settled, 1871, Johnson Co.

BURCH, J. W.
  settled in Jasper Co.

BURDETTE, T. L.
  settled in Callaway Co.

BURGESS, R. M.
  settled, 1842, Monroe Co.

BURGIN, H. S.
  settled, 1852, Harrison Co.

BURGIN, J. H.
  settled, 1852, Harrison Co.

BURKE, Charles R.
  settled in Adair Co.

BURKLEY, J.
  settled, 1866, Sullivan Co.

BURNER, J. S.
  settled, 1839, Livingston Co.

BURNETT, C.
  settled, 1876, Ray Co.

BURRIS, John J.
  settled, 1854, Chariton Co.

BURSON, H.
  settled, 1866, Newton Co.

BURTON, John W.
  settled, 1865, Lafayette Co.

BURTON, (family)
  settled in Howard Co.

BUSEY, Sarah
  settled in Saline Co.

BUSHNELL, Emanuell
  settled in Henry Co.

BUTLER, Thomas
  settled, 1836, Ralls Co.

BYERS, H. B.
  settled, 1852, Clark Co.

BYRD, W. H.
  settled, 1868, Marion Co.

C

CADLE, James
  settled, 1875, Franklin Co.

CAHILL, Perry
  1850 Census, Franklin Co.

CAHILL, Samuel
  1850 Census, Franklin Co.

CAIN, Jesse
  1850 Census, Franklin Co.

CALDWELL, F. M.
  settled, 1839, Cooper Co.

CALDWELL, John
  settled, 1840, Greene Co.

CALDWELL, John, Sr.
  1850 Census, Franklin Co.

CALDWELL, Mathew
  1850 Census, Franklin Co.

CALLAWAY, J. H.
  settled, 1846, Linn Co.

CALLIHAN, C. S.
    settled, 1854, Clark Co.

CALLISON, F.
    settled, 1845, Daviess Co.

CALVERT, (family)
    settled in Lincoln Co.

CALVERT, (family)
    settled in Pike Co.

CALVERT, Ziba
    settled, 1819, Marion Co.

CAMP, J.
    settled, 1875, Putnam Co.

CAMPBELL, G. W.
    settled, 1874, Newton Co.

CAMPBELL, J.
    settled, 1867, Callaway Co.

CAMPBELL, J.
    settled in Monroe Co.

CAMPBELL, J. D.
    settled, 1856, Putnam Co.

CANNEFAX, Chesley
    settled, 1831, Greene Co.

CANTLEY, John
    1850 Census, Franklin Co.

CARDER, F. M.
    settled, 1855, Knox Co.

CARLIN, Asa
    settled in Harrison Co.

CARLIN, William Marshall
    settled in Harrison Co.

CARLTON, T. R.
    settled in Callaway Co.

CARPENTER, Charles H.
    settled in Atchison Co.

CARPENTER, L. F.
    settled, 1854, Buchanan Co.

CARPENTER, (family)
    settled, 1869, Andrew Co.

CARR, J. E.
    settled, 1842, St. Charles Co.

CARRUTHERS, T. H.
    settled, 1831, Boone Co.

CARSON, E. J.
    settled, 1829, Marion Co.

CARSON, Wm.
    settled, 1840, Buchanan Co.

CARTER, Charles E.
    settled, 1852, Pike Co.

CARTER, J.
    settled, 1866, Linn Co.

CARTER, J. W.
    settled, 1849, Randolph Co.

CARTER, John
    settled in Cedar Co.

CARTER, John C., Jr.
    settled, 1852, Pike Co.

CARTER, John W.
    settled, 18--, Boone Co.

CARTER, L. H.
    settled, 1836, Ray Co.

CARTER, Miller (Mason)
    settled in Cedar Co.

CARTER, Thomas Miller
    settled, 1830, Linn Co.

CARTER, Tilamon
    settled, 1854, Greene Co.

CARTER, Wm. H.
    settled, 1849, Lafayette Co.

CARTER, W. L.
  settled, 1841, St. Charles Co.

CARTER, Wm. T.
  settled, 1839, Warren Co.

CASEY,
  settled in Cedar Co.

CASEY, Thomas
  settled in Cedar Co.

CASON, J. W.
  settled, 1843, Putnam Co.

CATRON,
  settled in Bates Co.

CAUFMAN, Margaret
  settled in Caldwell Co.

CAUL, Thomas
  settled, 1850, Putnam Co.

CAUTHORNE, B. R.
  settled in Audrain Co.

CHADWICK, A. F.
  settled, 1841, Knox Co.

CHADWICK, D. M.
  settled, 1842, Knox Co.

CHADWICK, Eli. D.
  settled, 1842, Knox Co.

CHAMBERLAIN, Wm. N.
  settled, 1870, Cooper Co.

CHAMBERS, John D.
  settled, 1855, Lafayette Co.

CHANCELLOR, B. M.
  settled, 1852, Howard Co.

CHANDLER, Henry
  settled, 1856, Greene Co.

CHANDLER, T. S.
  settled in Cooper Co.

CHAPMAN, George
  settled, 1839, Chariton Co.

CHAPMAN, Henry
  settled in Atchison Co.

CHAPMAN, J. E.
  settled in Callaway Co.

CHAPMAN, Walt.
  settled in Franklin Co.

CHEATHAM, Albert
  settled in Franklin Co.

CHEATHAM, Edwin
  settled in Franklin Co.

CHEATHAM, Henry
  1850 Census, Franklin Co.

CHEATHAM, Martha
  1850 Census, Franklin Co.

CHEATHAM, William
  1850 Census, Franklin Co.

CHENAULT, David H.
  settled in Atchison Co.

CHEVIS, G.
  settled, 1866, Macon Co.

CHILD, J. T.
  settled, 1866, Ray Co.

CHILDERS, I.
  settled, 1861, Sullivan Co.

CHILDS, Thomas W.
  settled in Atchison Co.

CHILES, Alfred M.
  1850 Census, Franklin Co.

CHILES, John G.
  1850 Census, Franklin Co.

CHILES, Wm. C.
  1850 Census, Franklin Co.

CHILTON, Joseph W.
    settled, 1840, Howard Co.

CHRISTIAN, ___
    settled in Cedar Co.

CHRISTIAN, D.
    settled, 1825, Pike Co.

CHRISTIAN, (family)
    settled in Lafayette Co.

CHRISTIE, D. W.
    settled, 1855, Lewis Co.

CHRISTIE, John F.
    settled, 1855, Lewis Co.

CLAPPER, J. F.
    settled, 1849, Monroe Co.

CLARK, Armstead
    settled, 1869, Holt Co.

CLARK, John P.
    settled, 1845, Audrain Co.

CLARK, M. N.
    settled, 1837, Pike Co.

CLARK, (family)
    settled in Linn Co.

CLARKSON, A. M.
    settled, 1859, Linn Co.

CLARKSON, Charles August
    settled in Chariton Co.

CLARKSON, J. S.
    settled, 1841, Boone Co.

CLARKSON, R. W.
    settled, 1856, Lafayette Co.

CLAYTON, S. A.
    settled, 1859, Harrison Co.

CLEMENTS, Richard H.
    settled, 1862, Chariton Co.

CLEMENTS, W.
    settled, 1870, Sullivan Co.

CLEVLAND, James
    settled, 1838, Livingston Co.

CLYMA, Wm. H.
    settled, 1870, Newton Co.

COCK, Wm. M.
    settled, 1833, Chariton Co.

COE, Edward M.
    settled in Knox Co.

COEN, Wm. S.
    settled in Clay Co.?

COFFER, T. W.
    settled, 1853, Andrew Co.

COLE, J. B.
    settled, 1881, Barton Co.

COLE, Jesse W.
    settled, 1818, Lafayette Co.

COLE, ___
    settled in Bates Co.

COLEMAN, John G.
    1850 Census, Franklin Co.

COLEMAN, T. H.
    settled, 1836, Pike Co.

COLLETT, J. H.
    settled, 1852, Macon Co.

COLLINS, David
    settled, 1847, Buchanan Co.

COLLINS, Wm. K.
    settled, 1831, St. Charles Co.

COMPTON, J. H.
    settled, 1839, Clay Co.

CONN, (family)
    settled in Lafayette Co.

CONNEL, F. W.
  settled in Randolph Co.

CONNER, S. P.
  settled, 1869, Adair Co.

CONSTABLE, L. N.
  settled, 1846, Mercer Co.

COOK, Mrs. E. H.
  settled, 1845, St. Charles Co.

COOK, P. A.
  settled in Monroe Co.

COOK, Winchester
  settled in Marion Co.

COOKSEY, V.
  settled, 1856, Mercer Co.

COONTZ, Jake
  settled, 1845, Jefferson Co.

COONTZ, R. E.
  settled, 1836, Marion Co.

COOPER, C.
  settled, 1851, Sullivan Co.

COOPER, G. M.
  settled, 1854, Clark Co.

COOPER, J. C.
  settled in Carroll Co.

COOPER, Wm. James
  settled, 1832, Lafayette Co.

COOTES, (family)
  settled in Cooper Co.

COPPAGE, Alfred (family)
  settled in Atchison Co.

COPPAGE, Alexander (family)
  settled in Carroll Co.

COPPAGE, William (family)
  settled in Henry Co.

COPPAGE, William (family)
  1850 Census, Pulaski Co.

COPPAGE, Wm. E. (family)
  settled in Carroll Co.

COPPAGE, (family)
  settled in Monroe Co.

COPPAGE, (family)
  settled in Maries Co.

COPPAGE, (family)
  settled in Washington Co.

COPPAGE, (family)
  settled in Crawford Co.

CORBIN, B. B.
  settled, 1849, Clay Co.

CORBIN, Champ C.
  settled, 1854, Lafayette Co.

CORBIN, Lewis (family)
  settled in Vernon Co.

CORLEY, E. B.
  settled in Callaway Co.

CORDER, C. H. (family)
  settled, 1865, Lafayette Co.

CORDER, Geo. W.
  settled, 1838, Lafayette Co.

CORDER, J. E.
  settled, 1856, Lafayette Co.

CORDER, Nathan
  settled, 1836, Lafayette Co.

CORDER, Polk
  settled, 1868, Lafayette Co.

CORLEY, George
  settled, 1843, Callaway Co.

CORMANY, Wm. D.
  settled, 1870, Andrew Co.

CORNELL, J. H.
  settled in Chariton Co.

COURTNEY, A. C.
  settled, 1840, Clay Co.

COWELS, James
  settled in Christian Co.

COWGILL, (family)
  settled, 1868, Jasper Co.

COX, Benjamin H.
  settled, 1850, Howard Co.

COX, L. C.
  settled, 1855, Carroll Co.

COX, Samuel L.
  settled, 1869, Lincoln Co.

CRAIG, Levi
  settled, 1867(?), Johnson Co.

CRAIGHEAD, L. Olive
  settled, 1829, Callaway Co.

CRAIGHEAD, W. A. B.
  settled, 1829, Callaway Co.

CRAIGHEAD, Wm.
  settled, 1836, Callaway Co.

CRAVENS, J. M.
  settled, 1839, Daviess Co.

CRAVENS, W. J.
  settled, 1867, Greene Co.

CRAWFORD, J. S.
  settled, 1840, Monroe Co.

CRAWFORD, Sarah C.
  settled, 1855, Randolph Co.

CREASY, J. A.
  settled, 1840, Carroll Co.

CREWS, B. S.
  settled, 1870, Lincoln Co.

CREWS, T. W. B.
  settled, 1865, Franklin Co.

CROCKETT, A. J.
  settled, 1837, Chariton Co.

CROCKETT, Hugh
  settled, 1836, Audrain Co.

CROMWELL, J. W.
  settled, 1855, Randolph Co.

CROWDER, Joel M.
  1850 Census, Franklin Co.

CROWDER, John M.
  1850 Census, Franklin Co.

CRUMBAUGH, Mrs. M. C.
  settled, 1854, Boone Co.

CRUMPACKER, D. H.
  settled, 1840, Sullivan Co.

CRUMPACKER, John
  settled, 1845, Putnam Co.

CRUZEN, J. C.
  settled, 1851, Carroll Co.

CULP, Wm.
  settled, 1868, Randolph Co.

CUMMINGS, H. J.
  settled, 1868, Newton Co.

CUNNINGHAM, C. G.
  settled, 1870, Audrain Co.

CUNNINGHAM, George P.
  settled, 1865, Jasper Co.

CUNNINGHAM, J. W.
  settled, 1843, Cooper Co.

CUNNINGHAM, L. P.
  settled, 1866, Jasper Co.

CURRIN, H. W.
  settled, 1865, Livingston Co.

D

DAGGS, W. R.
settled, 1837?, Clark Co.

DAIL, V. E.
settled, 1835, Linn Co.

DALHOUSE, Samuel F.
settled, 1867, Johnson Co.

DALTON, Rebbeca
settled, 1848, Lafayette Co.

DAMRON, J. D.
settled, 1844, Lincoln Co.

DANIEL, Samuel
settled, 1842, Lincoln Co.

DARLING, Wm.
settled, 1866, Cooper Co.

DAUGHERTY, J. J.
settled, 1867, Jasper Co.

DAVIDSON, ____
settled, 1843, Henry Co.

DAVIS, B. F.
settled, 1836, Monroe Co.

DAVIS, D. H.
settled, 1855, Daviess Co.

DAVIS, Elijah
1860 Census, Christian Co.

DAVIS, Elizabeth
settled in Christian Co.

DAVIS, George
settled, 1833, Pike Co.

DAVIS, Capt. J. J.
settled, 1857, Jefferson Co.

DAVIS, James
settled, 1832, Pike Co.

DAVIS, John
1860 Census, Cedar Co.

DAVIS, H.
settled, 1856, Schuyler Co.

DAVIS, P.
settled, 1856, Shelby Co.

DAVIS, Rebecca
settled in Christian Co.

DAVIS, Robert
settled, 1870, Audrain Co.

DAVIS, Robert T.
settled, 1855, Audrain Co.

DAVIS, W. F.
settled in Mercer Co.

DAVIS, W. H.
settled, 1843, Mercer Co.

DAWSON, J. R.
settled, 1867, Pike Co.

DAWSON, S. R.
settled, 1853, Pike Co.

DAWSON, Dr. W. E.
settled in Cedar Co.

DEARING, A. J.
settled in Marion Co.

DEARING, Wm. Q.
settled, 1849, Schuyler Co.

DEMORY, Josiah
settled, 1863, Macon Co.

DENNIS, Thomas L.
settled, 1846, Howard Co.

DENTON, H. F.
settled, 1858, Green Co.

DERRY, A. R.
settled, 1868, Carroll Co.

DESKINS, S. R.
settled, 1857, Linn Co.

DESMUKES, John E.
    settled, 1842, Howard Co.

DESPER, Forest G.
    1850 Census, Franklin Co.

DEVER, Hugh
    settled, 1848, Boone Co.

DeWITT, H. S.
    settled, 1865, Sullivan Co.

DEWS, Nancy
    settled in Lincoln Co.

DICKINSON, James P.
    settled, 1837, Pike Co.

DICKINSON, John Quaralles
    1850 Census, Franklin Co.

DIGGS, Betty
    settled in Chariton-Howard Co.

DIGGS, Francis W.
    settled in Howard Co.

DIGGS, Seneca
    settled in Chariton-Howard Co.

DILLARD, James W.
    settled, 1857, Pike Co.

DINGUS, Eliz.
    1850 Census, Franklin Co.

DINKLE?, ____
    settled in Saline Co.

DIX, Nancy R.
    settled, 1832, Cooper Co.

DIXON, A. J.
    settled, 1859, Lincoln Co.

DOBSON, Chas. L.
    settled, 1854, Linn Co.

DOBYNS, D. R. D.
    settled in Cedar Co.

DODSON, James D.
    settled, 1834, Lincoln Co.

DODSON, W. M.
    settled, 1875, Jackson Co.

DORTON, E. T.
    settled, 1856, Ray Co.

DOUGLAS, A. J.
    settled, 1837, Audrain Co.

DOWELL, E. M.
    settled in Monroe Co.

DOWNING, Henry
    settled, 1833, Schuyler Co.

DRACE, Lott M.
    1850 Census, Franklin Co.

DRAFFEN, J. W.
    settled, 1836, Cooper Co.

DRAFFEN, James
    settled in Cooper Co.

DRAFFEN, Wellington
    settled, 1836, Cooper Co.

DRAFFIN, Wm. R.
    settled, 1838, Cooper Co.

DRUMMOND, James P.
    settled, 1839, Daviess Co.

DUDLEY, C. J. and Stephen
    settled, 1835, Callaway Co.

DUFF, A. E.
    settled, 1866, Greene Co.

DUGGINS, Thomas C.
    settled in Saline Co.

DULEY, Anna
    settled, 1840, Harrison Co.

DUNAWAY, Wm.
    settled, 1857, Monroe Co.

DUNCAN, (family)
    settled in Cooper Co.

DUNCAN, W. H.
    settled, 1830, Boone Co.

DUNKERSON, S. J.
    settled, 1840, Pike Co.

DUNN, J. E.
    settled in Harrison Co.

DUNN, R. K.
    settled, 1866, Livingston Co.

DUNN, Samuel W.
    settled, 1875 or 1848?, Greene Co.

DURNIL, J. A.
    settled, 1840, Howard Co.

DUSENBERRY, F. M.
    settled, 1871, Livingston Co.

DUVALL, J. F.
    settled, 1844, Ray Co.

DUVALL, L.
    settled, 1844, Ray Co.

DUVALL, Nancy
    settled in Marion Co.

E

EAKEN, Samuel
    settled, 1864, Jefferson Co.

EAKEN, Samuel
    settled, 1840, Jefferson Co.

EARHART, P. M.
    settled, 1837, Marion Co.

EARLY, Easton
    settled, 1832, Pike Co.

EASLY, S. W.
    settled, 1868, Boone Co.

EDDENS, R. W.
    settled, 1867, Monroe Co.

EDDINS, B. C.
    settled, 1831, Howard Co.

EDDINS, W. J.
    settled, 1833, Howard

EDENS, George
    settled in Barry Co.

EDMONDS, G. H.
    settled, 1835, Shelby Co.

EDWARDS, David C.
    settled, 1871, Bates Co.

EDWARDS, John M.
    settled, 1842, Boone Co.

EDWARDS, John R.
    settled in Carroll Co.

EDWARDS, Wm. G.
    settled, 1835, Howard Co.

EHRDARDT, Henry
    settled, 1844, Chariton Co.

ELAM, Joe.
    settled, 1843, Chariton Co.

ELLINGTON, J. S.
    settled, 1837, Chariton Co.

ELLIOTT, Ira
    settled, 1840, Adair Co.

ELLIOTT, Thomas T.
    settled, 1837, Chariton Co.

ELLIS, Hezekiah
    settled in Marion Co.

ELLIS, Dr. W. H.
    settled, 1843, Cooper Co.

ELLY, B. F.
    settled, 1845, Callaway Co.

ELLY, E. B.
    settled, 1835, Callaway Co.

ELSEA, (family)
    settled in Lafayette Co.

ELSEA, John G.
    settled, 1841, Lafayette Co.

ELSON, ____
    settled in Greene Co.

EMERSON, Daniel
    settled in St. Charles Co.

EMMERSON, Z. T.
    settled, 1840, Pike Co.

ENGLISH, Elisha
    settled, 1862, Marion Co.

EPPERLY, Calvin P.
    settled, 1862, Jefferson Co.

ESTES, (family)
    settled in Vernon Co.

ESTILL, (family)
    settled in Howard Co.

EUBANK, (family)
    settled in Saline Co.

EVANS, Betty
    settled in Pettis Co.

EVANS, David C.
    settled in Bates Co.

EVANS, Fernando A.
    settled in Mo., county unknown

EVANS, John R.
    settled in Carroll Co.

EVANS, Wm. G.
    settled in Howard Co.

EVERLY, Samuel E.
    settled, 1866, Chariton Co.

EWING, (family)
    settled in Lafayette Co.

EWING, John J.
    settled, 1842, Chariton Co.

F

FAGG, Thomas J. C.
    settled, 1832, Pike Co.

FAIRFAX, C. P.
    settled, 1886, Cooper Co.

FANSLER, C.
    settled, 1866, Harrison Co.

FANT, J. L.
    settled, 1836, Warren Co.

FARRAR, Adeline
    1850 Census, Franklin Co.

FARRIS, Joseph M.
    settled, 1837, St. Charles Co.

FATTIG, H.
    settled, 1855, Worth Co.

FEAGANS, L. H.
    settled, 1854, Buchanan Co.

FELTY, G. T.
    settled, 1870, Lincoln Co.

FERGUS, James
    settled in Vernon Co.

FERGUSON, James
    settled, 1825, Chariton-Howard Co.

FERGUSON, W. J.
    settled, 1857, Bates Co.

FERGUSON, W. J.
    settled, 1835, Randolph Co.

FEWELL, R. Z.
    settled in Henry Co.

FICAS, Adam
    settled, 1837, Johnson Co.

FICKLIN, Horace B.
   settled in Randolph Co.

FIELDS, J. J.
   settled, 1867, Linn Co.

FIELDS, Mary
   settled in Cedar Co.

FIELDS, Nathan
   settled in Cedar Co.

FINCH, W. R.
   settled, 1842, Knox Co.

FINKS, Joe H.
   settled, 1850, Howard Co.

FIRESTONE, ___
   settled, 1853, Cedar Co.

FISHER, Jacob
   settled, 1838, Howard Co.

FISHER, John
   settled, 1853, Howard Co.

FISHER, Joseph
   settled in Howard Co.

FISHER, Michael
   settled, 1839, Boone Co.

FLEET, A. F.
   settled, 1873, Lafayette Co.

FLEET, Dr. John B.
   settled in Howard Co.

FLEMING, Capt. A. J.
   settled, 1847, Jefferson Co.

FLESHER, H. H.
   settled in Bates Co.

FLESHMAN, James D.
   settled, 1841, Putnam Co.

FLORY, Joseph
   settled, 1874, Holt Co.

FLOWERING, P. C.
   settled, 1854, Linn Co.

FLOYD, Elisha
   settled, 1846, Chariton Co.

FORBES, Mrs. Dorothy
   settled, 1856, Holt Co.

FORD, Miss L.
   settled, 1858, Ray Co.

FORE, Chas. A.
   settled in Linn Co.

FORE, P. M.
   settled, 1837, Linn Co.

FORSYTHE, L. E.
   settled in Jefferson Co.

FORT, Thomas C.
   settled, 1865, Caldwell Co.

FORTUNE, Martha
   settled in Bates Co.

FOSTER, Gasner Quarlles
   settled in Henry Co.

FOWLER, Christian E.
   settled in Barry Co.

FOWLER, R. H.
   settled, 1874, Audrain Co.

FOX, ___
   settled in Chariton-Howard Co.

FRANCE, C. B.
   settled, 1855, Buchanan Co.

FRANKLIN, S. H.
   settled, 1833, Chariton Co.

FRAY, Mrs. E. H.
   settled in Marion Co.

FREDRICK, P. E.
   settled, 1865?, Shelby Co.

FREEMAN, Samuel F.
    settled, 1875, Holt Co.

FRISTOE, Arthur B.
    settled in Buchanan Co.

FRISTOE, Mrs. Lucinda
    settled, 1854, Buchanan Co.

FROGGE, William R.
    settled, 1842, Buchanan Co.

FUDGE, Coleman
    settled in Bates Co.

FULKERSON, Dr. J. M.
    settled in Johnson Co.

FULKERSON, R. S.
    settled, 1849, Lafayette Co.

FULLHEART, Joel
    settled, 1862, Putnam Co.

FULLS?, Nelson
    settled in Cedar Co.

FULTON, J.
    settled, 1839, Knox Co.

FUQUA, John A.
    settled, 1843, Chariton Co.

FYFER, J. Tom
    settled, 1856, Boone Co.

G

GAINES, John W.
    settled, 1833, Howard Co.

GALL, David
    1850 Census, Franklin Co.

GALL, John, Sr.
    1850 Census, Franklin Co.

GALLIAN, ____
    settled in Greene Co.

GAMMON, William T.
    settled, 1869, Lafayette Co.

GARBER, Joel
    settled, 1866, Jasper Co.

GARDEN, Jno. H.
    settled, 1869, Johnson Co.

GARDENER, O. B.
    settled, 1855, Linn Co.

GARDNER, ____
    settled in Barry Co.

GARDNER, G. M.
    settled, 1856, Newton Co.?

GARLOCK, Andrew J.
    settled in Adair Co.

GARNETT, Edward G.
    settled in Saline Co.

GARNETT, Edward G.
    settled, 184-, Saline Co.

GARRETT, Levi J.
    settled, 1866, Lincoln Co.

GARRETT, R.
    settled, 1850, Warren Co.

GARRETT, W. B.
    settled, 1834, Callaway Co.

GARRETT, Wilson
    settled, 1865, Montgomery Co.

GARRETT, ____
    settled in Cedar Co.

GARRISON, Thomas E.
    settled, 1839, Shelby Co.

GARRISON, J. M.
    settled, 1839, Shelby Co.

GAUGH, William
    settled, 1839, St. Charles Co.

GAW, P. M.
    settled, 1818, Lafayette Co.

GAY, A. W.
   settled, 1840, Daviess Co.

GAY, James
   settled, 1840, Daviess Co.

GIBBONS, A. R.
   settled, 1867, Monroe Co.

GIBBS, D.
   settled, 1837, Livingston Co.

GIBBS, Peter D.
   settled in Chariton-Howard Co.

GIBSON, F. G.
   settled, 1869, Ray Co.

GIBSON, H. E.
   settled, 1867, Daviess Co.

GIBSON, J. S.
   settled, 1867, Newton Co.

GIBSON, John
   settled, 1867, Carroll Co.

GIBSON, Joseph
   1850 Census, Franklin Co.

GIBSON, T. B.
   settled, 1869, Cooper Co.

GIBSON, William Clay
   settled, 1860, Pettis Co.

GIESE?, Joachim
   settled, 1865, Jefferson Co.

GILBERT, W. S.
   settled, 1851, Callaway Co.

GILL, ____
   settled, 1844, Lewis Co.

GILL, John W.
   settled, 1836, Clay Co.

GILLESPIE, ____
   settled, 1842, Linn Co.

GILLMAN, W. J.
   settled, 1829, Callaway Co.

GILPIN, B. G.
   settled, 1854, Callaway Co.

GLASCOCK, Harvey
   settled, 1874, Ralls Co.

GLASCOCK, James
   settled in Ralls Co.

GLASCOCK, Jefferson
   settled, 1820, Ralls Co.

GLASGOW, James
   settled, 1855, Adair Co.

GLAZE, A. J.
   settled, 1845, Sullivan Co.

GLAZE, W. H.
   settled, 1845, Sullivan Co.

GLEN, David A.
   settled in Callaway Co.

GLEN, George
   settled, 1852, Holt Co.

GLICK, D.
   settled, 1864, Andrew Co.

GLICK, Joel
   settled, 1857, Holt Co.

GLICK, Joseph
   settled, 1857, Holt Co.

GOOD, Robert F.
   settled, 1857, Harrison Co.

GOODE, Edward
   1850 Census, Franklin Co.

GOODE, John
   1850 Census, Franklin Co.

GOODE, John
   1850 Census, Franklin Co.

GOODIN, A. V.
  settled, 1866, Greene Co.

GOODMAN, A. G.
  settled, 1836, Pike Co.

GOODRICH, J. C.
  settled, 1859, St. Charles Co.

GOODRICH, R. G.
  settled, 1856, Montgomery Co.

GOODRICH, W. W.
  settled in Bates Co.

GOODWIN, John T.
  settled, 1839, Lafayette Co.

GOODWIN, W. C.
  settled, 1866, Lafayette Co.

GOOLDY, Robert
  settled, 1874, Jasper Co.

GORDON, R. D.
  settled, 1836, Montgomery Co.

GOVER, ____
  settled in Callaway Co.

GRACE, J. A.
  settled in Livingston Co.

GRACE, Thomas J.
  settled, 1857, Chariton Co.

GRAFF, Ann
  settled in Mo., county unknown

GRAFF, George
  1850 Census, Cedar Co.

GRAHAM, M.
  settled, 1822, Boone Co.

GRAHAM, James J.
  settled, 1834, Johnson Co.

GRAHAM, John C.
  settled in Mo., county unknown

GRAHAM, John S.
  settled, 1841, Daviess Co.

GRAHAM, S. C.
  settled, 1834, Johnson Co.

GRAHAM, John G.
  settled, 1834, Johnson Co.

GRAHAM, ____
  settled in Cedar Co.

GRAVES, Thomas A.
  settled in Lewis Co.

GRAY, J.
  settled, 1855, Harrison Co.

GRAY, J. B.
  settled, 1824?, Callaway Co.

GRAY, Nancy J.
  settled, 1832, Boone Co.

GRAY, Hiaram (colored)
  settled, 1831, Cooper Co.

GRAY, T. J.
  settled, 1832, Boone Co.

GRAY, Wesley (colored)
  settled, 1831, Cooper Co.

GRAY, William E.
  settled, 1870, Greene Co.

GRAY, William H.
  settled in Henry Co.

GREEN, E. H.
  settled, 1855, Ray Co.

GREEN, M. T.
  settled, 1837, Daviess Co.

GREGG, John H.
  settled in Bates Co.

GREGG, Joseph G.
  settled, 1857, Pettis Co.

GREGORY, J. B.
    settled, 1835, Callaway Co.

GREGORY, R. F.
    settled, 1858, Mercer Co.

GREGORY, Roderick
    1850 Census, Franklin Co.

GREGORY, Roper?
    1850 Census, Franklin Co.

GREER, Spencer
    settled, 1862, Schuyler Co.

GRIFFIN, David
    settled, 1838, Ralls Co.

GRIFFITH, ___
    settled in Cedar Co.

GRIFFITH, Isaac
    settled, 1870, Holt Co.

GRIFFITH, James H.
    settled, 1870, Jasper Co.

GRIFFITH, W. T.
    settled in Holt Co.

GRIGGS, W. L.
    settled, 1858, Adair Co.

GRIMES, John
    settled, 1865, Newton Co.

GROOM, Elizabeth
    settled, 1854, Harrison Co.

GROVER, S. H.
    settled, 1875, Knox Co.

GROVES, William
    settled in Bates Co.

GULICK, D. W.
    settled, 1867, Jasper Co.

GUNN, William H.
    settled, 1858, Benton Co.

GURLEY, ___
    settled in Greene Co.

GUTHREY, John G.
    settled in Saline Co.

GUTHRIDGE, James
    settled, 1830, Chariton Co.

GWYN, Ursula
    settled, 1838, Monroe Co.

H

HACKER?, John R.
    settled in Benton Co.

HAGGERTY, Eliz.
    settled, 1856, Harrison Co.

HAISLIP, James N.
    settled, 1838, Montgomery Co.

HAISLIP, Robert S.
    settled in Christian Co.

HALE, William
    settled, 1845, Lafayette Co.

HALEY, J. M.
    settled, 1858, Pike Co.

HALL, Anderson
    settled, 1847, Holt Co.

HALL, David R.
    settled, 1875, Chariton Co.

HALL, D. N.
    settled, 1835, Boone Co.

HALL, Fred
    settled, 1875, Buchanan Co.

HALL, J. A.
    settled in Chariton-Howard Co.

HALL, J. G.
    settled, 1840, Lewis Co.

HALL, Stewart A.
    settled, 1818, St. Charles Co.

HALLENBACK, John
    settled in Holt Co.

HALTERMAN, James H.
    settled in Bates Co.

HALTERMAN, Michael
    settled, 1873, Carroll Co.

HAM, J. H.
    settled, 1870, Harrison Co.?

HAMILTON, A.
    settled, 1844, Knox Co.

HAMILTON, J. L.
    settled, 1867, Greene Co.

HAMILTON, J. M.
    settled, 1865, Chariton Co.

HAMILTON, Mason
    settled, 1839, Knox Co.

HAMMACK, William
    settled in Franklin Co.

HAMMER, J.
    settled, 1869, Worth Co.

HAMMER, B. F.
    settled, 1848, Lafayette Co.

HAMPTON, John P.
    settled, 1867, Lewis Co.

HAMPTON, W. G.
    settled, 1833, Montgomery Co.

HANAKER, A. C.
    settled, 1844, Holt Co.

HANCOX, M.
    settled, 1860, Carroll Co.

HANDY, Eliz.
    1860 Census

HANDLEY, John C.
    settled, 1839, Lafayette Co.

HANDY, Eliz.
    settled in Christian Co.

HANGER, C.
    settled, 1857, Monroe Co.

HANGER, John R.
    settled, 1851, Monroe Co.

HANGER, P. M.
    settled, 1863, Shelby Co.

HANNA, James K.
    settled, 1826, Howard Co.

HANNERSON, Reuben
    1850 Census, Franklin Co.

HARDEN, Joseph D.
    settled, 1838, Greene Co.

HARDING, Mrs. Lou.
    settled, 1833, Pike Co.

HARDMAN, Anthony
    settled, 1876, Holt Co.

HARLOW, John M.
    settled, 1870, Barton Co.

HARMON, James H.
    settled in Bates Co.

HARNETT, William A.
    settled, 1850, St. Charles Co.

HARPER, C. B.
    settled, 1830, Montgomery Co.

HARPER, William
    settled, 1864, Andrew Co.

HARRIS, A. W.
    settled, 1870, Callaway Co.

HARRIS, Anderson S.
    settled, 1846, Lafayette Co.

HARRIS, Fanny
  settled, 1853, Pike Co.

HARRIS, R. M.
  settled in St. Charles Co.

HARRIS, S.
  settled, 1855, Worth Co.

HARRIS, Samuel
  settled, 1860, Holt Co.

HARRIS, William
  settled, 1835, Pike Co.

HARRIS, William R.
  settled, 1838, Montgomery Co.

HARRISON, B. B.
  settled, 1867, Holt Co.

HARRISON, L. R.
  settled, 1836, Lafayette Co.

HARRISON, R. P.
  settled, 1859, Callaway Co.

HARRISON, W. D.
  settled, 1840, Andrew Co.

HART, J. S.
  settled, 1866, Sullivan Co.

HARVEY, B. B.
  settled, 1865, Linn Co.

HARVEY, C. C.
  settled, 1872, Randolph Co.

HATCHER, Thomas Edwin
  settled, 1830, Marion Co.

HATCHER, William
  settled, 1830, Marion Co.

HAUGHT, Peter
  settled, 1867, Greene Co.

HAWKINS, C. C.
  settled, 1851, Holt Co.

HAWKINS, George W.
  settled in Saline Co.

HAWKINS, Henrietta
  settled in Bates Co.

HAWKINS, J. C.
  settled, 1854, Pike Co.

HAWKINS, W. S.
  settled, 1849, Monroe Co.

HAYS, Wm. T.
  settled, 1844, Lafayette Co.

HEAD, B. S.
  settled, 1832, Randolph Co.

HEAD, John
  settled, 1831, Randolph Co.

HEAD, William
  settled, 1811, Howard Co.

HEATHERLY, Benjamin
  1850 Census, Franklin Co.

HEIZER, Cyrus
  settled, 1867, Johnson Co.

HEIZER, J. W.
  settled, 1836, Monroe Co.

HEIZER, Joseph
  settled, 1836, Monroe Co.

HELM, J. G.
  settled, 1864, Cooper Co.

HELSLEY, Wm. P.
  settled, 1871, Carroll Co.

HENDERSON, Eliz.
  settled, 1867, Cedar Co.

HENDERSON, John S.
  settled, 1823, Callaway Co.

HENDERSON, Joseph
  settled, 1834, Pike Co.

HENDLEY, H. W.
    settled, 18—, Franklin Co.

HENSHAW, J. P.
    settled, 1841, Johnson Co.

HENSLEY, M. P.
    settled, 1839, Boone Co.

HENINGER, ____
    settled, 1874, Macon Co.

HENINGER, S. G.
    settled, 1836, Monroe Co.

HEPLER, John R.
    settled, 1867, Cooper Co.

HEREFORD, Andrew C.
    1850 Census, Franklin Co.

HERNDON, Andrew J.
    settled, 1835, Chariton-Howard Co.

HERNDON, J. M.
    settled, 1857, Chariton Co.

HERNDON, John G.
    settled, 1838, Howard Co.

HERRING, W. J.
    settled, 1840, county unknown

HERRINGTON, Benjamin
    settled, 1858, St. Charles Co.

HERRINGTON, Wm. H.
    settled, 1858, St. Charles Co.

HERSHBERGER, Noah
    settled, 1839, Daviess Co.

HERSHBERGER, Peter
    settled in Daviess Co.

HESSER, B. S.
    settled, 1859, Pike Co,

HESSER, John F. N.
    settled, 1861, Pike Co.

HETRICH, Thomas
    settled, 1871, St. Charles Co.

HICKERSON, Hiram
    settled, 1849, Chariton-Howard C

HICKERSON, James W.
    settled in Howard Co.

HICKERSON, J. C.
    settled, 1871, Randolph Co.

HICKERSON, Jno. J.
    settled, 1868, Andrew Co.

HICKERSON, Jno. M.
    settled, 1841, Howard Co.

HICKERSON, Joseph W.
    settled in Chariton-Howard Co.

HICKEY, ____
    settled in Putnam Co.

HICKMAN, ____
    settled in Bates Co.

HICKMAN, R. G.
    settled, 1830, Monroe Co.

HIGGENBOTHAM, George W.
    settled, 1838, St. Charles Co.

HIGGERSON, C.
    settled, 1837, Cooper Co.

HIGGINBOTHAM, C. Y.
    settled, 1867, Warren Co.

HIGGINBOTHAM, E. H.
    settled, 1867, Lincoln Co.

HIGGINBOTHAM, J. W.
    settled, 1868, Lincoln Co.

HILL, C. A.
    settled in Henry Co.

HILL, D. H.
    settled in Bates Co.

HILL, Davis
    settled in Lafayette Co.

HILL, Eveline
    settled in Carroll Co.

HILL, J. G.
    settled in Jasper Co.

HILL, Martha E.
    settled, 1837, Lafayette Co.

HILL, R. E.
    settled, 1834, Clark Co.

HILL, Robert
    settled, 1844, Howard Co.

HILTON, Wm. S.
    settled in Barry Co.

HINER, ____
    settled in Saline Co.

HINES, Charles
    settled, 1855, Randolph Co.

HINES, Peter
    settled, 1855, Randolph Co.

HINES, W. D.
    settled, 1855, Randolph Co.

HINKLE, C. W. P.
    settled in Franklin Co.

HINKLE, Isaac
    1850 Census, Franklin Co.

HINKLE, M. P.
    settled, 1829, Franklin Co.

HITCH, G. B.
    settled, 1842, St. Charles Co.

HITE, ____
    settled in Henry Co.

HITT, D. L.
    settled in Atchison Co.

HIX, John
    settled, 1848, Randolph Co.

HIX, W. J.
    settled, 1848, Randolph Co.

HODGES, Mrs. Eliz.
    settled, 1853, Jackson Co.

HODGES, R. S.
    settled, 1839, Callaway Co.

HOFFMAN, James O.
    settled in Bates Co.

HOFFMAN, ____
    settled in Pettis Co.

HOGSETT, Wm. A.
    settled, 1868, Caldwell Co.

HOLLENBACH, John
    settled, 1872, Holt Co.

HOLLIDAY, J. W.
    settled, 1833, Shelby Co.

HOLMES, C. G.
    settled, 1854, Boone Co.

HOLSINGER, M. M.
    settled, 1855, Linn Co.

HOOK, J. T.
    settled, 1845, Lafayette Co.

HOOVER, Job
    settled, 1856, Holt Co.

HOOVER, J. H.
    settled, 1874, Andrew Co.

HOPE, T. W.
    settled, 1872, Jasper Co.

HOPKINS, E. W.
    settled, 1832, Callaway Co.

HORD, Alexander
    settled, 1837, Callaway Co.

HORD, R. L.
  settled, 1839, Callaway Co.

HORD, William
  settled, 1839, Monroe Co.

HORE, George W.
  settled, 1839, Randolph Co.

HORN, Samuel W.
  settled, 1860, Hickory-Cedar Co.

HORNER, Gustavus Brown
  settled in Franklin Co.

HORNER, Jhon D.
  settled, 1865, Cooper Co.

HORNER, Major
  settled, 1819, Howard Co.

HORTON, B. F.
  settled, 1847, Chariton Co.

HOUSTON, ____
  settled in Carroll Co.

HOWARD, Thomas
  settled in Chariton-Howard Co.

HOWE, George E.
  settled, 1867, Pike Co.

HOWERTON, James
  settled in Bates Co.

HOWERY, George W.
  settled in Bates Co.?

HOWLETT, R. E.
  settled, 1845, Cooper Co.

HUDSON, Repps B.
  settled, 1843, Carroll Co.

HUDSON, S.
  settled, 1851, Callaway Co.

HUFF, ____
  settled in Vernon Co.

HUGHS, A.
  settled, 1839, Callaway Co.

HUGHS, D. W.
  settled, 1845, Monroe Co.

HUGHS, David
  settled, 1835, Howard Co.

HULL, J. E.
  settled, 1839, Ray Co.

HULL, John R.
  settled in Randolph Co.

HUME, ____
  settled, 1844, Howard Co.

HUMPHREYS, ____
  settled, 1820, Callaway Co.

HUNDLEY, Henry
  1850 Census, Franklin Co.

HUNT, John
  1860 Census, Christian Co.

HUNTER, Wm. G.
  settled in Jefferson Co.

HUNTSMAN, Thomas
  settled, 1838, Randolph Co.

HURST, ____
  settled in Vernon Co.

HURT, Elisha
  1850 Census, Franklin Co.

HURT, J. H.
  settled, 1856, Mercer Co.

HURT, Ossomus
  settled, 1839, Saline Co.

HUSTON, George Webb
  settled in Lincoln Co.

HUTCHENS, J. C.
  settled, 1870, Greene Co.

HUTT, Thomas W.
  settled in Lincoln Co.

HUTTON, W. D.
  settled, 1840, Randolph Co.

I

INGE, James M.
  settled in Franklin Co.

IRBY, H. H.
  settled in Greene Co.

IRONS, W. A.
  settled in Monroe Co.

J

JACKSON, ____
  settled in Bates Co.

JACKSON, Christiana
  settled, 1871, Greene Co.

JACKSON, T. J.
  settled, 1874, Chariton Co.

JACKSON, Wm.
  settled, 1855, Cooper Co.

JACOBS, ____
  settled in Boone Co.

JACOBS, G. R., Jr.
  settled, 1853, Boone Co.

JACOBS, G. R., Sr.
  settled, 1842, Boone Co.

JACOBS, W. H.
  settled, 1852, Boone Co.

JAMES, ____
  settled in Macon Co.

JAMES, Asa
  settled, 1866, Marion Co.

JAMES, Jesse M.
  settled in Atchison Co.

JARRETT, David
  settled, 1840, Greene Co.

JEFFRESS, Elisha B.
  1850 Census, Franklin Co.

JEFFRIES, C. F.
  settled, 1819, Franklin Co.

JEFFRIES, Chas. Richard
  1850 Census, Franklin Co.

JEFFRIES, Cuthbert Swenson
  1850 Census, Franklin Co.

JEFFRIES, Elijah
  settled in Carroll Co.

JEFFRIES, Thomas B.
  settled, 1836, Lewis Co.

JEFFRIES, Whitehead Achillies
  1850 Census, Franklin Co.

JENKINS, John R.
  settled, 1836, Bates Co.

JENKINS, Wm. C.
  settled, 1874, Clark Co.

JENKS, S. J.
  settled, 1839, Daviess Co.

JENNETT, James H.
  1850 Census, Franklin Co.

JENNINGS, C. F.
  settled, 1873, Jasper Co.

JOHNSON, Benjamin C.
  settled, 1829, Marion Co.

JOHNSON, Israel
  settled in Randolph Co.

JOHNSON, John A.
  settled in Jasper Co.

JOHNSON, John W.
  settled, 1892, Jasper Co.

JOHNSON, P. B.
    settled in Franklin Co.

JOHNSON, Robert
    settled in Franklin Co.

JOHNSON, Robert
    settled, 1872, Jasper Co.

JOHNSON, S. R.
    settled, 1852, Linn Co.

JOHNSON, S. W.
    settled, 1860?, Franklin Co.

JOHNSON, T. D.
    settled, 1869, Harrison Co.

JOHNSON, Thomas J.
    settled, 1846, Franklin Co.

JOHNSON, V.
    settled, 1845, Franklin Co.

JOHNSON, William
    settled in Franklin Co.

JOHNSON, William W.
    settled, 1870, Franklin Co.

JONES, C. C.
    settled, 1831, Franklin Co.

JONES, Edward M.
    1850 Census, Franklin Co.

JONES, G. C.
    settled, 1862, Jefferson Co.

JONES, G. M.
    settled, 1865, Lafayette Co.

JONES, Isaac C. H.
    settled, 1876, Franklin Co.

JONES, J.
    settled, 1856, Harrison Co.

JONES, Col. J. F.
    settled, 1824, Callaway Co.

JONES, J. H.
    settled, 1870, Lafayette Co.

JONES, J. L.
    settled, 1869, Greene Co.

JONES, John
    1850 Census, Franklin Co.

JONES, N.
    settled in Warren Co.

JONES, R. H.
    settled, 1847, Greene Co.

JONES, R. P.
    settled, 1869, Greene Co.

JONES, Richard R.
    1850 Census, Franklin Co.

JONES, Stephen Miller
    settled in Franklin Co.

JUDY, Andrew
    settled, 1872, Holt Co.

JUSTICE, ____
    settled in Greene Co.

K

KAYLOR, Wm. M.
    settled, 1835, Lewis Co.

KEACH, John H.
    settled in Ralls Co.

KEATLEY, J. Wm.
    1850 Census, Franklin Co.

KEEBLE, Eliz. S.
    settled in St. Charles Co.

KEEN, Wm.
    settled in Ray Co.

KEETON, James
    settled in St. Charles Co.

KEITH, J. F.
    settled in St. Charles Co.

KEITH, R. R.
    settled in St. Charles Co.

KELCH, C. W.
    settled in Pike Co.

KELLER, P.
    settled, 1857, Andrew Co.

KELLY, George W.
    settled, 1841, Holt Co.

KELLY, James F.
    settled, 1836, Marion Co.

KELLY, Luke
    settled in Newton Co.

KELSICK, S. Y.
    settled, 1855, Callaway Co.

KEMP, _____
    settled in Pettis Co.

KEMP, Dudley
    settled, 1831, Callaway Co.

KEMPER, F. J.
    settled, 1844, Cooper Co.

KEMPER, French
    settled, 1832, Lincoln Co.

KEMPER, J. T.
    settled, 1838, Marion Co.

KEMPER, Shumate
    settled in Monroe Co.

KENNEDY, J. A.
    settled in Mercer Co.

KERN, J. W.
    settled, 1868, Clay Co.

KERR, J. M.
    settled in Monroe Co.

KERR, W. D.
    settled in Callaway Co.

KERRICK, R. A.
    settled in Marion Co.

KEYSER, J. F.
    settled in Henry Co.

KIBBLER, A. J.
    settled in Vernon Co.

KIDD, George W.
    settled, 1881, Lewis Co.

KIMBERLIN, F. W.
    settled, 1841, Andrew Co.

KIMBROUGH, John S.
    settled in Henry Co.

KIMLER, Chas. W.
    settled, 1837, Lincoln Co.

KIMLER, John T.
    settled, 1837, Lincoln Co.

KINCAID, J. H.
    settled, 1856, Livingston Co.

KINDIG, Samuel
    settled, 1858, Daviess Co.

KING, George Y.
    1850 Census, Franklin Co.

KING, Mrs. M. H.
    settled, 1847, Lafayette Co.

KINNER?, Eliz.
    settled in Bates Co.

KIRBY, Mill C.
    settled in Randolph Co.

KIRKPATRICK, J. (Reed)
    settled in Barton Co.

KIRKPATRICK, Z. W.
    settled, 1873, Carroll Co.

KNIGHT, W. J.
   settled, 1873, Jasper Co.

KOLLENBURN, J. J.
   settled, 1868, Jasper Co.

KOONTZ, Peter
   settled, 1868, Carroll Co.

KUECKELLAN?, Mrs. M.
   settled, 1837, Jasper Co.

KEN, W. D.
   settled, 1851, Callaway Co.

L

LACY, ____
   settled in Pettis Co.

LACY, J. L.
   settled, 1833, Marion Co.

LAIRD, D.
   settled in Chariton Co.

LAMKIN, S.
   settled, 1851, Marion Co.

LAMPKIN, Ethelbert
   settled in Henry Co.

LAMPKIN, Lucius
   settled in Bates Co.

LANDES, Isabelle
   settled in Pettis Co.

LANE, ____
   settled in Marion Co.

LANE, Dr. A.
   settled, 1854, Franklin Co.

LANE, A. V.
   settled, 1836, Boone Co.

LANE, George W.
   settled, 1827, Marion Co.

LANGDEN, J. N.
   settled in Bates Co.

LANGLEY, George
   settled, 1868, Chariton Co.

LARIMORE, A.
   settled, 1834, Audrain Co.

LARKIN, Izar
   settled, 1852, Jefferson Co.

LATHAM, ____
   settled in Pettis Co.

LAUCK, C. M.
   settled, 1857, Marion Co.

LAY, Mrs. C. B.
   settled, 1854, Chariton Co.

LAY, James H.
   settled in Benton Co.

LAYTON, A. S.
   settled, 1854, Christian Co.

LAZENBY, J. C.
   settled, 1869, Jasper Co.

LEAR, J.
   settled, 1855, Harrison Co.

LEATHERMAN, Z.
   settled, 1856, Lewis Co.

LEAVELL, H. D.
   settled, 1854, Clay Co.

LEE, ____
   settled in Macon Co.

LEE, E. Thomas
   settled in Lafayette Co.

LEE, John
   settled, 1819, Howard Co.

LEE, Reuben
   settled, 1855, Linn Co.

LEE, Richard
. settled in Lafayette Co.

LEFTWICK, J. P.
settled in Henry Co.

LEFTWICK, Jno. W.
settled, 1859, Carroll Co.

LEGG, J. P.
settled in Henry Co.

LEGGETT, J. B.
settled, 1857, Marion Co.

LELAND, John D.
settled in Howard Co.

LELAND, Sarah D.
settled in Howard Co.

LENOIR, S. D.
settled, 1854, Boone Co.

LEOPARD, James A.
settled, 1852, Daviess Co.

LE ROY, J. R.
settled, 1872, DeKalb Co.

LETCHER, Wm. H.
settled in Saline Co.

LEWIS, Abraham
settled in Pike Co.

LEWIS, Benjamin M.
settled in Lafayette Co.

LEWIS, Benjamin W.
settled, 1831, Howard Co.

LEWIS, Charles J.
settled in Lafayette Co.

LEWIS, James W.
settled, 1850, Chariton Co.

LEWIS, James W.
settled in Lafayette Co.

LEWIS, Mrs. James W.
settled, 1831, Howard Co.

LEWIS, Mahala
settled in Caldwell Co.

LEWIS, Thomas M.
settled in Lincoln Co.

LEWIS, Thomas W.
settled in Lafayette Co.

LEWIS, William
settled, 1866, Chariton Co.

LEWIS, William J.
settled, 1835, Lincoln Co.

LEWIS, William R.
settled, 1872, Bates Co.

LEWRIGHT, John Steptoe
1850 Census, Franklin Co.

LEWRIGHT, Wm. Price
1850 Census, Franklin Co.

LIGON, Daniel
settled, 1836, Lewis Co.

LILLARD, W. C.
settled, 1842, Lafayette Co.

LINDENBERGER, C.
settled in Pike Co.

LIPSCOMB, H. D.
settled, 1834, Marion? Co.

LITTLE, Alba
settled in Bates Co.

LITTLE, Geo. W.
settled in St. Charles Co.

LIVESAY, Fountain
settled in Lafayette Co.

LIVINGSTON, A. F.
settled in Monroe Co.

LLYONS, E.
    settled, 1838, Linn Co.

LOBBAN, W. P.
    settled in Randolph Co.

LOGAN, A. L.
    settled in Christian Co.

LONG, J. E.
    settled, 1869, Johnson Co.

LONG, James W.
    settled, 1876, Cooper Co.

LONG, Sarah
    settled in Monroe Co.

LONG, W. M.
    settled, 1866, Cooper Co.

LONG, William
    settled in Cooper Co.

LOUGH, Levi
    settled, 1870, Greene Co.

LOVE, James
    settled in Macon Co.

LOVE, James M.
    settled in Cedar Co.

LOVERMAN?, W. O.
    settled in Shelby Co.

LOVING, A. S.
    settled in Warren Co.

LOWNDES, W. O.
    settled in Shelby Co.

LUCAS, A. C.
    settled in Newton Co.

LUCK, H. L.
    settled, 1857, Lincoln Co.

LUCKETT, Thomas H.
    settled in St. Charles Co.

LUNCEFORD, ____
    settled in Cedar Co.

LUNCEFORD, J. W.
    settled in Newton Co.

LUSHER, Lewis
    settled, 1844, Chariton Co.

LUTTRELL, L. P. S.
    settled, 1830, Jackson Co.

LYELL, T. P.
    settled in Shelby Co.

LYON, James H.
    settled, 1867, Andrew Co.

LYON, Wm. J.
    settled, 1854, Cedar Co.

M

McBRIDE, A. T.
    settled, 1856, Harrison Co.

McBRIDE, James A.
    settled, 1849, Jackson Co.

McCALL, R. H.
    settled in Callaway Co.

McCALL, W. S.
    settled, 1834, Callaway Co.

McCALLISTER, K?
    1850 Census, Franklin Co.

McCALLISTER, T.
    settled, 1856, Sullivan Co.

McCARROLL, W. J.
    settled, 1870, Callaway Co.

McCARTY, John
    settled, 1871, Greene Co.

McCHESNEY, Thomas
    settled, 1842, Lafayette Co.

McCHESNEY, Thomas S.
    settled, 1842, Lafayette Co.

McCHESNEY, W. K.
    settled, 1859, Lafayette Co.

McCHESNEY, (Family)
    settled in Pettis Co.

McCLANAHAN, ___
    settled, 1856, Buchanan Co.

McCLEARY, J. S.
    settled, 1852, Montgomery Co.

McCLEOD, John Bell
    settled, 1857, Marion Co.

McCLINTIC, ___
    settled in Bates Co.

McCLINTIC, Moses
    settled, 1844, Marion Co.

McCLINTIC, Wm. S.
    settled, 1844, Marion Co.

McCLUNG, ___
    settled in Pettis Co.

McCLURE, Rufus A.
    settled, 1835, Greene Co.

McCLURE, Wm.
    settled in Pettis Co.

McCONKEY, (Family)
    settled, 1845, Gentry Co.

McCORMAC, Levi
    settled, 1865, Randolph Co.

McCORMACK, James
    settled in Bates Co.

McCORMICK, Isaac
    settled, 1838, St. Charles Co.

McCORMICK, John
    settled, 1846, Pike Co.

McCOWAN?, ___
    settled, 1875, Jasper Co.

McCOWEN, L.
    settled, 1877, Newton Co.

McCULLOCK, R. A.
    settled, 1831, Cooper Co.

McCULLOCK, Robert
    settled, 1835, Cooper Co.

McCULLOUGH, James
    settled, 1853, Chariton Co.

McCUTCHAN, J. N.
    settled, 1857, Monroe Co.

McCUTCHEN, Joseph N.
    settled, 1836, Lewis Co.

McCUTCHEN, Wm. M.
    settled, 1876, in Mo.

McDANIEL, Jennie
    settled in Atchison Co.

McDANIEL, Reuben E., Judge
    settled, 1841, Cooper Co.

McDANIEL, Wm.
    settled, 1865, Pike Co.

McDONALD, A. J.
    settled, 1857, Lafayette Co.

McDONALD, C. A.
    settled in Ray Co.

McDONALD, D. P.
    settled, 1875, Randolph Co.

McDONALD, Jno. B.
    settled, 1866, Lafayette Co.

McDONALD, M. F.
    settled, 1854, Ray Co.

McDOUGAL, H. C.
    settled, 1866, Daviess Co.

McELROY, John
    settled in Atchison Co.

McFADEN, R. F.
　settled, 1839, Knox Co.

McGEORGE, J. C.
　settled, 1860, Harrison Co.

McGOWAN, ____
　settled, 1833, Barton Co.

McHANEY, D.
　settled, 1849, Monroe Co.

McILHANEY, Marshall
　settled, 1846, Lafayette Co.

McKEE, J. H.
　settled, 1875, Shelby Co.

McKINNEY, ____
　settled in Barton Co.

McKINZIE, Polly
　settled, 1836, Boone Co.

McKLINTIC, J.
　settled, 1856, DeKalb Co.

McLEY, J. H.
　settled, 1850, Harrison Co.

McMILLIAN, D. V.
　settled in Benton Co.

McNEEL, Jno.
　settled, 1837, Lafayette Co.

McNUTT, Jno.
　settled, 1853, Monroe Co.

McPHATRIDGE, ____
　settled, 1881, Cooper Co.

McPHERSON, B.
　settled, 1854, Macon Co.

McQUEEN, W. P.
　settled, 1871, Carroll Co.

McQUIR, E. L.
　settled, 1830, Pike Co.

McREYNOLDS, Jno.
　1860 Census, Christian Co.

McWILLIAMS, Andrew
　1850 Census, Franklin Co.

MACE, Chris. Hanibal
　settled, 1856, Cedar Co.

MADDEN, G. W.
　settled, 1846, Clay Co.

MADDOX, James
　settled, 1834, Marion Co.

MADDOX, Thomas J.
　settled, 1838, Callaway Co.

MADDY, W.
　settled, 1859, Harrison Co.

MAGGART, S.
　settled, 1841, Sullivan Co.

MAGRUDER, W. B.
　settled, 1839, Shelby Co.

MAIDEN, N. L.
　settled, 1869, Greene Co.

MAIDEN, Noah L.
　settled in Barry Co.

MAINE, H. D.
　settled, 1868, Jackson Co.

MAJOR, ____
　settled in Lafayette Co.

MALLORY, J. H.
　settled, 1837, Lafayette Co.

MALLORY, L. M.
　settled, 1846, Carroll Co.

MALONEY, D. C.
　settled, 1860, Franklin Co.

MANNING, W. L.
　settled, 1837, Livingston Co.

MARKSBURY, ___
  settled in Pettis Co.

MARQUIS, Geo. W.
  settled, 1858, Cedar Co.

MARSH, John A.
  settled, 1841, Pike Co.

MARSHALL, ___
  settled in Pettis Co.

MARSHALL, Flemming
  settled, 1831, Cooper Co.

MARSHALL, H. D.
  settled, 1842, Putnam Co.

MARSHALL, Harriett
  settled, 1856, Holt Co.

MARTIN, Ann J.
  settled in Bates Co.

MARTIN, C. W.
  settled in Linn Co.?

MARTIN, C. W.
  settled, 1838, Lincoln Co.

MARTIN, Chas. Wm.
  settled in Linn Co.?

MARTIN, E. B.
  settled, 1867, Callaway Co.

MARTIN, G. P.
  settled, 1856, Schuyler Co.

MARTIN, J. P.
  settled, 1855, Warren Co.

MARTIN, S.
  settled, 1871, Warren Co.

MARTIN, W.
  settled, 1866, Clay Co.

MASON, Jno.
  settled, 1827, Chariton Co.

MASSEY, R. M.
  settled, 1871, Clay Co.

MASTERS, S. C.
  settled, 1869, Pike Co.

MATHEWS, Edwin F.
  settled, 1840, Pike Co.

MATSON, D. M.
  settled, 1837, Pike Co.

MATTOX, C. W.
  settled, 1858, Callaway Co.

MAUPIN, C. J. T.
  settled, 1849, Shelby Co.

MAUPIN, Chauncey C.
  settled in Henry Co.

MAUPIN, W. H.
  settled, 1835, Monroe Co.

MAXWELL, A. L.
  settled, 1836, Lafayette Co.

MAXWELL, Edley C.
  settled in Bates Co.

MAXWELL, J. N.
  settled, 1836, Lafayette Co.

MAXWELL, W. M.
  settled, 1837, Linn Co.

MAXWELL, W. P.
  settled, 1862, Daviess Co.

MAY, J. A.
  settled, 1842, Franklin Co.

MAY, Robert H., Sr.
  1850 Census, Franklin Co.

MAY, Stephen T.
  1850 Census, Franklin Co.

MAY, W. H.
  1850 Census, Franklin Co.

MAYS, S. H.
   settled in Randolph Co.

MAYWETHER, S. L.
   settled, 1829, Pike Co.

MEALER, James
   1850 Census, Franklin Co.

MEDSHER, Sarah
   settled, 1870, Greene Co.

MELVIN, A. O.
   settled, 1837, Franklin Co.

MENEFEE, ____
   settled, 1851, Ray Co.

MENEFEE, R. M.
   settled, 1860, Livingston Co.

MENTON?, Anderson
   1860 Census, Cedar Co.

MERRIWETHER, Mrs. M. C.
   settled, 1853, Pike Co.

METCALF, Rev. John T.
   settled in Howard Co.

METCALF, W. A.
   settled in Chariton Co.

MICKENS, E.
   settled, 1837, Ray Co.

MIERS, Elias
   settled, 1857, Lafayette Co.

MILAM, Daniel
   settled, 1832, Randolph Co.

MILLER, E. H.
   settled, 1873, Cooper Co.

MILLER, H. J.
   settled, 1859, Howard Co.

MILLER, J. W.
   settled, 1854, Daviess Co.

MILLER, James W.
   settled, 1862, Lafayette Co.

MILLER, R. H.
   settled, 1846, Clay Co.

MILLER, W. E.
   settled in Chariton-Howard Co.

MILLNER, ____
   settled in Pike Co.

MILLNER, Wm. P.
   settled in Pettis Co.

MILLS, Henry W.
   settled, 1840, Cooper Co.

MILLS, James C.
   settled in Adair Co.

MINEAR, Ellis
   settled, 1877, Schuyler Co.

MING, Wm. O.
   1850 Census, Franklin Co.

MINNICK, Isaac
   settled, 1841, Daviess Co.

MINOR, Edward
   settled, 1843, Cooper Co.

MINOR, N. P.
   settled, 1843, Pike Co.

MITCHELL, Alexander
   settled, 1842, Howard-Chariton

MITCHELL, C. P.
   settled, 1856, Monroe Co.

MITCHELL, J. B.
   settled, 1836, Macon Co.

MITCHELL, R. W.
   settled, 1859, Linn Co.

MITCHELL, Robert F.
   settled, 1873, Lafayette Co.

MONTAGUE, W. J.
    settled, 1873, Franklin Co.

MONTGOMERY, Hugh S.
    settled in Barry Co.

MOORE, Adolphus
    settled, 1857, St. Charles Co.

MOORE, Charles W.
    settled, 1876, Buchanan Co.

MOORE, George
    settled, 1874, Cooper Co.

MOORE, H.
    settled, 1875, Warren Co.

MOORE, Si M.
    settled, 1854, Chariton Co.

MOORMAN, Zachary B.
    settled, 1858, Carroll Co.

MOOREHEAD, Garrett W.
    settled, 1836, Ray Co.

MOOREHEAD, S. M.
    settled, 1836, Chariton Co.

MORGAN, J. J.
    settled, 1865, Cooper Co.

MORRIS, Charles W.
    settled, 1866, Pike Co.

MORRIS, Jno. T.
    settled in Pike Co.

MORRIS, R.
    settled, 1854, Harrison Co.

MORRIS, Wm.
    settled, 1847, Holt Co.

MORRIS, ____
    settled in Holt Co.

MORRISON, ____
    settled in Bates Co.

MORTON, N. B.
    settled, 1868, Cooper Co.

MOSELY, Wm.
    settled, 1828, Boone Co.

MOSER, Jacob
    settled in Holt Co.

MOSLEY, T.
    settled, 1839, Monroe Co.

MOSS, T. Benton
    settled in Jefferson Co.

MOTLEY, S. C.
    settled, 1838, Lincoln Co.

MOXLEY, Soloman R.
    settled, 1836, Lincoln Co.

MOYER, A.
    settled, 1865?, Linn Co.

MOYER, George
    settled, 1876, Andrew Co.

MOYES, Geo.
    settled, 1876, Andrew Co.

MURPHY, Travis
    settled in St. Charles Co.

MURRAY, E. M.
    settled, 1865, Franklin Co.

MURRY, S. F.
    settled, 1843, Pike Co.

MURY, Levi
    settled, 1855, Daviess Co.

MUSGRAVE, Arphaxed
    settled, 1840, Clay Co.

MUSSETTER, Sarah
    settled in Lafayette Co.

MYERS, B. W.
    settled, 1856, St. Charles Co.

N

NALLEY, James S.
    settled, 1840, Pike Co.

NALLEY, Thomas J.
    settled, 1845, Lincoln Co.

NANCE, A. W.
    settled in Gentry Co.

NEALE, Lewis
    settled, 1856, Lafayette Co.

NEALE, Penolope
    settled in Chariton-Howard Co.

NEALE, W. G.
    settled, 1849, Lafayette Co.

NEELY, Geo.
    settled, 1855, Cooper Co.

NEFF, T. B.
    settled, 1856, Putnam Co.

NELSON, A. M.
    settled, 1836, Cooper Co.

NELSON, E. D.
    settled, 1836, Cooper Co.

NELSON, R. H.
    settled, 1852, Jackson Co.

NEWBILL, ___
    settled in Pettis Co.

NEWHAM, S. K.
    settled, 1872, Ray Co.

NEWLAND, F.
    settled, 1867, Johnson Co.

NEWMAN, H. A.
    settled, 1856, Randolph Co.

NEWSOM, H.
    settled, 1820, Callaway Co.

NEWTON, L. A.
    settled, 1860, Greene Co.

NICHOLS, J.
    settled, 1873, Pike Co.

NICHOLSON, G. A.
    settled, 1834, Callaway Co.

NICKELL, Francis
    settled, 1865, Lafayette Co.

NOBLE, Joe
    settled, 1855, Callaway Co.

NOEL, J.
    settled, 1849, Holt Co.

NOEL, L. R.
    settled, 1870, Ray Co.

NOFFSINGER, Newton S.
    1860 Census, Cedar Co.

NOFFZINGER, D. C.
    settled, 1845, Ray Co.

NORTH, Flavius J.
    1850 Census, Franklin Co.

NORTH, James C.
    1850 Census, Franklin Co.

NORTHCRAFT, W. J.
    settled, 1838, Clark Co.

NORRIS, G.
    settled, 1856, Callaway Co.

NORTON, William
    settled, 1830, Pike Co.

NUNN, Catherine
    1850 Census, Franklin Co.

NUNN, John G.
    settled, 1829, Lewis Co.

O

OAK, George
    settled, 1858, Cooper Co.

O'BANION, Jno.
    1850 Census, Franklin Co.

OBANNON, W. S.
  settled, 1846, Chariton Co.

O'CONNER, G. W.
  settled in Marion Co.

ODER, Dr. George
  settled, 1870, Monroe Co.

OGDEN, H. T.
  settled, 1850, Pike Co.

O'KANE, Jno.
  settled, 1866, Pike Co.

OLD, Wm. T.
  settled, 1868, Boone Co.

OLIVAR, Morten V. B.
  settled, 1851, Lafayette Co.

OMES, H. J.
  settled, 1835, Monroe Co.

OMOHUNDRO, E. B.
  settled, 1875, Lincoln Co.

OMOHUNDRO, S. J.
  settled, 1875, Lincoln Co.

OREAR, J. B.
  settled in Jasper Co.

OREAR, Jesse
  settled, 1834, Boone Co.

ORNBURN, J. L.
  settled, 1838, Randolph Co.

OSBORN, Cyrus
  settled, 1837, Lafayette Co.

OSBORN, Geo. W.
  settled, 1837, Lafayette Co.

OSBORN, Wm.
  settled, 1850, Franklin Co.

OTEY, N. B.
  settled, 1866, Carroll Co.

OVERFELT, Elijah
  settled, 1845, Callaway Co.

OVERSTREET, ___
  settled in Pettis Co.

OWEN, Edward?
  settled, 1840, Lincoln Co.

OWEN, M. B.
  settled, 1882, Bates Co.

P

PACE, Jim L.
  settled in Bates Co.

PAGE, Geo. W.
  settled, 1860, Howard Co.

PAGE, R. A.
  settled, 1865, Cooper Co.

PAGE, T. N.
  settled, 1857, Daviess Co.

PAINTER, J.
  settled, 1837, Monroe Co.

PAINTER, S. H.
  settled, 1837, Monroe Co.

PALMER, Jno. W.
  settled, 1856, Buchanan Co.

PANKEY, Tom A.
  settled, 1856, Howard Co.

PARKER, Wm. P.
  settled, 1843, Lafayette Co.

PARISH, J. C.
  settled, 1859, Randolph Co.

PARSONS, ___
  settled in Pike Co.

PARSONS, J. W.
  settled, 1837, Shelby Co.

PARSONS, Wm. W.
    settled, 1839, St. Charles Co.

PASLEY, J. W.
    settled, 1867, Callaway Co.

PASLEY, R. D.
    settled, 1867, Callaway Co.

PATTENBURG, Rev. George
    settled, 1867, Lafayette Co.

PATTERSON, ___
    settled in Howard Co.

PATTERSON, J. W.
    settled, 1868, Putnam Co.

PATTERSON, W. H.
    settled, 1858, Linn Co.

PAULDING, W. R.
    settled, 1854, Macon Co.

PAXTON, Tom P.
    settled, 1873, Johnson Co.

PAYNE, ___
    settled in Pettis Co.

PAYNE, ___
    settled, 1847, Lincoln Co.

PAYNE, Cornelius
    1860 Census, Cedar Co.

PAYNE, J. F.
    settled, 1831, Chariton Co.

PAYNE, Jno. S.
    settled, 1867, Callaway Co.

PAYNTER, ___
    settled in Cedar Co.

PAYNTER, Chas. W.
    settled, 1857, Cedar Co.

PEACHER, J. W.
    settled, 1857, Greene Co.

PEACOCK, Jno. H.
    settled, 1855, Lafayette Co.

PEACOK, H. B.
    settled, 1857, Lafayette Co.

PECK, Jno. T.
    settled in Bates Co.

PENNY, Jno. H.
    settled, 1836, Randolph Co.

PERKINS, David
    1850 Census, Franklin Co.

PERKINS, Ira G.
    settled, 1833, Franklin Co.

PERKINS, J. H.
    settled, 1833, Franklin Co.

PERKINS, Jno. D.
    1850 Census, Franklin Co.

PERKINS, Jno. D.
    settled, 1854, Holt Co.

PERKINS, L. R.
    settled, 1856, Chariton Co.

PERKINS, Dr. P. H.
    settled, 1838, Linn Co.

PERKINS, W. B.
    settled, 1833, Franklin Co.

PERSINGER, James
    settled, 1849, Boone Co.

PETERS, Harrison
    1850 Census, Boone Co.

PETERS, Samuel
    settled, 1769, Cooper Co.

PEUGH, H.
    settled, 1860, Boone Co.

PEYTON, ___
    settled in Henry Co.

PEYTON, Mary Catherine Heath
    settled in Cooper Co.

PEYTON, Thomas R.
    settled, 1885, Cooper Co.

PHILLIPS, Ed
    settled, 1860, Pike Co.

PHILLIPS, S. W.
    settled, 1838, Chariton Co.

PHILLIPS, Wm. O.
    settled, 1829, Chariton Co.

PHILLIPS, Wm. T.
    settled, 1869, Greene Co.

PIERCE, ___
    settled in Atchison Co.

PIERCE, D. A. Cln?
    settled in Chariton-Howard Co.

PIERCE, M. P.
    settled in Knox Co.

PIERCE, Mary
    settled in Atchison Co.

PIERCE, Matilda
    1860 Census, Christian Co.

PIERCE, Richard R.
    settled, 1839, Howard Co.

PINKARD, Elias E.
    settled, 1866, Jasper Co.

PIPER, L. T.
    settled, 1839, Greene Co.

PIPER, Samuel
    settled, 1839, Greene Co.

PLEDGE, W. N.
    settled, 1831, Callaway Co.

PLUNKETT, J. D.
    settled in Callaway Co.

POAGE, G. A.
    settled, 1855, Daviess Co.

POAGE, Geo. A.
    settled in Bates Co.

POAGE, J. F.
    settled, 1852, Monroe Co.

POLITTE, Martha
    settled, 1835, Jefferson Co.

POLLARD, G. W.
    settled, 1832, Lincoln Co.

POLLARD, J. W.
    settled, 1869, Audrain Co.

POLLARD, Jno. M.
    settled, 1873, Jasper Co.

POLLARD, M. E.
    settled, 1872, Jasper Co.

POLLARD, W. J.
    settled in Jasper Co.

POLLARD, W. J.
    settled, 1872, Jasper Co.

POLLARD, Wm. H.
    settled, 1835, Pike Co.

POOL, James M.
    settled, 1832, Lafayette Co.

PORTER, A. K.
    settled, 1843, Clay Co.

PORTER, Charles M.
    settled in Lincoln Co.

PORTER, Charles V.
    settled, 1835, Lincoln Co.

PORTER, G. W.
    settled, 1866, Putnam Co.

PORTER, Gilchrist
    settled in Pike Co.

44

PORTER, Martin
    settled in Cooper Co.

PORTER, Tom B.
    settled, 1873, Carroll Co.

PORTER, Wm.
    settled, 1835, Lincoln Co.

PORTER, Wm. H.
    settled in Schuyler Co.

PORTERFIELD, J. W.
    settled, 1851, Andrew Co.

POSTON, Wm.
    settled, 1860, Knox Co.

POWELL, W. T.
    settled, 1843, Lincoln Co.

POWERS, Jno. A.
    1850 Census, Franklin Co.

PRATHER, A. E.
    settled, 1870?, Bates Co.

PRATHER, E. J.
    settled, 1839, Chariton Co.

PRATT, S.
    settled, 1831, Warren Co.

PREWITT, (Family)
    settled, 1829, Lincoln Co.

PRICE, Eliz.
    settled, 1831, St. Charles Co.

PRICE, Emory O.
    settled in Henry Co.

PRICE, Jno.
    settled, 1850, Andrew Co.

PRICE, Jno. H.
    settled, 1836, Greene Co.

PRICE, Col. Jno. H.
    settled in Greene Co.

PRICE, Jno. W.
    settled, 1833, Chariton Co.

PRICE, Peter
    settled, 1855, Holt Co.

PRICE, Pugh Williamson
    settled, 1823, Chariton Co.

PRICE, R. B.
    settled, 1850, Boone Co.

PRICE, R. M.
    settled, 1872, Andrew Co.

PRICE, R. M.
    settled, 1872, Audrain Co.

PRICE, T. J.
    settled, 1839, Cooper Co.

PRICE, Wm. H.
    settled, 1844, Chariton Co.

PRIEST, A. G.
    settled, 1852, Shelby Co.

PRIEST, H. H.
    settled, 1841, Ralls Co.

PRIEST, Jno. A.
    settled, 1841, Ralls Co.

PRIEST, M. J.
    settled, 1836, Shelby Co.

PRIEST, T. S.
    settled, 1841, Shelby Co.

PRIEST, W. M.
    settled, 1842, Monroe Co.

PRIESTLEY, ____
    settled in Benton Co.

PRITCHETT, J. M.
    settled, 1837, Warren Co.

PUGH, Calvin
    settled, 1837, Callaway Co.

PUGH, Madison
    settled, 1837, Callaway Co.

PUGH, Stephen
    settled, 1837, Callaway Co.

PUGH, (Family)
    settled, 1871, Bates Co.

PULLIAM, T. W.
    settled, 1835, Marion Co.

PULLIAM, Thomas,
    settled, 1838, Lewis Co.

Q

QUARRELLS, (Family)
    settled in Henry Co.

R

RAGLAND, J. K.
    settled, 1843, Cooper Co.

RAINES, Allen
    settled in Chariton-Howard Co.

RAINES, James S.
    settled in Chariton-Howard Co.

RAINS, A. M.
    settled, 1831, Marion Co.

RALLS, S. S.
    settled, 1857, Jackson Co.

RALSTON, E. S.
    settled, 1831, Cooper Co.

RANKIN, David
    settled, 1870, Adair Co.

RANKIN, Mrs. E. H.
    settled, 1837, Cooper Co.

RANKIN, James
    settled, 1837, Cooper Co.

RANKIN, T. C.
    settled, 1870, Harrison Co.

RANKIN, Wm.
    settled, 1870, Harrison Co.

RAWLINGS, W. H.
    settled, 1838, Shelby Co.

RAY, A. T.
    settled, 1856, Daviess Co.

RAY, Ephriam
    1860 Census, Christian Co.

RAY, Jno.
    settled in Christian Co.

RAY, Peter
    1850 Census, Franklin Co.?

REAMY, J. M.
    settled, 1842, Marion Co.

RECTOR, A. F.
    settled, 1870, Chariton Co.

RECTOR, B. J.
    settled, 1840, Ralls Co.

RECTOR, B. P.
    settled, 1845, Pike Co.

RECTOR, Jesse H.
    settled, 1839, Ralls Co.

REDWINE, Samuel L.
    settled in Barry Co.

REEDER, Austin
    settled in Bates Co.

REEDER, Joseph
    settled in Bates Co.

REEVES, ____
    settled in Jackson Co.

REID, A. C.
    settled, 1854, Harrison Co.

REID, I. M.
    settled, 1868, Linn Co.

REID, M. L.
    settled, 1874, Jasper Co.

REID, W. A.
    settled in Shelby Co.

REILEY, J. G.
    settled, 1857, Callaway Co.

RENNICK, ____
    settled in Holt Co.

RENOE, H. F.
    settled, 1829, Callaway Co.

REYNOLDS, Bedford
    settled, 1827, Callaway Co.

REYNOLDS, Cornelius (Family)
    settled in Bates Co.

REYNOLDS, Phillip
    settled, 1843, Saline Co.

RHOADS, Geo. J.
    settled in Saline Co.

RHODES, Si? S. T.
    settled in Marion Co.

RHODES, George Jud
    settled, 1841, Saline Co.

RICE, W. D.
    settled, 1854, Ray Co.

RICE, Wm. J.
    1850 Census, Franklin Co.

RICHARDSON, Nathan
    1850 Census, Franklin Co.

RICHARDSON, Phillip
    settled, 1853, Gentry Co.

RIGHT, Roland
    1850 Census, Franklin Co.

RILEY, Mrs. Ruth
    settled, 1838, Buchanan Co.

RILEY, Thomas
    settled in DeKalb Co.

RINEHARDT, Jno. W.
    settled, 1857, Lafayette Co.

RINEHART, S. C.
    settled, 1855, Knox Co.

ROACH, E. G.
    settled, 1840, Pike Co.

ROACH, Thornton
    settled, 1854, Johnson Co.

ROARK, Michael
    1850 Census, Franklin Co.

ROBB, Jno. Michael
    settled in Chariton-Howard Co.

ROBBINS, G. H.
    settled, 1854, Chariton Co.

ROBBINS, Howard
    settled, 1801?, Christian Co.

ROBERTS, Archibald S.
    1850 Census, Franklin Co.

ROBERTS, Edward James
    1850 Census, Franklin Co.

ROBERTS, James R.
    1850 Census, Franklin Co.

ROBERTSON, ____
    settled in Greene Co.

ROBERTSON, Hiram
    settled in Chariton-Howard Co.

ROBERTSON, J. M.
    settled, 1830, Randolph Co.

ROBINSON, C. W.
    settled, 1856, Macon Co.

ROBINSON, Geo. W.
    settled, 1852, Pike Co.

ROBINSON, J. H.
    settled in Newton Co.

ROBINSON, T. W.
    settled in Macon Co.

RODGERS, W. H.
    settled, 1869, Shelby Co.

ROGERS, Jno.
    settled, 1863, Randolph Co.

ROGERS, Mrs. P. F.
    settled, 1841, Greene Co.

ROGERS, R. D.
    settled, 1859, Greene Co.

ROOTES, L. J.
    settled, 1840, Callaway Co.

ROSE, A. P.
    settled, 1866, Greene Co.

ROSE, B.
    settled, 1852, Putnam Co.

ROSE, W. O.
    settled, 1848, Howard Co.

ROSE, Z. L.
    settled, 1869, Pike Co.

ROSEN, S. S.
    settled in Howard Co.

ROTHGEB, S. B.
    settled, 1855, Cooper Co.

ROTHWELL, Jno. C.
    settled, 1859, Johnson Co.

ROYALTY, J. J.
    settled, 1835, Pike Co.

ROYER, Geo.
    settled, 1863, Caldwell Co.

ROYSTON, Jno. H.
    settled in Henry Co.

RUCKER, Ambrose
    1850 Census, Franklin Co.

RUCKER, M. J.
    settled, 1852, Chariton Co.

RUDASILL, ____
    settled in Atchison Co.

RUPERT, M. C.
    settled, 1838, Callaway Co.

RUSK, W. H.
    settled, 1870, Jasper Co.

RUSSELL, J.
    settled, 1858, Clay Co.

RYAN, Daniel
    settled, 1856, St. Charles Co.

RYAN, George M.
    settled, 1849, St. Charles Co.

S

St.CLAIR, Edward S.
    settled, 1857, Howard Co.

St.ROBERTS, H. C.
    settled, 1871, Greene Co.

SALLEE, Pleasant
    settled, 1848, Greene Co.

SAMPLE, G. O.
    settled, 1871, Pike Co.

SANDERS, ____
    settled in Mo.

SANDERS, D. W.
    settled, 1872, Pike Co.

SANDERSON, James A.
    settled, 1850, Pike Co.

SANDERSON, Jno.
    settled, 1874, Pike Co.

SANDRICH, Geo.
    settled, 1865, Jefferson Co.

SAPPINGTON, ____
    settled in Saline Co.

SAPPINGTON, J. A.
    settled, 1857, Ralls Co.

SAUFLEY, (Family)
    settled in Saline Co.

SAUNDERS, D. G.
    settled, 1851, Livingston Co.

SAUNDERS, Jno.
    settled, 1841, Chariton Co.

SAUNDERS, O. B.
    settled, 1854, Andrew Co.

SAVAGE, J. J.
    settled, 1855, DeKalb Co.

SAYERS, A.
    settled in Linn Co.

SAYERS, Jno. L.
    settled, 1838, Greene Co.

SAYERS, M. S.
    settled, 1845, Linn Co.

SAYERS, Thomas W.
    settled, 1840, Greene Co.

SCHOOLER, Ezra Heath
    settled in Atchison Co.

SCHROCK, A. J.
    settled, 1854, Linn Co.

SCHURTZ?, S.
    settled, 1844, Clay Co.

SCOTT, Dr. A. K.
    settled, 1855, Daviess Co.

SCOTT, Alexander
    settled, 1835, Pike Co.

SCOTT, B.
    settled, 1855, Linn Co.

SCOTT, James
    settled, 1843, Holt Co.

SCOTT, Jno. P. (Family)
    settled, 1828, Saline Co.

SCOTT, R. A.
    settled, 1859, Chariton Co.

SCOTT, R. M.
    settled, 1836, Monroe Co.

SCOTT, Sarah J.
    settled Atchison Co.

SCRIGGS, Wm. H.
    settled, 1845, St. Charles Co.

SCRUGGS, W. C.
    settled, 1853, Cooper Co.

SCULL, Mrs. Louisa
    settled in Buchanan Co.

SEAMANS, J. D.
    settled, 1840, Sullivan Co.

SEATON, Jno. R.
    settled, 1854, Pike Co.

SEDWICK, B. W.
    settled, 1857, Holt Co.

SEE, Noah
    settled, 1838, Mercer Co.

SEIBERT, J. W.
    settled, 1871, Macon Co.

SELECMAN, S. R.
    settled, 1844, Andrew Co.

SETTLE, A.
    settled in Bates Co.

SETTLE, C. J.
    settled, 1859, Audrain Co.

SETTLE, H. P.
    settled, 1844, Ray Co.

SETTLE, J. D.
   settled, 1862, Buchanan Co.

SETTLE, M. B.
   settled, 1839, Monroe Co.

SETTLES, D.
   settled, 1858, Boone Co.

SEWELL, F. L.
   settled, 1864, Jackson Co.

SEWELL, John D.
   settled, 1838, Boone Co.

SHACKLETT, Robert
   settled, 1836, Marion Co.

SHAFER, H. P.
   settled, 1873, Harrison Co.

SHAFROTH, Andrew
   settled, 1835, Howard Co.

SHANNON, Wm. L.
   settled, 1844, Livingston Co.

SHARP, James A.
   settled, 1837, Marion Co.

SHARP, Richard N.
   settled, 1831, Marion Co.

SHARP, S. N.
   settled, 1858, Pike Co.

SHAW, A. W.
   settled in Howard Co.

SHAW, W. W.
   settled, 1847, Linn Co.

SHAW, Wm. Webb
   settled in Linn Co.

SHEARER, Simeon
   settled in Vernon Co.

SHELTON, A. M.
   settled in Bates Co.

SHELTON, Jacob
   settled in Montgomery Co.

SHELTON, James David
   settled, 1829, Lincoln Co.

SHELTON, Peachy G.
   settled, 1837, Lincoln Co.

SHEPHERD, J. M.
   settled, 1845, Johnson Co.

SHEPHERD, Jonah H.
   settled in Chariton-Howard Co.

SHEPHERD, M. A.
   settled, 1855, Pettis Co.

SHEPHERD, W. G.
   settled, 1861, Putnam Co.

SHEWALTER, J. D.
   settled, 1848, Lafayette Co.

SHIELDS, E. O.
   settled, 1850, Chariton-
            Howard Co.

SHINN, Austin
   settled, 1848, Carroll Co.

SHINN, Asa
   settled, 1867, Marion Co.

SHINN, N.
   settled, 1869, Linn Co.

SHIRKEY?, S. B.
   settled, 1869, Ray Co.

SHORE, Jno. T.
   settled, 1866, Cooper Co.

SHROUPER, Jno. W.
   settled, 1868, Lafayette Co.

SHULTS, A. M.
   settled, 1853, Linn Co.

SHUMATE, J. T.
   settled, 1835, Marion Co.

SHUMATE, James
    settled, 1834, Johnson Co.

SILOUSE, Jake
    settled, 1862, Holt Co.

SIMCO, Jno. M.
    settled, 1835, Callaway Co.

SIMCO, R. B.
    settled, 1835, Callaway Co.

SIMMONS, B. F.
    settled, 1853, Lafayette Co.

SIMONS, James T.
    settled, 1837, St. Charles Co.

SIMPSON, W. T.
    settled, 1868, Macon Co.

SISSONS, A. C.
    settled, 1842, Clark Co.

SISSONS, A. M.
    settled in Marion Co.

SISSONS, W. J.
    settled, 1838, Pike Co.

SKELTON, C. W.
    settled, 1855, DeKalb Co.

SLAGEL, James
    settled in Gentry Co.

SLAGEL, S.
    settled, 1855, Randolph Co.

SLAGLE, J. M.
    settled, 1878, Gentry Co.

SLAUGHTER, Alfred
    settled, 1871, Cooper Co.

SLAUGHTER, Martin
    settled, 1844, Lafayette Co.

SLAUGHTER, T.
    settled, 1863, Harrison Co.

SLEMP, Wm. T.
    settled in Atchison Co.

SLONE?, James T.
    settled, 1875, Greene Co.

SMALLWOOD, R. J.
    settled, 1865, Holt Co.

SMELSEY, Sam
    settled, 1854, Clark Co.?

SMILEY, Hugh
    settled, 1869, Monroe Co.

SMILEY, James
    settled, 1841, Monroe Co.

SMITH, A. J.
    settled, 1838, Pike Co.

SMITH, Catherine
    settled, 1853, Johnson Co.

SMITH, Mrs. C. E.
    settled, 1835, Callaway Co.

SMITH, Dan
    settled, 1845, Schuyler Co.

SMITH, E. W.
    settled, 1866, Monroe Co.

SMITH, F. D.
    settled, 1857, Lafayette Co.

SMITH, G. L.
    settled, 1857, Shelby Co.

SMITH, Henry
    settled, 1868, Ralls Co.

SMITH, Hosea
    settled, 1841, Chariton-Howard C

SMITH, J. G.
    settled, 1844, Randolph Co.

SMITH, J. H. B.
    settled, 1873, Sullivan Co.

SMITH, James? H.
   settled, 1856, Cooper Co.

SMITH, Jno. A.
   settled, 1834, Marion Co.

SMITH, Jno. N.
   settled, 1838, Buchanan Co.

SMITH, Joseph
   settled, 1832, Marion Co.

SMITH, Joshua F.
   settled in Franklin Co.

SMITH, J. T.
   settled, 1838, Pike Co.

SMITH, Lucinda
   settled in Bates Co.

SMITH, K. G.
   settled, 1857, Mercer Co.

SMITH, Mary
   settled, 1846, Marion Co.

SMITH, Mary O.
   settled, 1849, Chariton-Howard Co.

SMITH, Nathan A.
   settled in Pettis Co.

SMITH, P. R.
   settled in Newton Co.

SMITH, P. T.
   settled in Newton Co.

SMITH, R. Y.
   settled, 1834, Pike Co.

SMITH, S. I.
   settled, 1865, Audrain Co.

SMITH, Sam L.
   settled, 1855, Lafayette Co.

SMITH, Thomas M.
   settled, 1836, Marion Co.

SMITH, Thomas T.
   settled, 1845, Jackson Co.

SMITH, Wm. H.
   settled, 1832, Pike Co.

SMITH, W. J.
   settled, 1838, Chariton-Howard Co.

SNEED, ____
   settled in Pettis Co.

SNYDER, J. H.
   settled, 1866, Mercer Co.

SNYDER, James A.
   settled in Chariton-Howard Co.

SNYDOR, H. C.
   settled in Lafayette Co.

SOUTHERLAND, W. D.
   settled, 1835, Linn Co.

SPARKS, J. A.
   settled, 1846, Monroe Co.

SPARKS, W. M.
   settled, 1851, Monroe Co.

SPEED, Wm. Pope, Jr.
   settled in Cooper Co.

SPELLMAN, J. A.
   settled, 1847, Boone Co.

SPENCE, E. C.
   settled, 1837, Marion Co.

SPENCER, Perry
   1860 Census, Cedar Co.

SPENCER, ____
   settled, 1866, Chariton Co.

SPINDLE, I. C.
   settled, 1860, Greene Co.

SPIVEY, Levi M.
   settled, 1857, Caldwell Co.

52

SPRAGUE, A. D.
  settled, 1843, Marion Co.

SPURLOCK, G. N.
  settled, 1868?, Andrew Co.

SPURLOCK, M. M.
  settled in Ray Co.

STABUS, Christian
  settled in Chariton Co.

STAFFORD, G. S.
  settled, 1855, Clark Co.

STAFFORD, ____
  settled in Henry Co.

STALCUP, Wm.
  settled, 1835, Monroe Co.

STALLEY, C. P.
  settled in Bates Co.

STALTON, D. E.
  settled, 1856, Putnam Co.

STANDIGER, T.
  settled, 1851, Linn Co.

STANLEY, James W.
  1850 Census, Franklin Co.

STANLEY, Theodore
  settled in Pettis Co.

STAPLES, Dr. T. E.
  settled in Cooper Co.

STARKE, Dryden
  settled, 1834, Cooper Co.

STARKE, J. D.
  settled, 1843, Cooper Co.

STATON?, N. G.
  settled in Putnam Co.

STAUBUS, Christian?
  settled, 1870, Chariton Co.

STEMMONS, W. F.
  settled in Jasper Co.

STEPHENS, G. W.
  settled, 1856, Linn Co.

STEPHENS, Larry C.
  settled in Cooper Co.

STEVENS, A. S.
  settled in Callaway Co.

STEVENS, A. W.
  settled, 1866, Lafayette Co.

STEVENS, Charles H.
  settled, 1836, Lewis Co.

STEWARD, Judge M. A.
  settled in Henry Co.

STEWART, Ausbon
  settled, 1839, Montgomery Co.

STEWART, Thomas
  settled, 1840, Pike Co.

STEWART, W. H.
  settled, 1843, Lewis Co.

STILL, E. C.
  settled, 1837, Macon Co.

STIPES, E. H.
  settled, 1869, Carroll Co.

STOCKTON, Mary S.
  settled in Pettis Co.

STOKES, (Family)
  settled, 1850, Holt Co.

STONE, ____
  settled, 1863, Johnson Co.

STONE, G. H.
  settled, 1843, Linn Co.

STONE, H. G.
  settled, 1866, Linn Co.

STONE, L. C.
  settled, 1855, Warren Co.

STONE, L. D.
  settled, 1852, DeKalb Co.

STONE, M. F.
  settled, 1852, DeKalb Co.

STONE, M.
  settled, 1840, Sullivan Co.

STONE, Ted
  settled, 1825, Marion Co.

STONEBERGER, J.
  settled, 1837, Warren Co.

STRATTON, D. Jno.
  settled, 1856, Chariton Co.

STREET, Jno. M.
  settled, 1838, Carroll Co.

STREIT, Jno. A.
  settled, 1840, Cooper Co.

STROTHER, Susan
  settled, 1858, Pike Co.

SULLINS, Jno.
  settled in Franklin Co.

SULLIVAN, H. M.
  settled, 1853, Chariton Co.

SULSER, A.
  settled, 1856, Putnam Co.

SURFACE, Jno. W.
  settled, 1870, Jasper Co.

SURFACE, Sam
  settled, 1841, Daviess Co.

SUTHERLIN, Nathan
  settled, 1836, Cooper Co.

SWARTZ, S. B.
  settled, 1869, Harrison Co.

SWINNEY, Tom A.
  settled, 1847, Howard Co.

SWINNEY, Wm. D.
  settled, 1858, Howard Co.

SWISHER, Maurice
  settled in Knox Co.

SWISHER, Noah
  settled, 1857, Marion Co.

T

TAGGART, J. J.
  settled, 1858, Johnson Co.

TAGGART, J. J., Jr.
  settled, 1858, Johnson Co.

TALIAFFERO, Robert P.
  settled, 1854, Pike Co.

TALLEY, Jno.? A.
  settled in St. Charles Co.

TANNER, Ben N.
  settled in Chariton Co.

TATE, Jim
  settled, 1842, Marion Co.

TATUM, Geo. H.
  settled, 1855, Howard Co.

TATUM, Jno.
  settled in Chariton-Howard Co.

TAYLOR, Dan
  settled in Shelby Co.

TAYLOR, J. T.
  settled, 1854, Ray Co.

TAYLOR, James S.
  settled, 1868, Mercer Co.

TAYLOR, Jno. H.
  settled, 1871, Jasper Co.

TAYLOR, Thornton
  settled in Chariton-Howard Co.

TERRILL, James
    settled, 1836, Randolph Co.

TERRY, Ben D.
    1850 Census, Franklin Co.

TEVIS, D. W. B.
    settled, 1858, Lafayette Co.

THARP, W. S.
    settled, 1859, Sullivan Co.

THEODORE, Stanley
    settled, 1850, Atchison Co.

THISTLE, Sam T.
    settled, 1840, Johnson Co.

THOMAS, ____
    settled in Lafayette Co.

THOMAS, Jno. L.
    settled in Jefferson Co.

THOMPSON, A.
    settled, 1866, Livingston Co.

THOMPSON, Calvin
    settled, 1872, Jackson Co.

THOMPSON, Elizabeth R.
    settled, 1844, Greene Co.

THOMPSON, J. P.
    settled, 1844, Ray Co.

THOMPSON, John H.
    1850 Census, Franklin Co.

THOMPSON, R. R.
    settled, 1836, Cooper Co.

THOMPSON, Robert
    settled, 1840, Carroll Co.

THOMPSON, S. P.
    settled, 1865, Buchanan Co.

THOMPSON, W. B.
    settled, 1869, Johnson Co.

THOMPSON, W. J.
    settled, 1833, Franklin Co.

THOMPSON, W. L.
    settled, 1850, Randolph Co.

THORNKILL, ____
    settled in Vernon Co.

THORNKILL, Nelson
    settled in Callaway Co.

THORNTON, ____
    settled in Vernon Co.

THORNTON, Evaline
    settled in Bates Co.

THORNTON, W. A.
    settled, 1856, Lafayette Co.

THORNTON, Dr. Wm. T.
    settled in Henry Co.

THREKELD, Eliz.
    settled, 1857, Audrain Co.

THROCKMORTON, R. T.
    settled, 1835, Audrain Co.

THURMAN, Allen
    settled, 1853, Pike Co.

THURMOND, James
    settled, 1832, Pike Co.

TIMBROOK, H.
    settled, 1853, Shelby Co.

TIMMS, J. H.
    settled, 1857, Clay Co.

TINDALL, Obediah
    settled in Mo.

TINSLEY, Addison
    settled, 1849, Pike Co.

TINSLEY, James R.
    settled, 1849, Pike Co.

TINSLEY, S. B.
    settled, 1864, Howard Co.

TIPP, T. F.
    settled, 1869, Monroe Co.

TISDALE, R. H.
    settled, 1843, Chariton Co.

TISDALE, Woodson
    settled, 1830, Boone Co.

TOLSON, ____
    settled in Howard Co.

TOMLINSON, J. B.
    settled, 1850, Newton Co.

TOMPKINS, D. S.
    settled in Cooper Co.

TOMPKINS, Junius
    settled, 1850, Lewis Co.

TOOTHMAN, D.
    settled, 1879, Newton Co.

TORREYSON, J. R.
    settled in Audrain Co.

TORREYSON, Tom T.
    settled, 1866, Audrain Co.

TOTTEN, S. H.
    settled, 1868, Holt Co.

TOWLER, R. F.
    settled, 1830, Marion Co.

TOWLES, A. L.
    settled, 1865, Lewis Co.

TRACY, ____
    settled, 1866, Holt Co.

TRAMMEL, G. W.
    settled in Atchison Co.

TRENT, W. W.
    settled, 1856, Cooper Co.

TREVEY, Robert
    settled in Henry Co.

TRIGG, Frank
    settled, 1845, Lafayette Co.

TRIMBLE, J. M.
    settled, 1873, Audrain Co.

TRIMBLE, James W.
    settled, 1857, Monroe Co.

TRIMBLE, Rev. W. W.
    settled, 1868, Callaway Co.

TRIPLETT, ____
    settled, 1838, Franklin Co.

TRIPLETT, J. C.
    settled, 1853, Putnam Co.

TRIPLETT, W. L.
    settled in Knox Co.

TRIPLETT, Wm. P.
    settled, 1839, Franklin Co.

TUCK, ____
    settled, 1830, Pettis Co.

TUCK, Wm.
    settled, 1830, Greene Co.

TUCKER, D. M.
    settled, 1830, Callaway Co.

TUCKER, Rev. Hartwell
    settled, 1849, Jackson Co.

TUCKER, James R.
    settled, 1855, Macon Co.

TUCKER, W. W.
    settled, 1821, Atchison Co.

TUGGLE, Jno. A.
    settled, 1839, Daviess Co.

TULEY, E. M.
    settled, 1851, Marion Co.

TULEY, Elisha
  settled, 1851, Marion Co.

TULL, Henry
  settled, 1849, Buchanan Co.

TULL, Judge Jno. A. S.
  settled in Lafayette Co.

TURNER, D. H.
  settled, 1836, Pike Co.

TURNER, F. J.
  settled, 1868, Livingston Co.

TURNER, F. N. S.
  settled, 1838, Pike Co.

TURNER, Geo. S.
  settled, 1835, Pike Co.

TURNER, Lucinda
  settled, 1849, Linn Co.

TURNER, Maria
  settled, 1866, Jackson Co.

TURPIN, Mrs. Isabelle
  settled, 1841, Pike Co.

TURPIN, Mrs. M. F.
  settled, 1840, Carroll Co.

TURPIN, R. L.
  settled, 1869, Carroll Co.

TWYMAN, Wm. I.
  settled, 1860, Chariton Co.

TYLER, Henry W.
  settled, 1865, Buchanan Co.

TYLER, John I.
  settled, 1865, Buchanan Co.

TYLER, Richard
  1850 Census, Franklin Co.

TYMAN, ____
  settled in Jackson Co.

V

VAN BIBBER, Mrs. Eliz.
  settled, 1837, Buchanan Co.

VAN BIBBER, Maj. Isaac
  settled in Callaway Co.

VAN BUSKIRK, B.
  settled, 1854, Putnam Co.

VANDEVENTER, W. H.
  settled in Audrain Co.

VANDIVER, J. L.
  settled, 1840, Shelby Co.

VANDIVER, S. A.
  settled, 1840, Shelby Co.

VANDIVER, T. L.
  settled, 1849, Chariton Co.

VANDIVER, W. A.
  settled, 1837, Shelby Co.

VAN NORT, C. W.
  settled, 1841, Shelby Co.

VAN TRUMP, Dan
  settled, 1865, Carroll Co.

VAN TRUMP, J.
  settled, 1859, Ray Co.

VARNER, Isaac
  settled, 1865, Lafayette Co.

VARNER, Joe
  settled, 1855, Cooper Co.

VARNES, ____
  settled in Bates Co.

VAUGHAN, Beverly
  settled, 1847, Greene Co.

VAUGHAN, C. B.
  settled, 1858, Carroll Co.

VAUGHAN, Eliz.
  settled, 1854, Holt Co.

VAUGHAN, Geo.
    settled in Barton Co.

VAUGHAN, Jno.
    settled in Mo.

VAUGHAN, Jones
    settled, 1854, Holt Co.

VAUGHAN, N.
    settled, 1837, Andrew Co.

VAUGHAN, N.
    settled, 1837, Boone Co.

VAUGHAN, Gen. Richard C.
    settled in Lafayette Co.

VIA, M. L. A.
    settled,1828, Mo.

VICKAR, Ben F.
    settled in Lafayette Co.

VINCENT, W. H.
    settled, 1857, Lafayette Co.

VINEYARD, C. W. S.
    settled, 1834, Jefferson Co.

VIOLETT, Edward
    settled, 1855, Johnson Co.

VIRTS?, Henry J. J.
    settled in Mo.

W

WADDLE, John J.
    settled in Lafayette Co.

WADE, Jefferson
    settled, 1875, Newton Co.

WAGNER, G. B.
    settled in Pike Co.

WALE, Dr. H. H.
    settled, 1842, Jasper Co.

WALKER, Ana
    settled in Henry Co.

WALKER, B. J.
    settled, 1859, Jasper Co.

WALKER, F. John
    settled, 1848, Monroe Co.

WALKER, G. H.
    settled in St. Charles Co.

WALKER, J.
    settled, 1862, Clay Co.

WALKER, J. P.
    settled, 1839, Macon Co.

WALKER, James B.
    settled in St. Charles Co.

WALKINS, F. G.
    settled, 1867, Callaway Co.

WALL, Samuel
    settled in Saline Co.

WALLER, F.
    settled, 1862, Clay Co.

WALTERS, J. D.
    settled, 1853, Lafayette Co.

WALTHALL, W. B.
    settled, 1865, Callaway Co.

WALTON, Handon Olney
    1850 Census, Franklin Co.

WALTON, J. W.
    settled, 1868, Howard Co.

WALTON, M. L.
    settled, 1832, Chariton Co.

WALTON, T. H.
    settled, 1832, Chariton Co.

WALTON, Wm. E.
    settled in Bates Co.

WAMPLER, Isaac
    settled, 1868, Holt Co.

WARD, James M.
  settled, 1855, Daviess Co.

WARD, L. R.
  settled, 1833, Barton Co.

WARD, L. R.
  settled in Barton Co.

WARD, T. B.
  settled, 1838, Greene Co.

WASH, R. E.
  settled, 1857, Johnson Co.

WASHINGTON, (Family)
  settled, 1868, Johnson Co.

WATSON, J. S.
  settled, 1840, Callaway Co.

WAUGH, Robert I.
  settled in Howard-Chariton Co.

WAYLAND, Eli
  settled, 1820, Chariton Co.

WAYLAND, J. H.
  settled, 1838, Randolph Co.

WAYLAND, J. H.
  settled, 1821, Howard Co.

WAYLAND, Jerimiah
  settled, 1828, Clark Co.

WAYLAND, Marvin N.
  settled in Chariton-Howard Co.

WAYLAND, Wm.
  settled, 1824, Howard Co.

WAYLAND, Wm.
  settled, 1869, Howard Co.

WEAMS, Bernal?
  1850 Census, Franklin Co.

WEATHERFORD, Sarah
  1860 Census, Christian Co.

WEBB, Geo. W.
  settled, 1838, Monroe Co.

WEBB, J. E.
  settled, 1869, Cooper Co.

WEBB, J. Garland
  settled, 1836, Lafayette Co.

WEBB, James B.
  settled, 1844, Greene Co.

WEBB, Wm. C.
  settled, 1836, Lafayette Co.

WEBER, Micajah
  settled, 1835, Clark Co.

WEEKS, J. H.
  settled, 1851, Callaway Co.

WEEKS, S. T.
  settled, 1851, Callaway Co.

WEEKS, W. P.
  settled, 1851, Warren Co.

WELCH, Thomas A.
  settled, 1866, Carroll Co.

WELDON, W. B.
  settled, 1856, Harrison Co.

WELDON, Z.
  settled, 1856, Harrison Co.

WELLS, E. D.
  settled in Audrain Co.

WELLS, E. P.
  settled, 1873, Mercer Co.

WELLS, H. F.
  settled, 1837, Lincoln Co.

WELLS, J. B.
  settled, 1856, Audrain Co.

WELLS, Peter
  settled, 1857, Howard Co.

WELLS, W. S.
   settled, 1860, Buchanan Co.

WENGER, Sam M.
   settled in Benton Co.

WEST, Mrs. Virginia
   settled, 1837, Boone Co.

WESTON, Everett
   settled, 1837, Buchanan Co.

WHALEY, David
   settled, 1835, Callaway Co.

WHEELER, Malcom
   settled, 1820, Franklin Co.

WHEELER, R. J.
   settled, 1832, Linn Co.

WHEELER, Mrs. Kate
   settled, 1870, Johnson Co.

WHITE, A. P.
   settled, 1854, Knox Co.

WHITE, D. B.
   settled, 1836, Howard Co.

WHITE, Gilaman
   settled, 1859, Clark Co.

WHITE, Horace Y.
   1850 Census, Franklin Co.

WHITE, M. W. S.
   settled in Knox Co.

WHITE, T.? M.
   settled, 1869, Audrain Co.

WHITE, Thomas B.
   settled, 1861, Carroll Co.

WHITE, Wm. C.
   settled, 1842, Lafayette Co.

WHITE, Wm. M.
   settled, 1870, Daviess Co.

WHITLOCK, Tom E.
   settled, 1850, Pike Co.

WHITTEN, Jacob M.
   settled, 1869, Howard Co.

WHITTEN, John P.
   settled in Chariton-Howard Co.

WHITTEN, Thomas
   settled, 1855, Howard Co.

WICKS, N. D.
   settled, 1857, Pettis Co.

WICKS, Ras.?
   settled, 1858, Howard Co.

WIEDNYER?, Jno. M.
   settled in Henry Co.

WILHITE, ____
   settled in Bates Co.

WILKERSON, ____
   settled, 1836, Pettis Co.

WILKINSON, A.
   settled, 1854, Johnson Co.

WILKINSON, J.
   settled, 1855, Johnson Co.

WILKINSON, S. W.
   settled, 1839, Franklin Co.

WILKINSON, T. P.
   settled, 1842, Chariton Co.

WILKINSON, T. S.
   settled, 1838, Franklin Co.

WILLIAMS, Festus E.
   settled, 1866, Pike Co.

WILLIAMS, Geo.
   settled, 1835, Howard Co.

WILLIAMS, N. G.
   settled, 1871, Jackson Co.

WILLIS, Robert H.
    settled in Saline Co.

WILLOUGHBY, _____
    settled in Bates Co.

WILLS, Jno. Thomas
    settled in Howard Co.

WILLS, W. W.
    settled, 1831, Howard Co.

WILSON, F. T.
    settled, 1845, Monroe Co.

WILSON, R. M.
    settled, 1837, Shelby Co.

WILSON, S. B.
    settled, 1884, Gentry Co.

WINDSOR, J.
    settled, 1866, Howard Co.

WINDSOR, Loften
    settled, 1847, Cooper Co.

WINE, Leroy
    settled, 1842, Macon Co.

WINGFIELD, L.
    settled, 1873, Jasper Co.

WISLEY, J. D.
    settled in Chariton-Howard Co.

WITACRE, J. F.
    settled, 1877, Adair Co.

WITACRE, J. T.
    settled, 1879, Adair Co.

WITHERS, Henry M.
    settled, 1871, Jackson Co.

WITTEN?, Owen R.
    settled, 1850, Pike Co.

WITTEN?, W. M.
    settled, 1859, Daviess Co.

WOLFF, L. C.
    settled, 1856, Sullivan Co.

WOLVERTON, J. S.
    settled, 1857, Randolph Co.

WOMACK, Allen
    settled, 1854, Callaway Co.

WOMMACK, Richard
    settled, 1823, Linn Co.

WONDERLY, W. W.
    settled, 1858, Knox Co.

WOOD, _____
    settled in Lafayette Co.

WOOD, C. W.
    settled, 1831, Franklin Co.

WOOD, David P.
    1850 Census, Franklin Co.

WOOD, E. P.
    settled in Mo.

WOOD, N. W.
    settled, 1860?, Callaway Co.

WOOD, F. P.
    settled, 1871, Pike Co.

WOOD, J. E.
    settled, 1857, Ray Co.

WOOD, J. Ward
    settled in Marion Co.

WOOD, James R.
    settled, 1831, Franklin Co.

WOOD, L. S.
    settled, 1868, Shelby Co.

WOOD, Thomas
    settled in Mo.

WOOD, Maj. W. L.
    settled, 1844, Johnson Co.

WOODSON, Blake L.
    settled, 1877, Jackson Co.

WOODSON, Geo. T.
    settled, 1841, St. Charles Co.

WOODSON, J. C.
    settled, 1852, Pike Co.

WOODSON, Tom P.
    settled, 1855, Pike Co.

WOOLRIDGE, ____
    settled in Cooper Co.

WORRELL, R. B.
    settled, 1856, Monroe Co.

WRIGHT, Adams
    settled, 1837, Howard Co.

WRIGHT, C. M.
    settled, 1857, Mercer Co.

WRIGHT, G. W.
    settled, 1836, Ralls Co.

WRIGHT, Joe. E.
    settled, 1874, Ralls Co.

WRIGHT, R. H.
    settled, 1847, Pike Co.

WRIGHT, S. W.
    settled, 1842, Schuyler Co.

WRIGHT, Townsend
    settled in Chariton-Howard Co.

WRIGHTMAN, T. J.
    settled, 1866, Greene Co.

Y

YAGER, Thomas W.
    settled, 1840, Randolph Co.

YATES, T. B.
    settled, 1856, Daviess Co.

YOAKUM, Cread
    settled, 1887, Mercer Co.

YOAKUM, George
    settled in Bates Co.

YOUNG, ____
    settled, 1836, Lafayette Co.

YOUNG, J. T.
    settled, 1854, Linn Co.

YOWELL, J. B.
    settled, 1837, Monroe Co.

YOWELL, Robert G.
    settled, 1856, Monroe Co.

Z

ZIEGLER, ____
    settled, 1867, Holt Co.

62

ADDENDA PART I

Page Column Entry

13	1	5	Add:	Settled, 1867.
13	2	10	Add:	Settled, 1843.
22	2	5	Add:	Settled, 1836.
30	2	14	Add:	Settled, 1833.
31	1	1	Add:	Settled, 1868.
37	1	11	Add:	Settled, 1834.
40	1	3	Add:	Settled, 1868.
43	1	17	Add:	Settled, 1818.
48	2	8	Add:	Settled, 1863.
52	2	4	Add:	Settled, 1868, Callaway Co.
55	1	16	Add:	1855, and read: Boone Co. for Atchison Co.
57	1	7	Add:	Boone Co., after 1828.

ERRATA PART I

2	1	9	Read:	Settled, 1831.
4	1	10	Read:	"Sr." after BATES
6	1	15	Read:	"J" for "P", and add: Settled, 1858.
7	2	15	Read:	1866 for 1856.
16	2	8	Read:	James for "J" and Wellington for "W".
17	2	17	Read:	E. G. for E. B.
18	2	14	Read:	William for "W".
22	1	15	Read:	Graham, P. M.
28	2	7	Read:	Humphreys, W. F.
31	1	4	Read:	Audrain Co. for Andrew Co.
33	1	8	Read:	1844 for 1854.
39	1	8	Read:	Lock B. for Zachary B.
45	2	3	Read:	1868 for 1856.
49	1	14	Read:	Lincoln Co. for Linn Co.
49	1	15	Read:	Lincoln Co. for Linn Co.
50	2	6	Read:	Smilieu for Smiley.
55	2	15	Read:	Boone Co. for Atchison Co.
60	2	4	Read:	Lincoln Co. for Linn Co.

PART II

VIRGINIA COUNTIES FROM WHICH SETTLERS CAME AND THE MISSOURI COUNTIES IN WHICH THEY LIVED.

From Patrons' Lists in Missouri Atlases

compiled by

A. Maxim Coppage III

ACCOMAC COUNTY

Melvin	Franklin

ALBEMARLE COUNTY

Abell	Daviess
Brown	Callaway
Brown	Montgomery
Burgess	Monroe
Caruthers	Boone
Dameron	Lincoln
Dodson	Lincoln
Draffen	Cooper
Fagg	Pike
Ferguson	Randolph
Gardner	Linn
Gentry	Pettis
Hall	Lewis
Hall	Boone
Harden	Greene
Harris	Montgomery
Hensley	Boone
Herring	Callaway
Johnson	Franklin
Johnson	Linn
Kirby	Randolph
Lane	Boone
Leavell	Clay
Lewis	Lincoln
Lobban	Randolph
McCullock	Cooper
Maupin	Henry
Maupin	Shelby
Morris	Callaway
Mury	Daviess
Porter	Saline
Reiley	Callaway
Shakelford	DeKalb
Sharp	Marion

Simco	Callaway
Terrill	Randolph
Thomas	Jefferson
Tompkins	Lewis
Via	Boone
Wash	Lafayette
Wayland	Randolph
Wells	Lincoln
Wood	Franklin
Wood	Lafayette

ALLEGHANY COUNTY

Given	Randolph
Persinger	Boone

AMELIA COUNTY

Ligon	Lewis

AMHERST COUNTY

Berford	Lewis
Duncan	Boone
Goodrich	Montgomery
Higginbotham	Lincoln
Martin	Clay
Old	Boone
Omohundro	Lincoln
Tucker	Callaway
Wood	Franklin

APPOMATTOX COUNTY

Thornkill	Callaway
Watkins	Callaway
Watkins	Callaway

AUGUSTA COUNTY

Anderson	Clark
Bull	Harrison
Carson	Putnam
Cook	Monree
Dalhouse	Johnson
Estill	Howard
Fisher	Howard
Flory	Holt
Glen	Holt
Graham	Boone
Ham	Harrison
Hanger	Monroe
Harlow	Barton
Heizer	Monroe
Henderson	Callaway
Hogsett	Caldwell
Humphrey	Callaway
Kerr	Monroe
Kindig	Monroe
McCutchan	Monroe
McCutchen	Lewis
Maupin	Monroe
Miller	Daviess
Oder	Monroe
Patterson	Putnam
Scott	Chariton
Sewell	Boone
Smiley	Monroe
Spindle	Greene
Stabus	Chariton
Sullivan	Chariton
Trimble	Callaway
Trimble	Monroe
Wilson	Saline
Wright	Ralls

ALEXANDRIA -- ARLINGTON

Langley	Chariton
Mercer	Jackson
Stevens	Lewis

BATH COUNTY

Bratton	Boone
Callihan	Clark
Davis	Shelby
Davis	Schuyler
Gray	Boone
Hill	Callaway

Laird	Chariton
McClintic	Bates

BEDFORD COUNTY

Allen	Callaway
Austin	Carroll
Boswell	Boone
Clayton	Harrison
Creasy	Carrell
Douglas	Audrain
Ewing	Lafayette
Gilpin	Callaway
Goldy	Jasper
Hardman	Holt
Leftwick	Carroll
Mattox	Callaway
Nance	Gentry
Noble	Callaway
Omes	Monroe
Overfelt	Callaway
Pollard	Jasper
Saunders	Livingston
Shaw	Lincoln
Staples	Putnam
Stevens	Callaway
Turpin	Carroll
Weeks	Callaway
Whittington	Callaway
Wingfield	Jasper
Wright	Randolph

BOTETOURT COUNTY

Allen	Daviess
Allen	Pike
Baker	Franklin
Bean	Greene
Brown	Linn
Crawferd	Randolph
Denton	Greene
Firestone	Cedar
Fullheart	Putnam
Hughs	Monroe
Kimberlin	Andrew
Noffsinger	Cedar
Vaughan	Andrew
Wrightsman	Greene

BRUNSWICK COUNTY

Johnson	Franklin
Webb	Greene

BUCKINGHAM COUNTY

Corley	Callaway
Johnson	Franklin
Lewis	Chariton
Lewis	Howard
Maddox	Callaway
Moyer	Linn
Sallee	Greene
Spencer	Chariton
Wheeler	Howard

CAMPBELL COUNTY

Anderson	Callaway
Bristow	Carroll
Cannefax	Greene
Crumpacker	Putnam
Herndon	Chariton
Hunter	Franklin
Hunter	Jefferson
Lee	Lafayette
Martin	Lincoln
Moorman	Carroll
Owen	Lincoln
Phillips	Chariton
Plunkett	Callaway
Thompson	Carroll
Triplett	Franklin
Towles	Lewis
Weber	Chariton

CAROLINE COUNTY

Barlow	Harrison
Luck	Lincoln
Massey	Clay
Newton	Greene
Smith	Johnson

CARROLL COUNTY

Johnson	Franklin
Mallory	Daviess
Robbins	Clark
Stone	Franklin

CHARLOTTE COUNTY

Coleman	Franklin
May	Franklin
Mosley	Monroe
Price	Boone
Roberts	Franklin
Watson	Callaway

CHESTERFIELD COUNTY

Flowering	Linn
Hatcher	Marion
Hix	Randolph
Lyons	Linn
Nicholson	Callaway

CLARKE COUNTY

Orear	Boone

CULPEPER COUNTY

Cook	Chariton
Coppage	Henry
Duncan	Cooper
Duvall	Ray
Edwards	Boone
Elly	Callaway
Garnett	Saline
Graves	Lewis
Green	Ray
Harper	Montgomery
Hawkins	Monroe
Hickerson	Andrew
Hines	Randolph
Hopkins	Callaway
Hord	Callaway
Jeffries	Lewis
Kemper	Lincoln
Lear	Harrison
McDonald	Ray
McGowan	Barton
Major	Lafayette
Menefee	Livingston
Porter	Pike
Pulliam	Lewis
Reeves	Jackson
Russell	Clay
Settle	Audrain
Sparks	Montgomery

Spellman	Boone	Clarkson	Linn
Thomas	Lafayette	Coppage	Carroll
Tucker	Boone	Coppage	Atchison
Tutt	Lafayette	Daniel	Lincoln
Vaughan	Carroll	Dearing	Schuyler
Wale	Jasper	Diggs	Howard
Willis	Saline	Dodd	Ralls
		Dowell	Monroe

CUMBERLAND COUNTY

Alderson	Jefferson	Downing	Schuyler
Allen	Chariton	Eddins	Monroe
Blanton	Linn	Edmonds	Shelby
Larimore	Audrain	Fant	Warren
Wilkinson	Chariton	Garrison	Shelby
		Glascock	Ralls
		Glascock	Marion
		Gulick	Jasper

ESSEX COUNTY

Brown	Howard	Guthridge	Chariton
Cauthorn	Audrain	Hampton	Lewis
McGeorge	Harrison	Hickerson	Randolph
Mitchell	Ch.-Howard	Hickerson	Howard
Mitchell	Linn	Hurt	Saline
		Keeble	St. Charles
		McKinzie	Boone

FAIRFAX COUNTY

Blackburn	Callaway	Martin	Callaway
Carter	Boone	Mickens	Ralls
Clark	Holt	Moxley	Lincoln
Coffer	Andrew	Murphy	St. Charles
Ferguson	Ch.-Howard	Nelson	Cooper
Fleming	Jefferson	O'Bannon	Chariton
Fox	Ch.-Howard	Parr	Monroe
Gill	Cooper	Payne	Callaway
Lane	Marion	Payne	Lincoln
Lane	Pike	Payne	Marion
Selecman	Andrew	Priest	Monroe
Stewart	Lewis	Priest	Shelby
Windsor	Cooper	Priest	Ralls
		Rector	Monroe
		Rector	Shelby
		Rector	Ralls

FAUQUIER COUNTY

Ashby	Chariton	Reid	Monroe
Ball	Pike	Reid	Shelby
Baylis	Ralls	Rogers	Cooper
Beal	Clay	Rogers	Shelby
Blackwell	Carroll	Rupert	Callaway
Bowie	Ralls	Saunders	Chariton
Busey	Saline	Settle	Ray
Butler	Ralls	Sisson	Pike
Chancellor	Howard	Smith	Marion
Chapman	Chariton	Smith	Monroe
		Smith	Monroe
		Smoot	Marion
		Sparks	Monroe

Strother	Pike
Triplett	Putnam
Waddle	Pike
Waller	Clay
Wine	Macon
Wine	Marion

FLOYD COUNTY

Light	Cedar

FLUVANNA COUNTY

Black	Clark
Clements	Chariton
Haislip	Montgomery
Harrison	Callaway
Johnson	Marion

FRANKLIN COUNTY

Adkins	Boone
Allen	Callaway
Ashbire	Livingston
Bell	Callaway
Bon Durant	Warren
Boone	Ch.-Howard
Boothe	Callaway
Bradley	Callaway
Brooks	Callaway
Burdett	Callaway
Craighead	Callaway
Dudley	Callaway
Freeman	Holt
Gilbert	Callaway
Gwyn	Monroe
Hodges	Callaway
Kemp	Callaway
Lavender	Montgomery
McCall	Callaway
Marshall	Putnam
Martin	Warren
Pasley	Callaway
Pemberton	Adair
Pinkard	Jasper
Pollard	Jasper
Webb	Monroe
Weeks	Warren
Wright	Mercer

FREDERICK COUNTY

Besker	Ralls
Christie	Lewis
Dunaway	Monroe
Elsea	Lafayette
Gibson	Carroll
Griffin	Ralls
Griffith	Jasper
Hiner	Saline
Holliday	Shelby
Hoover	Andrew
Hudson	Callaway
Loughead	Putnam
McCleod	Marion
McCormac	Randolph
Magruder	Shelby
Metcalf	Chariton
Price	Holt
Shepherd	Ch.-Howard
Smith	Mercer
Van Nort	Shelby
Vasse	Randolph
Watson	Lewis
Young	Linn

GILES COUNTY

Biggs	Greene
Cooksey	Mercer
Hale	Livingston

GLOUCESTER COUNTY

Mitchel	Howard

GOOCHLAND COUNTY

Green	Daviess
Minor	Pike
Pledge	Callaway
Priest	Ralls
Tuggle	Daviess
Vaughan	Lafayette

GRAYSON COUNTY

Pugh	Linn
Schooler	Atchison

Stone	Linn

GREENE COUNTY

Finks	Howard
Good	Harrison
Loving	Warren

HALIFAX COUNTY

Anderson	Montgomery
Bates	Franklin
Bates	Ray
Brogan	Randolph
Bruce	Audrain
Carlton	Callaway
Chandler	Greene
Crews	Lincoln
Hawkins	Franklin
Hendley	Franklin
Hughs	Callaway
Jennings	Montgomery
Lenoir	Boone
McCarty	Greene
Powell	Lincoln
Reynolds	Callaway
Scott	Monroe
Stewart	Lewis
Street	Carroll
Tatum	Callaway
Throckmorton	Audrain
Trammel	Boone
Tuck	Greene
Weston	Buchanan
Wilkinson	Franklin
Wommack	Lincoln

HENRICO COUNTY

Bourquenat?	Saline
Eubank	Greene

HENRY COUNTY

Arnold	Clark
Bassett	Monroe
Burris	Chariton
Edwards	Howard
Edwards	Warren
Jarrett	Greene
Martin	Warren
Nunn	Lewis

Pace	Bates
Perkins	Linn
Smith	Schuyler
Staples	Cooper
Tucker	Jackson
Wells	Mercer

HIGHLAND COUNTY

Stewart	Montgomery

KING GEORGE COUNTY

Holmes	Boone

LOUDOUN COUNTY

Hammer	Worth

LOUISA COUNTY

Bagby	Holt
Diggs	Ch.-Howard
Gibson	Cooper
Lasley	Cooper
Mitchell	Monroe
Perkins	Holt
Perkins	Randolph
Perkins	Franklin
Smith	Randolph
Thompson	Franklin
Tisdale	Boone
Wood	Franklin

MADISON COUNTY

Blakenbaker	Ch.-Howard
Blakley	Monroe
Field	Clay
Finks	Howard
Hoffman	Bates
Hord	Monroe
Jones	Callaway
McCallister	Sullivan
Taliaffero	Cooper
Tatum	Ch.-Howard
Tipp	Monroe
Wayland	Ch.-Howard
Wayland	Clark
Yager	Randolph
Yowell	Monroe

MECKLENBURG COUNTY

Boyd	Greene
Brame	Henry
Cadle	Franklin
Jeffries	Franklin
Vaughan	Greene

MONTGOMERY COUNTY

Baskerville	Bates
Beckner	Greene
Berry	Putnam
Biggs	Greene
Cooper	Sullivan
Gordon	Montgomery
Hall	Chariton
Harrison	Audrain
Henderson	Cedar
Howerton	Bates
Savage	De Kalb
Surface	Jasper

NELSON COUNTY

Brooks	Andrew
Jackson	Chariton
Jacobs	Boone
Jenkins	Bates
Johnson	Ch.-Howard
Shields	Pike
Shields	Ch.-Howard
Tucker	Randolph
Turner	Linn
Wood	Pike

NORTHUMBERLAND COUNTY

Booth	Boone
Hull	Randolph
Lampkin	Bates
Lampkin	Henry
Leland	Howard

ORANGE COUNTY

Ancell	Randolph
Blakley	Chariton
Collins	St. Charles
Fyfer	Boone
Goodlett	Henry

Hawkins	Saline
Head	Randolph
Lay	Randolph
Lewis	Chariton
Mansfield	Randolph
Mason	Chariton
Peacher	Greene
Porter	Carroll
Porter	Clay
Quensberry	Saline
Reynolds	Saline
Rhoads	Saline
Robertson	Randolph
Rogers	Randolph
Rucker	Chariton
Smith	Audrain
Southerland	Linn
Threkeld	Audrain
Twyman	Chariton
Wayland	Chariton
Webb	Howard
Webb	Cooper
Whitlock	Pike
Wright	Ralls

PAGE COUNTY

Britton	Lincoln
Brubaker	Cooper
Burner	Lafayette
Carpenter	Andrew
Fristoe	Buchanan
Gibbons	Monroe
Griffith	Holt
Hershberger	Daviess
Keyser	Henry
McCullough	Chariton
Murray	Franklin
Rothgeb	Cooper
St. Roberts	Greene
Sedwick	Holt
Stoneberger	Warren
Varner	Lafayette
Wood	Callaway

PATRICK COUNTY

Edens	Barry
Harris	Worth
Hudson	Carroll
Jones	Sullivan

Manning	Livingston	Wells	Lincoln
Slaughter	Harrison		

PITTSYLVANIA COUNTY

Blanks	Linn
Carter	Greene
Carter	Lincoln
Carter	Warren
Dews	Lincoln
Garnett	Lincoln
Gregory	Callaway
Hampton	Montgomery
Harper	Audrain
Irby	Greene
Jones	Warren
Patterson	Linn
Pollard	Lincoln
Pritchett	Warren
Shelton	Lincoln
Shelton	Montgomery
Stewart	Warren
Walton	Howard
Weldon	Harrison

*

PRINCE EDWARD COUNTY

Adams	Callaway
Baldwin	Henry
Dail	Linn
Ellington	Chariton
Elam	Chariton
Fore	Linn
Fuqua	Chariton
Pankey	Howard
Powers	Franklin
Price	Chariton
Rogers	Greene
Walthall	Callaway
Walton	Chariton
Woolridge	Saline

PRINCE WILLIAM COUNTY

Compton	Clay
Davis	Audrain
Keach	Ralls
McDaniel	Cooper
McDaniel	Saline
Mathews	Randolph
Mosely	Boone
Renfroe	Callaway

RICHMOND
(City and County)

Bell	Bates
Bon Durant	Warren
Child	Ray
Cootes	Cooper
Cox	Carroll
Ellis	Cooper
Evans	Pettis
Helsick	Callaway
Lee	Linn
McDonald	Randolph
Saunders	Andrew
Stanley	Pettis
Van Bibber	Buchanan
White	Bates

ROANOKE COUNTY

Jones	Greene
Kern	Clay
McClanahan	Buchanan
Payne	Chariton
Politte	Linn
Ray	Daviess
Richards	Gentry
Walker	Clay

ROCKBRIDGE COUNTY

Clarkson	Ch.-Howard
Henderson	Pettis
Hickman	Monroe
Jenks	Daviess
McClure	Pettis
McCutchen	Lewis
McNutt	Monroe
Ornburn	Randolph
Shafer	Harrison
Shaw	Randolph
Taylor	Mercer
Trimble	Audrain
Turpin	Carroll

* ## POWHATAN COUNTY

Branch	Greene

ROCKINGHAM COUNTY

Arey	Jasper
Beasley	Boone
Bowman	Ray
Brenneman	Jasper
Brock	Carroll
Dever	Boone
Dinkle	Saline
Freeland	Montgomery
Garber	Jasper
Gregory	Mercer
Holsinger	Linn
Keller	Audrain
Kirkpatrick	Carroll
Koontz	Carroll
Lough	Greene
Newham	Ray
Noel	Holt
Saufley	Saline
Scull	Buchanan
Shirkey	Ray
Sisson	Clark
Smallwood	Holt
Smelsey	Clark
Stokes	Holt
Van Trump	Carroll
Van Trump	Ray
Wampler	Holt
Welch	Carroll

RUSSELL COUNTY

Alexander	Linn
Browning	Linn
Dorton	Ray
Hamilton	Chariton
Hart	Mercer
Horton	Chariton
Price	Greene
Robbins	Chariton
Thompson	Ray

SCOTT COUNTY

Bledsoe	Jefferson
Dixon	Lincoln
Eaken	Jefferson
Hilton	Barry
Mace	Cedar

SHENANDOAH COUNTY

Baker	De Kalb
Bashor	Andrew
Everly	Chariton
Fansler	Harrison
Glick	Andrew
Glick	Holt
Helsley	Carroll
Hines	Randolph
Huston	Lincoln
Johnson	Randolph
Long	Monroe
Moore	Chariton
Silouse	Holt
Surface	Daviess
Varner	Lafayette

SPOTSYLVANIA COUNTY

Allen	Pike
Alsop	Howard
Ames	Jefferson
Anderson	Pike
Bronaugh	Clay
Corbin	Clay
Layton	Christian
Penny	Randolph
Rootes	Callaway

STAFFORD COUNTY

Blackburn	Harrison
Ficklin	Randolph
Fisher	Howard
Gill	Clay
Hore	Randolph
Lane	Franklin
Rose	Putnam

SURRY COUNTY

Speed	Cooper

TAZEWELL COUNTY

Brooks	Harrison
Currin	Livingston
Deskin	Linn
Gibson	Daviess
Grieves	Atchison

Harmon	Bates
Harrison	Holt
Higginbotham	Warren
Jones	Harrison
Love	Macon
Maxwell	Bates
Maxwell	Daviess
Maxwell	Linn
Milan	Randolph
Rogers	Harrison
Sayers	Linn
Sayers	Greene
Shannon	Livingston
Thompson	Livingston
Ward	Greene
Wilson	Gentry
Wynn	Daviess

WARREN COUNTY

Balthis	Chariton
Fristoe	Buchanan
Gardener	Johnson
Loughead	Putnam
Settles	Boone

WASHINGTON COUNTY

Chapman	Callaway
Cooper	Carroll
Duff	Greene
Fields	Linn
Glen	Caldwell
Head	Howard
Houston	Carroll
Little	Boone
Livingston	Monroe
McChesney	Lafayette
McClure	Greene
Madden	Clay
Maiden	Barry
Marshall	Holt
Montgomery	Barry
Piper	Greene
Porterfield	Andrew
Scott	Holt
Smith	Ralls
Wheeler	Franklin

WESTMORELAND COUNTY

Hutt	Lincoln
Lyell	Shelby

WYTHE COUNTY

Bridgemon	Holt
Buck	Greene
Cormany	Andrew
Davis	Monroe
Felty	Lincoln
Frogge	Buchanan
Hill	Carroll
Howard	Ch.-Howard
Pugh	Callaway
Reeder	Bates

MISCELLANEOUS

Blackwell	Southwest Va. to Jeffers
Clark	Winchester to Lincoln
Robertson	Near Washington, D. C.
Smith	Mint Springs, Va., to Pe

PART III

1850 CENSUS RECORDS OF SOME MISSOURI COUNTIES

SHOWING NAMES OF HEADS OF FAMILIES BORN IN VIRGINIA

compiled by

A. Maxim Coppage III

BOONE COUNTY

Barnett, Athanasus	42
Barnett, Jesse E.	45
Barnett, William	36
Basye, James	29
Duncan, Spicey	51
(incomplete)	

BUTLER COUNTY

Balis, James	35
Booten?, Dr. Wm.	40
Cheatham, Robert	41
Con, Mary	62
Davis, Thomas	42
Eudaby, John	39
Ferguson, Nimrod	47
Gravens, Charles	39
Haines, John	40
Helm, John	67
Inman, Polly	37
Kearby, Nancy	19
Roberts, George	18
Roberts, Moses	27
Roberts, Thomas	21
Rowe, Jane	27
Scott, Eve	49
Scott, John	17
Seal (Teal), Thomas	50
Spurlock, John	47
Vandover, Theodrick	33
Vandover, William	35
Vinson, Archibald	43
Walton, John	44
Watson, Catherine	46

CAMDEN COUNTY

Abott, Amy	52
Baker, William	41

Brooks, Samuel	67
Clark, Daniel	56
Clayton, John W.	36
Cobb, James	35
Coffee, Kissiah	69
Coloney?	49
Crain, Francis	54
Eakin, Saul	39
Folia?, Thomas	57
Foster, Williamson	66
Hampton, Thomas	49
Hit, John	65
Hobbs, John	18
Holdren, Morel?	51
Hurst, L. B.	63
Jackson, Richard	53
Lints	60
Lowell, Jesse	54
Merideth, David	58
Morgan, Thomas	76
Newberry, William	55
North, Elizabeth	65
North, Nathan	40
North, Thomas	65
Northrip, William	50
Oder, John	40
Osborn, Ambrose	76
Parish, Thomas	60
Richardson, Thomas	12
Robinson, George	48
Russell, George	78
Snider, John	59
Starr, Aaron	51
Stone, James	48?
Tinsley, William	61
Tucker, Fields	46
Webb, Arah	67

74

DODGE COUNTY
(merged with Putnam before 1860)

Basket, Robert K.	35
Bonce?, Garnet?	71
Calfee, John	17
Calfee, William	47
Castuk?, Nancy	77
Castuk?, William	54
Crumpacker, John	17
Crumpacker, John	65
Hadin, William	87
Landis, John B.	40
Rodgers, Lewis I.	52
Shanklin, William	40
Wadkins, William	69

DUNKLIN COUNTY

Buckwith, Eliza	47
Callaway, James	30
Cauldy?, El___	57
Clifton, Hardy?	28
Huston (Austin?), John	44
Lane?, Jesse	56
Marsh, John	30
Moore, Howard	57
Moore, Jesse	23
Moore, William	25
Parkinson, Robert	45
Shelton, Gilbert	64
Welch, Sarah	44
___ssy, Nathaniel	30

GASCONADE COUNTY

Allen, William Y.	35
Arthur, John B.	35
Branson, Valentine	39
Branson, William	47
Ca___, ____	63
Davis, Peter	27
Elridge, Nesmond	51
Fisher, Nichols?	22?
Haines, Lester	35
Hanna?, A.	33
Harrison, John B.	41
Humphrey, Benjamin	30
Jenkins, Hedgeman	55
M___, Charles	46
Mc___, Edward	55

McMillian, Daniel	30
McMillian, John	48
Mason, Thompson	41
Maupon, William	63
Powell, Thomas L.	41
Powell, William	17
Price, Samuel	69
Reynolds, Charles	52
Robinson, John	21
Scantling?, Robert S.	30
Sharkly, Thomas	55
Smith, Isaac	46
Smoth?, Thomas W.	37
Souden, Jacob	60
Stemp, Leonard	21
Stemp, Perry	26
Stradford, ____	49
Thomas, John	67
Ticklett, ____	43

LACLEDE COUNTY

Bidderhack, Daniel	57
Burten?, William	33
Craddock, Richard R.	17
Cradock, E___m	54
Davis, George V.	39
Davis, Robins?	41
Denis, Isaac	28
Dunne?, Thomas	57
Finch, William	40
Fletcher, Daniel A.	44
Harrison, James W.	42
Housewright, ____	28
Huff, Peter	52
Hugh?, William	45
Hu___lanb?, James	51
Northrip, A.	55
Osborn, Nelson	16
Osborn, Stephen	48
Paradise, John	65
Peary?, Burwell	75
Rodgers, Nathaniel K.	35
Sanders, William	44
Smith, William H.	50
Thurman, John	46
Traylor, Henry M.	32
Traylor, Peter	68
Vernon, Miles	63
Williamson, Isaac	47
Wineby?, Jennings	35

MISSISSIPPI COUNTY

Bailey, Charles	20
Beckwith, Marmaduke	43
Beckwith, Quiros	50
Beckwith, Richard	51
Beckwith, Underwood	55
Brown, Ellen	43
Chiverdaker, Isaiah	21
Clannahan, A. M.	53
Dalton, Timothy	34
Daugherty, Isaiah	21
Daugherty, Mary	45
Daugherty, Wm.	23
Ellis, Richard	53
Gilbert, Amos	39
Gillispie, Lewis H.?	20
Goode, W. W.	22
Hardin, Richard	40
Hays, J. B. S.	
Howell, Allen	36
Howell, C.	45
Jones, John F.	34
Keen?, Samuel	50
Lockheart, J. A. (fem.)	23
Lunstall, John	83
Lunstall, Lynch	50
Millar, Abe	70
Millar, Abe	34
Myars, Sarah	53
Newman, A. R.	37
Oaks, Rebecca	50
Overton, James M.	40
Parker, Samuel	42
Poindexter, Dr. Lewis	24
Ramsey, Rebecca	50
Robeson, Prudence	39
Sayers, Wm.	55
Stout?, Hezekiah	68
Taylor, M. F.	43
Thomas, Jane	40
Thomas, Wm.	37
Waugh, James R.	32
White, Robert	40
Winn?, John P.	41
___, E.	54

OZARK COUNTY

Blankenship, Wm. H.	25
Brow__?, Thomas S.	37
Bundyne, Amos	70

Campbell, James	42
Fleetwood, Isaac	40
Flores, Abijah	48
Flores, Isaac	74
Fritz, John	23
Gouldy, Charles	49
Herndon, George	56
Hughes, Leith	51
Hutph___?, Joseph	54
McVey, James?	64
Ply, Jacob	29
Riley, Zachiniah?	60
R___, Nathaniel	50
Sievert?, Peter	36
Stone, Fleming	
Stone, Thomas	55
Stone, Wm.	28
Thomas, Kinnel?	51
Todd, Preston	36
Wilson, ____	62
Young, John	

POLK COUNTY
(not completely searched)

Abbott, Joseph	65
Able, John	40
Ailstock, George H.	39
Alexander, Alexander M.	53
Alexander, Charles M. L.	13
Alexander, Claborne	26
Alexander, David L.	16
Alexander, Edmund M.	25
Alexander, James	19
Anderson, Nathaniel	32
Ball, William C.	29
Barkley, Samuel	48
Becker, Preston	68
Blakley, John	50
Blakley, Robert	79
Bland, Elliott	36
Bolt, Charles	55
Childers, James	73
Churnley, Robert	64
Crump, Madison	39
Davis, Bales	32
Derogrett, John	60
Devin, Clayton	56
Devin, John	34
Devin, Wm. R.	60
Dillaplain, John	50
Dowell, George L.	67

Ewing, Arthur	47	Luk?, William	63
Evans, Robert	52	McMullian, Thomas	69
Falkins, James	47	Miller, John	69
Fausher, Wm.	46	Milton, Joel	51
Flint, Ezekiel	42	Mitchell, Samuel	44
Flint, Samuel	8	Nelson, Susan	14
Flint, Wm.	35	Newberry, Joseph	40
Frieze, Jacob	63	Newport, Richard	55
Goodson, Joushia	59	Norris, Moses	44
Gordon, Noah	72	Oaks, Charles F.	50
Green, Wm.	36	Payne, John M.	35
Hambilton, Elijah	59	Prewitt, Richard	84?
Hambilton, Isaiah	51	Reed, Sarah	68
Hagerman, Benjamin	36	Reed, Thompson	40
Haiegsore?, John R.	36	Riley, Abraham	57
Harper, Zachens?	60	Riley, Catherine	51
Hendricks, Gibson	55	Robertson, Rice	39
Hess, Noah	41	Scaggs, Richard	69
Heydon, Nancy	76	Shinell, Samuel R.	53
Holden, Bledsoe	56	Smith, Daniel V.	53
Horn, Peter	65	Smith, Richard	70
Hughes, Leonard	65	Therman, ____	
		Thomas, Joseph	45
PULASKI COUNTY		Vinson, Anna	55
		Wayman, John	45
Arthur, Wm.	54	Wayman, Thomas	43
Baker, Henry	46	Westlake, Polly	54
Blakenship, Julia	38	Wright, Isaac?	64
Bryant, Richard B.	35	Wynn, Richard	55
Bryant, Willie O.	50		
Click, Robert	37	**REYNOLDS COUNTY**	
Cliburne, Andrew	22		
Colter, Thomas	60	Asher, David	91
Coppedge, William	81	Bailey, Morgan	58
Cowrie?, Robert B.	22	Black, George	36
Cox, Amos?	73	Black, Robert	33
Cradwich, Peter?	72	Boyd, John	48
Deer, Lovell	48	Brooks, James	36
Dodd, Josiah	63	Byers, John	53
Douglas, Samuel	36	Carpenter, James Y.	45
Edgar, John E.	68	Cotton, Aaron	70
Evans, Archibald	69	Dennison, Joseph	42
Fisher, John	37	Ford, Charles	43
Fuler, Siemon	42	George, A. G.	44
Green, Thomas	24	Hanger, Samuel	28
Grigsby, Samuel	45	Helvy, Jacob	60
Hanks, Rowley	30	Helvy, John	37
Hood, William	30	Helvy, Wm.	15
Howell, James	33	Hurst, Daniel	60
Johnson, Thomas	66	Latham, Ed	28
Kitchen, Anthony	72	Latham, Jno.	5

Latham, Moses	2	Radford, Millender	29?
Latham, Robert	34	Satterfield, Ed M.	89
Latham, Wm.	13	Shaw, Nancy	46
McMillian, Edward	45	Slade, James A.	35
Miner, Labbon	59	Stricklan , John C.	50
Murrel?, Joseph	60	Stricklan, Thomas	44
Norris, John	26	Tanner, Wm.	47
Nuckles, Thomas D,	30	Wadlow, Elijah	43
Pennington, Reeany	37	Williams, Wm. G.	48

ADDENDA PART II

ALBEMARLE COUNTY

Henry	Callaway
Vineyard	Jefferson
Wood	Johnson

FAUQUIER COUNTY

Clarkson	Boone
Kemper	Monroe

ORANGE COUNTY

Nelson	Cooper
Stephens	Linn

BEDFORD COUNTY

Turner	Livingston

ERRATA PART II

p. 63, column 1
Read: Damerson, Lewis Co., for Lincoln Co.
Read: Dodson, Lewis Co., for Lincoln Co.

p. 64, column 1
Read: Kindig, Daviess Co., for Monroe Co.
Read: Smileiu for Smiley.
Read: Staubus for Stabus.
column 2
Read: Gooldy for Goldy.
Read: Ormes for Omes.

p. 70, column 2
Read: Politte, Jefferson Co., for Linn Co.

PART IV

TOMBSTONE INSCRIPTIONS, OBITUARIES, CENSUS AND OTHER RECORDS

compiled by

Ilene Sims Yarnell

Mt. Nebo Church of God, 5 miles N.W. of Versailles, Mo., organized 25 Oct., 1891, Howcreek Township, Morgan Co., Mo. This church is inactive at present; the cemetery is fenced; the church yard and cemetery are mowed regularly. Mrs. Lewis Jones, Versailles, Mo., resides near this little country church.

WILLIAM HUGHES	ELIZA HUGHES
Born Buckingham Co., Va., 1774	Born Buckingham Co., Va., 1784
Died Morgan Co., Mo., 1844	Died Morgan Co., Mo., 1854
age 70 yrs.	age 70 yrs.

Concord Church, organized 10 May, 1817, Concord Cemetery, 6 miles S. of Boonville, in Cooper Co., Mo. Luke Williams, b. Aug., 1776, Colony of Virginia, settled in Cooper Co., Mo., 1816, was the first minister to preach at this Concord Baptist Church. (Cooper Co., Mo., Atlas, 1877, p. 17; "History of Cooper Co., Mo.," by Levens and Drake, 1876, pp. 58, 61, 112.

ALL ON ONE TOMBSTONE

Conrad Harness, born Hardy Co., Va., March 27, 1811; married Elizabeth Ann Tucker April 9, 1835; died March 29, 1898.
Edward Bates Harness, Aug. 22, 1856; June 25, 1901.
Laura H. Harness, April 11, 1942.
Elizabeth Ann Tucker Harness, born in Hampshire Co., Va., April 13, 1817; died May 3, 1897.

Hopewell Union Church Cemetery, rural, E. of Versailles, Mo. This church was organized in 1866 in Moreau Township and is active at the present time with Rev. Walter Miller, Minister. (1963) A picture of this church will be included in the book "Missouri Historical Sites," by the State Historical Society, Columbia, Mo.

MORELAND AND HUNTER LOT

Mark, son of William Cyrus and Elizabeth Susan Gunn, Aug. 14, 1851; Aug. 23, 1865, 14 yrs.
Elizabeth Susan (Moreland), 2nd wife of Shores P. Hunter, Sept. 14, 1831; June 29, 1917, born in Lynchburg, Va.

Isabell P. Moreland, born 1813, Amherst, Va.; d. Aug. 29, 1904.

Elizabeth Lee, wife of Andrew Moreland, born May 21, 1796, Amherst, Va.; d. 1868.

Andrew Moreland, born 1782, Lancaster Co., Va.; died 1859.

W. F. Moreland, born in Amherst Co., Va., Aug. 1, 1828; married to M. M. Williams, March 8, 1859; died March 25, 1885.

Cline Family Cemetery near the Henry Grupe farm, Florence, Morgan Co., Mo. This cemetery was in the field across the road from Mr. Grupe's home and he faithfully cared for this plot during his lifetime but he died Oct., 1962, at age 83.

Doctor Jacob Cline, born Va.; came to Morgan Co., Mo., before 1843; died Nov. 22, 1864, age 53 yrs. 2 m. 25 d.

Tabitha Ard, wife of Jacob Cline, born Ky., Oct. 11, 1807; d. Nov. 14, 1878.

These are mentioned in Baker's "History of Morgan Co., Mo.," 1907, p. 94.

Versailles, Mo., Cemetery

Peter R. Burns, Mason, born July 23, 1818, Va.; died Morgan Co., Mo., May 6, 1890.

Christiana Argenbright, born Augusta Co., Va., Aug. 23, 1776; died Morgan Co., Mo., June 19, 1867.

John Argenbright, born April 1, 1799, Augusta Co., Va.; died May 30, 1860, age 61 y. 2 m. (Stone broken into.)

Catherine J., wife of John Argenbright, born Aug. 23, 1804, Augusta Co., Va.; died Oct. 5, 1872, Morgan Co., Mo. 68 y 1 m 12 d.

Dooley Cemetery, rural, S.W. of Eldon, Miller Co., Mo.

James Dooley, born Bedford Co., Va., Feb. 14, 1760. Emigrated to Maury Co., Tenn., 1800. In 1829, he moved to Miller Co., Mo. He died Nov. 26, 1863.

Woods Cemetery, private, on a farm in Moreau Township, East of Versailles, Mo. This farm was owned several years ago by Rixey Eckert of Versailles. The cemetery may be seen from Highway 52. The house on this farm is one of the earlier homes in this county and is included in "Missouri Historical Sites."

Dr. P. G. Woods, born Dec. 19, 1844, Franklin Co., Va., son of Samuel H. Woods and wife, Sicily (Patterson) Woods, who came to Morgan Co., Mo., Dec., 1855.

Samuel H. Woods, born May 28, 1798; d. July 13, 1876.

Wife, Sicily Patterson Woods, born July 3, 1807; died Aug. 28, 1868.

Cemetery of Olive Branch Baptist Church, established in 1892, S. of Syracuse, Morgan Co., Mo. It was inactive for several years but is starting services again as a Mission. (1963)

Elmyra Hampson, born in Va., about 1842, died _____.

BUNCETON, MO., CEMETERY

Benjamin Franklin Doran, born March 8, 1837, Hampshire Co., Va. Note: Benjamin Franklin Doran, son of Lucy Green (Fry) and Joseph Doran.

Joseph Doran, son of Sarah (Reed), b. Va., and Alexander Doran (born Jan. 28, 1760, Morris Co., N. J.; died May 26, 1844; served in Rev. War).

Sarah Doran, dau. of Alexander and Sarah (Reed), married Sept. 30, 1819, Thomas Moore, Sr. (b. 1774), as his second wife and had three children born in Va.: Rebecca Moore, John Moore and Eliza Moore. These children are buried in Morgan County, Mo.

Benjamin Letchworth of the Virginia Continentals, born Hanover Co., Va., Oct. 17__; married in Va., 1782. Rev. War Soldier. Private under Capt. Thomas Johnson and Colonels Hugh Mercer and Thomas Marshall. Received pension. Grave was marked by a big tree in Shawnee Bend on Osage River near Versailles, Mo. Grave was moved when Lake of the Ozark was made. A descendant, Dorsey Letchworth, lives in Versailles.

OBITUARIES

Mrs. Elizabeth Hord, aged 85, died Feb. 20, 1897, near Harrisburg, Mo. She was wife of Daniel Hord and came from Virginia in the 1830's. She had a son, T. B. Hord.

Dr. John T. Bailey, aged 73, died in 1897, at the home of a daughter, Mrs. W. N. Wine of Fayette, Mo. He was born Jan. 1, 1824, Campbell Co., Va., and came to Boone Co., Mo., in 1837, and moved to Howard Co., Mo., in 1854. He was a member of the Knights Templar and the Christian Church.

O. W. Carter died July 4, 1921, Fortuna, Mo.; burial in Masonic Cemetery, Tipton, Mo. He was born April 13, 1830, Danville, Va., and married Dec. 30, 1888. His son is Virgil Carter, a Dry Goods Merchant of Fortuna, Mo.

Mary Charles, dau. of Andrew and Jane Atkeson, died Christmas Day, 1952, age 92 years. She was born in Charleston, W. Va., Feb. 21, 1840; resided at Tipton, Mo., where she was a charter member of the Methodist Church. She married John D. Charles, Sept. 19, 1870.

Dr. J. Denzil Bowles, son of W. T. Bowles, born Richmond, Va., July 24, 1873; died Sept. 20, 1912; buried in Masonic Cemetery, Tipton, Mo. He married Nora Snodgrass. He came to Tipton, Mo., in 1873.

Hiram Kaylor Hobbs died June 22, 1946, at Fortuna, Mo., age 83. He was born April 5, 1865, Abbingdon, Va., and married Jan. 10, 1894, Nancy Cunningham, who died June 20, 1931. He remarried Sept. 1, 1932, Mrs. Orthe Strother. He belonged to Flag Springs Baptist Church, Moniteau Co., Mo., and is buried in its cemetery.

J. F. Woodyard died Jan. 28, 1933, Fortuna, Mo. He was born April

28, 1853, in Wood Co., W. Va., and married Sarah Boggs in 1875. He came to Fortuna during the mining boom. They had 10 children.

Josiah B. Williams, born Jan. 2, 1806, Norfolk, Va.; died Feb. 3, 1882, at Versailles, Mo., age 72 y 1 m 1 d.

Elizabeth Madole Williams, born Logan Co., Va., April 21, 1813; died Versailles, Mo., April 18, 1868, age 54 y. 20 d. Josiah B. and Elizabeth (Madole) Williams were married Nov. 17, 1831; their children were all born in Logan Co., Ky.; moved to Morgan Co., Mo., 1851. (Elizabeth Madole had two brothers, Samuel and Hiram Madole, and one sister, Mrs. Polly Madole Clayton Adcock, all settled in Morgan Co., Mo.)

FOSTER BIBLE RECORD

Minggo Foster, born Aug. 24, 1884 (operated the elevator at Clarksburg, Mo.)

In this Bible was the death notice of Miles Allee, maternal grandfather of Minggo Foster. Services held at the Baptist Church, Sunday, Nov. 6, 1898; buried in the Allee Cemetery 5 miles N.W. of California, Mo.

I was told that Minggo Foster's father was Lashley Foster. This Bible is the possession of Mrs. Minggo Foster, Clarksburg, Mo.

Ref.: "History of Missouri," 1889. Moniteau Co. section, p. 908. Miles Allee, born Feb. 7, 1822. His father, William Allee was born in Ky. and came to Mo. in 1821. William married Nancy Hill, born in Va.

1850 CENSUS, MORGAN CO., MO.

74.	William Ellis	65 Va.
	Nancy	57 Va.
	Mary	25 Va.
	Harriet	23 Va.
	James	22 Va.

1850 CENSUS, MILLER CO., MO.

63.	William Philips	56 Ky.
	Lucinda	55 Va.
	John	18 Ky.
	Thomas	17 Mo.
	Susan	14 Mo.
	Elisa	12 Mo.
	Henry	9 Mo.
	Philadelphia	5 Mo.

1850 CENSUS, MONITEAU CO., MO.

163.	Robert Allison	48 Va.
	Mary	42 Va.
	John	18 Va.
	Martha	14 Mo.

Hannah	13 Mo.	270.	Stephen Adair	37 Va.
Charles	11 Mo.		Marian	32 Ala.
Nancy	2 Mo.		William	14 Mo.
Judith	7 Mo.		Nancy	10 Mo.
Rheda	4 Mo.		Thurston	7 Mo.
			Porter	5 Mo.

1860 CENSUS, MORGAN CO., MO.

731.	John Hanby	82 Va.	625.	Syracuse, Mo.	
	Cecil	57 No. Car.		Hickman Estes	55 Ky.
	John	12 Mo.		Martha Estes	54 Ky.
	Mary	9 Mo.		Mary Estes	81 Va.
				Martha Sims	27 Mo.
867.	Jacob Arisman	65 Pa.		Henry Sims	26 Mo.
	Malinda	55 Va.		Jim	7 Mo.
	Frank	15 Mo.		Eliza	2 Mo.
				Nancy Custin	19 Ohio
624.	W. H. Porter	45 Va.			
	Amanda	39 Ky.	755.	Elijah Shanklin	61 Va.
	Mary	18 Mo.		Ann	61 Ky.
	B	14 Mo.		Ivy	37 Ky.
	Lin C	9 Mo.		John	24 Mo.
	Bentin B.	3 Mo.		Mary	21 Mo.
	William H.	1 Mo.		Elijah	19 Mo.
				M. McCoy	16 Mo.

Note: Alexander McCoy m. Oct. 12, 1842, Morgan Co., Mo., to Ivy Shanklin by Rev. J. G. Berkley, minister of the United Baptist Church.

263.	William S. Ball	38 Va.	262.	Rev. J. M. Chaney	51 Ky.
	Matilda	32		Sarah A.	42 Va.
				Charles D.	14 Ky.
260.	John Ball	34 Va.		James M.	12 Ky.
	Joley	25 Mo.		Mary E.	10 Ky.
	Elizabeth A.	5 Mo.		Jno. B.	7 Ky.
	James W.	Mo.		James P.	2 Ky.
				(male)	4/12 Ky.
261.	Jamison Ball	Va.			

Note: Rev. J. M. Chaney is buried in Morgan Co. in Freedom Baptist Church Cemetery, where he once preached. This church was organized in 1844 and is still active in 1963.

1173.	Joseph Doran	56 Va.
	Dicy	52 Va.
	Lucy (dau.)	15 Va.
	Amanda	12 Va.

MISCELLANEOUS RECORDS

Abram and Mary (Baker) Willson were born in Virginia and moved to
Tennessee, where he died in 1834, leaving his widow with eight children:
Robert, Louisa, Malvina, Julia Adaline, Benjamin F., Samuel M., Mary B.
and Jane R. Willson. Mrs. Abram Willson came to Morgan Co., Mo., in
1837 as a pioneer. Reference: Leader-Statesman, Versailles, Mo., Jan.
13, 1961. Article by Mrs. Gerald Yarnell, Versailles, Mo.

William Temple Cole married Nellie Boundes of Wythe Co., Va. (Dan
Stephens History. Publ. 1936.)
William Temple Cole, Jr., married Hannah Allison and had nine chil-
dren. Hannah Allison Cole, 1764-1843, Pioneer of Cooper County, Mo.
Grave marked by Pilot Grove Chapter, Daughters of the American Revolution,
1932. She is buried south of Bellair, Cooper Co., Mo., by the side of No.
5 Highway by the Hannah Cole Park. She left many descendants. See:
"William Temple and Hannah (Allison) Cole" by officers of the Missouri
Cole Association. Publ. 1943. Mrs. Farrie Cole, Otterville, Mo., is
President of the Cole Association (1963).

General George R. Smith

A two-page article appeared in the Centennial Edition of the Sedalia
Democrat, Sedalia, Mo., Oct. 16, 1960.
General George R. Smith, founder of Sedalia, Mo., born in Va., Aug.
17, 1804; married April 24, 1827, to Melita Ann Thomson, dau. of General
David Thomson. Gen. Smith died July 11, 1879. His wife preceded him in
death on April 22, 1861.

Virginia Natives of a Later Era

William Moore, born May 30, 1889, Bristol, Va., son of Asa and Cor-
delia Shupp Moore; married in 1927 to Gladys Dowler in Weeping Water,
Nebr. Died at age 74. Obituary appeared in the Sedalia Capital, Sedalia,
Mo., April 10, 1964.

John H. Bryan, 75, of Hamilton, Mo., was born in Singers Glen, Va.,
and had lived in Hamilton for 45 years. Obituary appeared in the Kansas
City (Mo.) Star, Dec. 18, 1963.

Mrs. Mary Soto, 81, of Summit, Mo., was born in Wheeling, W. Va.,
and had lived in Summit for 35 years. Obituary in the Kansas City (Mo.)
Times, March 12, 1964.

Roy R. Humphrey, 75, of Smithville, was born in Ronsford, Va., and
had lived in Clinton and Clay Counties, Mo., for 70 years. Obituary in
the Kansas City (Mo.) Star, March 20, 1964.

Mrs. Hannah Agnes Jarvies, 91, of Kansas City, was born in Fairfax
Co., Va., and lived in Kansas City for 70 years. Obituary in the Kansas
City Times, Jan. 2, 1964.

Luther McClure Gates, 76, of Parkville, was born in West Virginia and lived in Parkville. Obituary in the Kansas City (Mo.) Times, March 16, 1964.

Miss Mary Roberts Edwards, 86, of Kansas City, was born in Grayson Co., Va., and came to Kansas City when she was three years old. Obituary in the Kansas City (Mo.) Times, March 31, 1964.

Mrs. Linda Gertrude McNeese, 80, Lee's Summit, was born in Virginia and had lived in Harrisonville, Mo., 12 years, and in Lee's Summit, 4 years. Obituary in the Kansas City (Mo.) Times, Jan. 8, 1964.

Mrs. Ada Moore Williams, 86, of Galt, a daughter of early Grundy County settlers and a descendant of a Jamestown, Va., colonist. Obituary in the Kansas City (Mo.) Times, Nov. 11, 1963.

Denver Thurston Hannen, 73, of Kansas City, was born in Evelyn, W. Va., and lived in Kansas City 40 years. He served in World War I. Obituary in the Kansas City (Mo.) Times, Feb. 22, 1964.

Ernest W. Hess, Sr., 64, of Smithville, Mo., was born in Roane Co., W. Va., and lived in Smithville about 60 years. He served in World War I. Obituary in the Kansas City (Mo.) Times, March 6, 1964.

Lemuel G. Ballard, Sr., 75, of Independence, Mo., was born in Monroe Co., W. Va., and lived in Independence eight months. Obituary in the Kansas City (Mo.) Star, March 6, 1964.

Mrs. Effie Virginia Grose, 89, of Kansas City, was born in Virginia and lived in Kansas City 50 years. Obituary in the Kansas City (Mo.) Times, Jan. 6, 1964.

Albert Ballard, 81, of Kansas City, was born in West Virginia and lived in Kansas City 35 years and in Lenexa seven years. Obituary in the Kansas City (Mo.) Times, March 9, 1964.

Alec L. Cruikshanks, 85, of Olathe, was born in West Virginia and lived in Omaha before moving to Olathe in 1935. Obituary in the Kansas City (Mo.) Times, April 6, 1964.

Mrs. Nancy Misenhelter, 99, of Hamilton, Mo., was born in Holiday Cove, Va., and lived in Hamilton most of her life. Obituary in Kansas City (Mo.) Times, Jan. 11, 1964.

Mrs. Cornelia Fuller, 94, of 3604, the Paseo, was born in Franklin Co., Va., and lived in Kansas City for 75 years. Obituary in the Kansas City (Mo.) Star, May 24, 1964.

Alexander and Sarah (Reed) Doran Family Bible Record

(Now in possession of Mr. Jacob Edwin Cole, Real Estate Broker, living in
Belleville, Kansas. Copied by Ilene Sims Yarnell, Versailles, Mo., from
a photostat of the Bible Record. She is a descendant of the Doran-Moore
line listed below, and Genealogical Recorder of Niangua Chapter D.A.R.,
Camdenton, Mo.)

BIRTHS

Alexander Doran, Jan. 28, 1760. (Notation was made, "Probably born in
   New Jersey, his father's family moved to Patterson Creek, Hampshire
   Co., Va.")
Sarah Reed, born Oct. 13, 1765.
Sarah Doran, born Dec. 23, 1791.
William Doran, born Feb. 24, 1794.
Elizabeth Doran, born May 27, 1796.
John Doran, born Aug. 28, 1798.
James Doran, born Jan. 9, 1802.
Joseph Doran, born July 8, 1804; died July 23, 1868, buried Oak Grove Cem-
   etery, Versailles, Mo.
Peter Doran, born Nov. 26, 1806.
Alexander Doran, born Jan. 22, 1809.
Daniel Doran, born Feb. 28, 1826.
Sarah Doran, born Sept. 24, 1827.
David Doran, born Sept. 9, 1830.
Louisa Doran, born May 3, 1833.
Alexander Doran, born Sept. 11, 1835.
Samuel Doran, born Feb. 1, 1838.
Nancy Carmichael, born July 6, 1818.
Hannah Doran, born June 17, 1799. (Notation "Grandmother wife of William.")
Hannah Elizabeth Doran, born July 17, 1856.
Mary Jane McNemar, born July 20, 1834.

DEATHS

Sarah Reed died July 16, 1808.
Alex. Doran, Jr., was drowned April 8, 1834.
Alexander Doran, son of Joseph Doran, was drowned June 13, 1836.
Sarah Doran died the 14th of Sept., 1836.
Alexander Doran died May 26, 1844. (Notation "Uncle Sam's grandfather.")
Peter Doran died Dec. 28, 1843.
William Doran died Jan. 7, 1850.
Hannah Doran died Aug. 24, 1850.
Sarah Loy died March 7, 1855.
Louisa Rupe died Sept. 26, 1871.
Alexander Doran died April 18, 1887, at Decatur, Ill.
David Doran died July 14, 1905.
Mary Jane Doran died July 26, 1913.
Frank Rupe died 1927 or 1928.
Samuel Doran passed on Nov. 11, 1932, age 94 years.

MARRIAGES

Alexander Doran and Sarah Reed, married March 20, 1791.
Elizabeth Doran and Joseph Smith, married Dec. 28, 1815.
John Doran and Rhoda Baker, married Sept. 30, 1819.

Sarah Doran and Thomas Moore, married Oct. 14, 1824. (Morgan Co., Mo.,
   Pioneers)
William Doran and Hannah Carmichael, married May 5, 1825.
Samuel Doran and Mary McDonald, married June 9, 1872.
Joseph Doran and Lucy G. Frye, married Sept. 27, 1827. (Both buried
   Oak Grove Cemetery, Morgan Co., Mo.)
James Doran and Rhoda Ruckman, married April 8, 1830.
Peter Doran and Rebecca Dicks, married Sept. 3, 1835.
Nancy Carmichael and Thomas Ruckman, married Jan. 6, 1838.
Sarah Doran and William Loy, Jr., married Dec. 24, 1846.
David Doran and Mary Jane McNemar. (Could last letter be n -- McNeman?)

                      Family of John Robinson

From "Historical Atlas of Westmoreland County, Va.," by David W. Eaton.

      John Robinson, born in Westmoreland Co., Va., married Susan McClana-
han, daughter of Reverend William McClanahan and Mary Marshall, in Culpeper
Co., Va., and removed to the Greenville District, So. Car., and in 1810
moved to Bourbon Co., Ky., and finally settled in 1825 in Boone Co., Mo.
He died in Boone Co., Mo. They had 11 children as follows:
   1. John, died single in Ohio in service of the United States in
       the War of 1812.
   2. Gerrard, married his cousin, Ann McClanahan, and moved to Howard
       Co., Mo., and left children.
   3. William, married ____ Sims and settled in Howard Co., Mo., and
       left issue.
   4. Maxmillian, married ____ Butler, settled in Boone Co., Mo., and
       left issue.
   5. Sidney, born about 1805 in Greenville District, So. Car., married
       his cousin, Susan McClanahan, moved to Morgan Co., Mo., and left
       issue.
   6. Benjamin F., married first ____ McClanahan; married second, ____
       Alcock, and settled in Texas.
   7. Louis Marshall, married ____ Benson, removed to California.
   8. Francis, married ____ Benson, removed to California and left
       issue.
   9. Richard H., married ____ Sibley, settled in California and
       left issue.
  10. Elizabeth, married Stephen Bedford, lived in Boone Co., Mo.,
       and left issue.
  11. Alexander Marshall Robinson, born in Greenville, So. Car., Nov.
       17, 1802, died in Platte City, Mo., in 1894. He married first,
       1822, Louisa Bayse, daughter of Lisbon Bayse, Bourbon Co., Ky.
       After her death he married, second, Catherine A. Hughes, daugh-
       ter of William Hughes, of Bourbon Co., Ky. She died in 1884,
       in Platte Co., Mo. He was a state Senator several terms. An-
       other brother, in Morgan County, Mo., was a candidate for state
       Senator against Major William Monroe, and Major Monroe was elec-
       ted.

John McClanahan who came to Missouri with the Robinson family, settled
in Morgan Co., Mo., having come from Kentucky. He married in Kentucky,
Priscilla Chisholn, and in their family was born John Marshall McClanahan,
Nov. 14, 1846. He was married Feb. 28, 1871, to Nannie T. Anthony, at the
home of Anderson W. Anthony, by Rev. James Edward Sims. He died July 21,
1927. He left issue:

    Vallie Blanch, born Aug. 6, 1874.
    Vergie Bernice, born Nov. 13, 1879; died Nov. 4, 1925.
    Harold Anthony Robinson, born Jan. 5, 1882.
    Samuel Livingston, born April 19, 1884.
    Priscilla Lillian, born June 14, 1888.

HE PAID $400 FOR 40 ACRES DOWNTOWN

Experiences of a Virginia Settler in Missouri. Kansas City (Mo.) Star,
Oct. 2, 1963.

Recently, a 56-page folio, typewritten and entitled "The Fabulous
Forty Acres," was dropped on the desk of The Star's feature editor. It
proved to be a detailed history of the various shifts of downtown parcels
of real estate involving the Bryant estate from the birth of Kansas City
to 1950, the year the folio was compiled by Alvin S. McCoy, veteran member of The Star's editorial staff.

The leading paragraphs relate the story of the 40 acres which com-
prise the area between Ninth and Twelfth, the alley between Main and Baltimore on the west, and the alley between McGee and Oak on the east.
This tract was purchased for $400 by Thomas A. Smart, farmer, looking for
a suitable spot to settle his family—a wife and two small daughters.
Taking the long view of this fortuitous purchase, McCoy risks a comparison
with Peter Minuit's alleged purchase of Manhattan Island from the Indians
for the equivalent of $25 in guilders.

Smart, from whom the Bryants are descended, had come up-river from
Callaway County in the fall of 1836 to visit his brother James, who had
previously homesteaded in the area on a government grant.

Tom built his home in a clearing, having purchased the 40 acres from
Oliver Caldwell in 1841 for $10 an acre. Smart opened a store on the le-
vee in 1839, a log cabin, and it thrived—Indians and traders bought blan-
kets, tobacco, powder, sugar, cloth, ribbons, beads and grocery staples.

Actually, Smart's purchase of the tract was the third. Henry Chiles
and Caldwell had purchased the tracts from Uncle Sam in June of 1833,
paying $1.25 an acre. Later, Chiles and his wife sold their interest to
Caldwell for $280 ($7 an acre).

Six months after Smart's first purchase, he bought from Caldwell an
additional 40 acres on the east for $250; they were bounded, as of today,
by Ninth and Twelfth, the alley between McGee and Oak, and the alley between Holmes and Charlotte. This total of 80 acres was what comprised
the Smart farm.

Smart was a Virginian by birth and the farm labor on the tract was
performed by slaves. Mrs. Amanda Graves, Smart's older daughter, inter-
viewed by The Star in 1911, when she was 82, said of those pioneer days:
"The road from our house to the store practically followed the route

of Main Street. My father left that side of the farm unfenced and made
a sort of highway of it. The brush was so thick at first that he had his
Negroes blaze a trail for us children.

"Our first home, a beautiful place, occupied the square between Eleventh and Twelfth Streets, Main and Grand. It stood near the center, about
where Walnut Street is now, and faced north. It was two stories in height,
with a wide hall in the center and a long ell in the rear. People from
everywhere visited us, and every summer a barbecue was held in the front
yard. Our horse lot and stables were on the site of Emery, Bird, Thayer."

Kansas City, in those days, was dense forest and ravines. Deer and
wild turkey were common, and the crack of a hunter's rifle echoed through
the woods. Split-rail fences surrounded the little clearings. Neighbors
were the first Kansas Citians--the McGees, the Jarboes and the Evans families, and the French settlement along the river with its Prudhommes, Rummels, Chouteaus and Grand Louis families.

Mrs. Graves recalled the flood of 1844 which covered the bottom lands.
One of the Chouteau families took to horse and found refuge with the Smarts;
it was lots of fun for the children, Mrs. Graves recalled:.

"Weeds and uncultivated lands stretched between the few farm houses.
The only school in this wild territory was taught in Father Roux's log parish house (Eleventh and Pennsylvania), afterwards known as Father Donnelly's.
Twelfth Street, then a neighborhood lane, was our road to school."

It is of record that in 1849, when the gold rush in California poured
thousands of persons through the town of Kansas, tragedy struck. A group
of some 300 Belgians had arrived by ship up the river from New Orleans,
and had formed a settlement in the East Bottoms. Cholera, in a raging,
virulent form, broke out in their midst.

Some of the 1849 graves of children remain in Union cemetery as reminders of that epidemic.

Mrs. Elizabeth Martin of "Martin's Hotel," Versailles, Mo., was born
in 1826, Patrick Co., Va.; died 1930; married Samuel Martin, born 1814;
died 1906; both buried in Versailles Cemetery. They moved to Versailles
in 1853.

The Martin Hotel was built in 1879 and in 1963 is operated by a nephew,
Foster Brown, member of the oldest continuous hotel family in one location
in Missouri.

Ref.: "Early American Inns and Taverns," by Elise Lathrop. Tudor
Publishing Co., New York. 1946.

MISSOURIANS PAY TRIBUTE TO A VIRGINIA NATIVE

Titus W. Beasley, professor of history and political science, was honored by Southwest Baptist College, Bolivar, Mo., on Jan. 30, 1964. He was
presented a gold plaque in recognition of his 32 years of service at the
college.

Announcement was made that the new half million dollar dormitory for
men had been named the Titus W. Beasley Hall.

Prof. Beasley was born in Hollywood, Va., ten miles from Appomattox
within three miles of the surrender grounds in an old log cabin built be-

fore the Civil War.

VIRGINIAN BECAME HORSE-AND-BUGGY BOOK SELLER

Mary Hosbrook was born in 1866 in Virginia and moved to Kansas City in 1901 to sell books for a dealer, Blair W. Kincaid, to whom she was married two years later.

Mrs. Mary Kincaid made the rounds of her book customers for many years by street car, horse and buggy and motor car, using the latter only after the self-starter was developed.

She was an art teacher for four years at the Stonewall Jackson Institute at Abingdon, Va. Recognition came to her ability in art and woodcarving when one of her paintings was hung in the Corcoran Art Gallery in Washington, and she carved the panels of the pipe organ in Music Hall in Cincinnati.

Ref.: "It Says Here," by Bill Moore, Kansas City Star, Oct. 11, 1962.

FAMILY LIVES IN SAME HOME 114 YEARS

Robert Hugh Miller, a Virginian by birth, moved to Liberty, Mo., in 1846 to found the Liberty Tribune which has been published continuously, missing only one issue in September, 1861.

June 26, 1848, Robert H. Miller married Miss Enna F. Peters, who died Dec. 3, 1867, leaving four children. May 3, 1871, he married Miss Lulu Wilson, daughter of John Wilson of Platte County.

Mrs. Ida Miller Dye is one of the three daughters who are still living in 1963. Mrs. Dye was born 87 years ago in the Miller home of brick and logs, "Forest Hill," on Wilson Street in Liberty, Mo. She is the present owner and occupant of the mansion which has been occupied by the same family for 114 years.

Ref.: "Liberty Link with 1850 Survives Fire," by Mrs. Sam H. Ray, Kansas City Star. (Date not on clipping.)

Mr. James Ellis Murray, P. O. Box 506, Rogers, Ark., has compiled a Murray Genealogy and in 1961 published "The Genealogy of the James Ball Family of Fauquier Co., Va."

Nancy Ball, dau. of James and Nancy (___), born Oct. 8, 1792, married William Ellis in Fauquier Co. She died in Missouri in 1845.

"Missouri Baptist Biography," by Maple and Rider. Vol. 3, p. 252.

Dr. Milton McCoy was from Virginia and of Scotch-Irish ancestry. He was a dentist and lived in Tipton, Mo., and Boonville, Mo. He was born in 1824 and died in 1886.

Sedalia (Mo.) Democrat. April 26, 1964. Contributed by the Pettis County Historical Society.

Dorothy (Dorthea) Henry, wife of George Dabney Winston, was an 1840 resident of Pettis County. A daughter of Patrick Henry of Virginia, she and a son lived near the home of her daughter, Elvira. Elvira was the wife of Col. James William Crenshaw, also a native of Virginia. Col. Crenshaw entered land and was also a land purchaser in the area. Mrs. Winston entered land in the southwest part of the county.

"At 102, She Links City with Its Beginnings," is the title of a long feature article by John Edward Hicks, in the Kansas City (Mo.) Star, May 28, 1964.

Memories, legends and family lore of more than a century were recalled a few days ago by a woman who saw the Civil War come to an end and watched this city grow from a riverfront town to its present proportions.

Mrs. Virginia Harris Thornton, 102 today, is related by blood and marriage to several families whose names are linked prominently with the beginnings of Westport and Kansas City. She was born at the farm home of a grand-uncle, the Rev. Edward Thompson Peery, for whom Peery Avenue is named, in what became the northeast sector of Kansas City.

Mr. Peery had been the first Methodist Episcopal missionary to the Delaware Indians, serving from 1833 to 1837 in a log church on the site of the present White Church community in Wyandotte County. He had married Jane Chick, daughter of Col. William Miles Chick, and they had served the Shawnee, Delaware, Kickapoo, Pottawatomi and Wyandot Indians. He also was presiding elder of the Cherokee nation.

Giving up their missionary work in 1847, they came here and built a home in the deep forest on his farm at what now is Ninth and Harrison Streets. Mrs. Thornton's parents, Dr. William Warren Harris and Nellie McCoy Harris, were married in 1859 by Mr. Peery. The ceremony took place at Woodside, country estate of the bride's father, John Calvin McCoy, founder and first postmaster of Westport and one of the founders of Kansas City. His father, the Rev. Isaac McCoy, Baptist missionary, had come to this area in 1827. The John Calvin McCoy farm was situated, according to present boundaries, south from Linwood Blvd. to Thirty-eighth Street, and west from Troost Avenue to Robert Gillham Road.

Nellie's mother, McCoy's first wife, had been Virginia Chick, daughter of Col. William Miles Chick, early-day merchant and first postmaster of Kansas City, whose home on Pearl Street, near the river, had been among the elite. Legend says he carried the postoffice in his hat.

Mrs. Thornton's father, handsome young Dr. Harris, had come to old Westport from Lynchburg, Va., having just been graduated from the medical school of the University of Pennsylvania. A scholarly man, speaking five languages, he also was a graduate of the University of Virginia. Nellie McCoy was a leader of Westport's younger set.

She m. Robert Taliaferro Thornton, whose father had large land holdings between Lee's Summit and Blue Springs. They were married in Rich Hill, Mo., and moved to Kansas City where Mr. Thornton opened a drug store at Fifteenth Street and Virginia Avenue.

McCOY BIBLE RECORDS

These records are owned by Mrs. L. E. Wood of Eminence, Mo., daughter
of Mrs. Caroline Parsons. They were copied by Velma Novotny, 109 South
Inka, Pratt, Kansas, and sent to us by Mrs. Gerald D. Yarnell, Versailles,
Mo.

Samuel McCoy born the 12th of May, 1786.
Elizabeth Graves born the 30th of Jan., 1796, married 1809.

BIRTHS OF THE CHILDREN OF SAMUEL AND ELIZABETH McCOY.

1. John McCoy born the 17th day of April, 1810. (Ancestor of Mrs. Novotny.)
2. William McCoy born the 22nd day of April, 1812.
3. Ervin McCoy born the 21st day of April, 1814.
4. Nancy McCoy born the 2nd day of May, 1816.
5. Alexander McCoy born the 31st day of Aug., 1818.
6. James McCoy born the 24th day of Jan., 1821.
7. Milton McCoy born the 24th day of Jan., 1824.
8. Elizabeth McCoy born the 1st day of April, 1827.
9. Martha McCoy born the 23rd day of April, 1829.
10. Simpson McCoy born 20th day of Nov., 1831. (Grandfather of Mrs. L. E. Wood, Eminence, Mo.; resided Syracuse, Mo.)
11. Samuel McCoy born the 16th of Nov., 1837.

DEATHS

James McCoy died the 4th of June, 1846.
Samuel McCoy (Father) died the 16th of Sept., 1846.
Alexander McCoy died the 8th of Sept., 1843, age 25 years, 8 days.
John McCoy died — date unknown.
Elizabeth McCoy (Mother) died the 7th of April, 1878.
Milton McCoy died the 22nd of Sept., 1886. (Was doctor at Boonville, Mo.)
Samuel McCoy died the 28th of June, 1892.
William McCoy died the 1st day of Jan., 1899. (Home, Syracuse, Mo.)
Nancy McCoy Shrewsburg died 17th of Oct., 1901. (Lived in California.)
Simpson McCoy died 27th of Nov., 1907. (Home, Syracuse, Mo.)
Elizabeth McCoy Huddleson died 30th of March, 1916.
Martha McCoy Burford died 15th of March, 1922. (Home, Syracuse, Mo.)
Ervin McCoy died the 8th day of Jan., 1899.

Ref.: "History of Howard and Cooper Co., Mo.,"1883, Nat. Historical Soc.,
St. Louis, Mo. Page 897 mentions Dr. Milton McCoy, son of Samuel
McCoy of Charlottesville, Va.

"History of Missouri," illustrated, Goodspeed Publishing Co.,
1889, Morgan County Section, page 1071, mentions Simpson W. McCoy.

PART V

THE VIRGINIA GAZETTE, WILLIAMSBURG, VIRGINIA

From the Weekly Genealogy Page of

Dorothy Ford Wulfeck

4897. (A) BLACKORBY-PALMER-MOORE. Grigsby Blackorby m. Elizabeth Palmer who was born 1781 in Virginia. She may have been a widow. Their son, Henry Blackorby, b. 1820 in Virginia. What county? He m. 21 Sept., 1844, Henry Co., Ky., Nancy M. Moore and moved to Pike Co., Mo. Was Nancy the dau. of Jeremiah Moore, b. 1795? And was Grigsby Blackorby the son of Grigsby Blackorby, Sr., and grandson of Nathaniel? Want locations for these. (Mrs. B. H. Hadler, 5917 Myrtle Ave., Long Beach 5, Calif.) Aug. 2, 1957.

MY FIRST THREE GENERATIONS, SHEPHERD FAMILY. Compiled by Jewell Lofland Crow (Mrs. Edmon L.), 3225 Lovers Lane, Dallas 25, Texas. Aug. 30 and Sept. 6, 1957. (B) Susannah Shepherd, dau. of Augustine (1730-1796) and Sarah (Shelton) of Amherst Co., Va.; m. 7 Aug., 1804, Amherst Co., Joseph Clements Roberts. They had Shelton Roberts, b. 1805, m. Jane Moon; Polly Roberts, b. 1807; Henry Garland Roberts, b. 1809, m. his half-cousin, Mildred Jane Henry, widow of Dr. Jonathan B. Henry, and dau. of Henry Dawson Roberts, merchant and Post Master of Faber (Nelson Co.), Va.; Saryan Roberts, b. 1811, m. John Jackson; Joseph Austin Roberts, b. 1814; Susan B. Roberts, b. 1819, m. John Bethel and moved to Missouri.

MY FIRST THREE GENERATIONS. Compiled by John R. Martin, 1914 No. 4th St., St. Joseph, Mo. Sept. 24, 1957. Joseph Thomas Martin, b. 1 Jan., 1811, Va.; d. 23 Aug., 1880, Polk Co., Mo., son of Orson and Elizabeth (Sadler) of Cumberland and Henry Counties, Va.; m. Martha Frances Mayes. Some of his brothers and sisters were: Samuel Hudson Martin, b. 20 Feb., 1813; d. Collins, St. Clair Co., Mo., 14 May, 1873; m. 1834, Dorothy Branch Allen, dau. of William Allen and Martha C. Jones. (See "Your Family and Mine, Descendants of William Allen," by John R. Martin, 1956, for complete list of descendants.) Elizabeth Jane, b. 17 Jan., 1820; d. Caplinger Mills, Cedar Co., Mo., m. 7 May, 1838, John Milton Barding. (Excerpt)

4958. (A) DANIEL-FOX. Want parents of Estridge Daniel, b. 15 May, 1782, Va.; d. 6 Nov., 1852, Montgomery Co., Ky.; m. when? where? Mary Samantha Fox, b. 1783, Va.; d. near Mexico, Mo., 1863. Who were her parents? Had six children, one of whom was James Quincy Daniel, b. 17 Dec., 1824, Mt. Sterling, Ky.; d. 5 Oct., 1901, Fairport, Mo. (Mrs. Alicia Pearl Mayer, 4226 Chamoune Ave., San Diego 15, Calif.) Oct. 11, 1957.

5029. (A) SEAVER-CROBERGER-DODGE. Want any record on Henry Seaver, father of Jacob Seaver, b. 15 Jan., 1773; d. 1826; m. Esther Croberger. Children: William Seaver, b. 1800, died in infancy; Jeremiah Seaver, b. 10 Nov., 1801, Scott Co., Va., m. Nancy ____, removed to Mo., had a large family, including a son James who was a physician; Henry Seaver, b. 13 Dec.,

1803 and had no children; Joseph Seaver, b. 12 Sept., 1805, Scott Co., Va., m. Sarah Dodge and moved to Switzerland Co., Ind.

5038. DAVIS-STARNS(STEARNS). Want parents of George Starns, b. ca 1794, Va.; m. Nancy ___, b. ca 1799; removed to Mo. where he owned the first mill at Noel or Pineville, Mo. Children: John, David, Martin, George W., Nancy A., Mary Ann, b. 1839, Pineville, Mo., m. John Wesley Davis, b. 19 Dec., 1840, Fayetteville, Ark., d. 21 June, 1900 at Gore, Okla., son of Solomon Davis and Winifred (Freeman) Davis. Want par. of wife of George Starns, also. (Mrs. Alvena Attebery, 650 Hill Villa Drive, Layton, Utah) Jan. 10, 1958

5043. (A) CHANDLER-SQUIRES. William Monroe Chandler m. Sarah Squires, b. 1795, Va. (1850 Census, Lawrence Co., Ark.) She d. 1850-60. Dau. Minerva Chandler, b. 1830, Mo.; when 10-12 years old moved with her parents to northeastern Ark. Mr. Chandler took charge of a barrel factory at Pocahontas, Randolph Co., Ark., and died prior to 1850. Want anc. of Sarah Squires.

MY FIRST THREE GENERATIONS, THE PRILLAMAN FAMILY. Compiled by Mrs. James W. Rogers, Jr., 5012 56th Place, Rogers Heights, Hyattsville, Md. March 28, 1958. William Melvin Snidow, b. 1 May, 1788; d. 3 Dec., 1864, son of Philip (1756-1792) and Barbara (Prillaman) of Blacksburg, Va.; m. 13 Oct., 1822, Cabell Co., (West) Va., to Chloe Ann Freeley, b. 1 Nov., 1804; d. 23 June, 1848. They rem. in autumn of 1837 to Madison, Monroe Co., Mo. Had eight children. (Excerpt)

5204. TAYLOR-SOUTHWORTH. John Taylor, b. Morgantown, Va. (now W. Va.); d. St. Louis, Mo., of cholera, about or after 1830; m. Lucretia (or Lydia) Southworth, b. 1773; d. 1845, Senecaville, Ohio, at home of son, Thomas Taylor. Children were: Sarah m. ___ Hale; James d. unmd.; George m. Mary ___, res. St. Louis, Mo., in 1830; Lucretia m. ___ Buchanan, perhaps a cousin of Pres. Buchanan; Rev. Thomas, b. 1801, m. Jane Rosemond, res. Senecaville, Ohio; Henry, b. Morgantown, W. Va., about 1803, m. bef. 1840, Harriet Jackson Thompson, as son, Norvell, was born in that year.

Have quite a collection of Southern Taylor data, none of which contains parentage of John Taylor of Morgantown, W. Va. His par. and anc. very much desired. (Miss Myrtle Jillson, 56 Montgomery St., Waterbury 8, Conn.) June 20, 1958.

5213. (A) SEARS. Want data on par. of Thomas Sears, b. ca 1790, Va.; m. Margia ___, b. Va. Want her anc. They rem. to Ill., where children, William and Rachel, were born, and then to Ky., where Milton G. was born, and then to Randolph Co., Mo., ca 1829. Thomas Sears d. 1870-80. (Mrs. W. K. Waugh, 1403 Park, Norfolk, Neb.) June 20, 1958.

5221. MATHEWS-SMITH-ORDWAY-CULBERTSON-CUMMINS. Edward Mathews was sent by Thomas Jefferson, then Gov. of Va., with supplies to relieve Ft. Jefferson on the Mississippi River. He floated past the fort in the dark and went on to New Orleans where the Spanish confiscated his goods and

put him in irons. Later sent him back to Virginia. Early in 1800, he returned to the Mississippi River with his sons: Edward, Jr., Charles, Joseph, James and Allen, and settled in what is now Mississippi Co. Edward
Matthews, Jr., m. 1805, Elizabeth Smith in Mo. Edward Mathews, Jr., d. 16
Aug., 1832. Joseph Mathews' wife was Priscilla ___. New Madrid, Mo.,
court records show Joseph Matthews and wife, Priscilla, sold 200 acres of
land, April 8, 1816, for $170. This land being on Lake LeBoeff in Tywappity
Township. June 11, 1816, Edward N. Matthews sold to Albert Gallaten 200
acres of land south of Lake LeBoeff which was head-right of Joseph Matthews,
granted to him by the Spanish Government. Edward Matthews, Sr., m. (2)
Mary Ordway. When was he born and where in Virginia was his home and who
were his parents? Joseph Matthews moved to Claiborne Co., Miss.; m. 15
Oct., 1817, a widow, Sarah (Cummins) Culbertson, whose husband had been
Rev. soldier John Culbertson. Joseph Mathews d. 1826. (Mrs. Clem Wilson,
Rte. 3, Box 123, Hot Springs, Ark.) July 4, 1958.

5242. McALLISTER-OCHILTREE-CLIFTON-BIBB-GARLAND. Want proof or clues
concerning the anc. of Garland McAllister, b. 4 March, 1793, Va.; d. 1 Aug.,
1857, Gasconade Co., Mo.; m. 30 May, 1811, Rockingham Co., Va., Mary Ochil-
tree, b. 14 Feb., 179-, Va., dau. of Matthew, son of Michael of Augusta
Co., Va.; d. 13 Aug., 1864, Gasconade Co., Mo. Can give list of their
children, marriages and residences if others are searching.
    Louisa Co., Va., records indicate many desc. of William McAllister,
b. 1764, wife Elizabeth, who had the name of Garland McAllister. Have many
records to exchange if anyone can assist me in proving connections on above-
named Garland McAllister. One of the executors of the will of William Mc
Allister, 1764, Louisa Co., Va., was Nathaniel Garland, prob. his bro.-in-
law. William had sons: John, Alexander, William and others who were not
named. He had a son-in-law, Thomas Thompson. (Mrs. W. T. Bishop, 616 W.
6th St., Sedalia, Mo.) July 11, 1958.

5256. (B) LEWIS-STEWART-BOONE. Can anyone prove the par. of James
Lewis, b. 25 Sept., 1770, Va.; d. ca 1840 in Jackson Co., Mo.; m. prob. in
1786, Annie Stewart? One of their sons, William Lewis, m. Elvira Sloane.
Annie Stewart was dau. of John Stewart and Hannah Boone, sis. of the fron-
tiersman, Daniel Boone. Annie, b. 1770, Wilkes Co., No. Car. Can anyone
give par. of John Stewart, b. ca 1742; d. 1769/70; m. 14 Feb., 1756, Hannah Boone? It is thought he was killed by Indians when alone on an expedition in the wilderness. He was a frequent companion of Daniel Boone.
(Mrs. Elvin E. Lea, 4015 Butler Ave., Fresno 2, Calif.) July 25, 1958.

5259. COCKERILL. Want info on Simon Cockerill, Sr., b. ca 1745, res.
Russell Co., Va.; d. in Missouri; m. Magdalene ___. Who was she and when
and where did they marry? Want par. of both. Several sons settled in
Breathitt Co., Ky. Simon was a Baptist Minister. (Mrs. John L. Hicks,
Jr., 310 Pepper Drive, Lexington, Ky.) Aug. 1, 1958.

5301. YORK-LINGENFELTER-WINGATE-PAXTON-EADS-HILLMAN-BRAGG. Want anc.
of John York, b. ca 1748, Va.; entered Army, 1776, in Orange Co., Va.; m.
Nancy ___. Who was she? Listed 1785 Census, Orange Co., Va.; rem. to
Ky. bef. 1805; drew Rev. War pension. Did he reside in Ind. bef. 1805?

Children: (1) Nancy m. 1805, Fayette Co., Ky., George Lingenfelter; rem.
to Clay Co., Mo., ca 1823. (2) Eliza m. 1808, Fayette Co., Ky., Jacob
Lingenfelter. (3) Polly m. 1809, John Collins Wingate. (4) Bartlett m.
1817, Fayette Co., Ky., Agnes Paxton, and d. 1853, Anderson Co., Ky. (5)
Newman m. 1816, Nancy Bads and rem. to Clay Co., Mo. Prob. (6) Armistead,
b. 1771, Orange Co., Va.; m. there, 1801, Joannah Hillman. Prob. (7) Jen-
ny m. 5 Nov., 1801, Orange Co., Va., Moore Bragg. I have names of children
of Nancy and George Lingenfelter and Polly and John Collins Wingate. Would
like names of descendants of other children. Newman York in 1830 Census,
Clay Co., Mo. Where did he go from there? I do not believe this family
was connected with the Yorks of North Carolina unless it was very early.
(Nadine Hodges, 4310 Highway No. 7, Apt. 206, Minneapolis, Minn.) Sept.
26, 1958. 1964 address: 705 W. 38th St., Kansas City 11, Mo.

MY FIRST THREE GENERATIONS, KITCHEN FAMILY. Compiled by Robert L.
Steenrod, 3600 W. Diversey Ave., Chicago 47, Ill. Jan. 9, 1959. Daniel
Kitchen, son of William of Fairfax Co. and Loudoun Co., b. 1753, Fairfax
Co., Va.; d. 25 Jan., 1823, Fairfax Co., Va.; m. 1 Feb., 1786, Cameron
Parish, Loudoun Co., Va., Mary "Molly" Barker, b. 1762; d. after 1840.
Daniel was a Rev. War soldier and pensioner. Children:

1. John, b. ca 1787; d. after 1838.
2. William, b. 1789-90; d. 1850-60, in Fairfax Co., Va.; m. 19 May,
   1818, Georgetown, D. C., by Rev. Birch, to Elizabeth I. Butler,
   b. 19 July, 1797, in Va.; d. 13 Feb., 1875, near Herndon, Fairfax Co., Va. Children: Kitty M., Nancy W. m. John H. Slack,
   John H. and Charles William m. Harriet Ann ____.
3. Amelia, b. ca 1792; m. 1810-20, ____ Ward.
4. Caleb, b. ca 1794, alive ca 1845.
5. Weston, b. 1795; d. 8 March, 1872, Pleasant Ridge, Weston Township, Platte Co., Mo.; m. (1) Rhoda Lee who d. ca 1835; m. (2)
   Susan ____, b. 1803 in Ky.; d. after 1870. Children (by 1st
   wife): Mary m. Joseph Reddick; Nancy m. William T. Brashears;
   Elizabeth; Daniel; Sarah A.; George m. ____ Burnham. (by 2nd
   wife) Weston, Jr., Lewis C. and Jemima.
6. Elisha, b. ca 1797, living 1838, of Cameron Parish, Loudoun Co.,
   Va.; m. by 1830, ____ ____, b. 1800-10; prob. d. 1830-33.
7. Henry, b. 1800, alive 1850, Marshall Township, Platte Co., Mo.;
   m. ca 1826, Catherine "Kitty" Butler, b. ca 1806, Va.; rem. to
   Mo., 1827-31, was in St. Louis by 1834, then rem. to Platte Co.
   Children: Charles W. m. Lou A. Miller; John T.; Susan A. m.
   James Ira Gabbert; James B. m. Josephine Gabbert; Richard J.;
   Kitty; Julia m. Moses Norris; Nelly m. Frank Sprague; Henry, Jr.;
   Minerva m. James McMinnis.
8. A son, b. ca 1802; d. 1810-20.
9. Nancy, b. ca 1804, alive in 1838.
10. Daniel, Jr., b. ca 1804-6; d. 1850-60, Rush Township, Buchanan
    Co., Mo.; m. Nancy ____, b. ca 1803-4, Tenn. or So. Car., alive
    in 1860, no known children.
11. Mary "Polly", b. 1809; alive in 1838.

5405. (A) BEASLEY-COON-TIPPETT-WALL. Reuben Beasley served in 11th Va. Regiment. Can this record be proven as of Reuben Beasley of Culpeper Co., Va., who is said to have had the following family: wife, Alice; sons: Thomas; Reuben; Cornelius, b. 1780, Va., d. 1871, Saline Co., Mo.; Charles E., b. 1790, Va., d. in Saline Co., Mo.; daus.: Nancy Coon, Patsy Tippett, Betsy Wall, and another? (Mrs. Wm. T. Bishop, 616 W. 6th St., Sedalia, Mo.) Feb. 6, 1959.

5411. LAFFOON-FOSTER-WILLIAMS-WEST. Wish to correspond with any descendant of Laffoon Family of Brunswick Co., Va., or anyone descended from Fallon, Foster, Williams, West. My maternal gr-parents, Harden West and wife, Katherine Williams, dau. of George and Elizabeth H. (Foster) Williams, who m. 1806, Brunswick Co., Va. Harden was the son of Abner West and Sarah Laffoon. Need par. of Abner and Sarah. They m. and lived in Pendleton Co., So. Car., until 1814, when they migrated to Hopkins Co., Ky., with 4 children: Ellen, William, Harden and John Laffoon. Ca 1831, the Wests migrated to Osage Co., Mo., where they died. George Williams rem. to Caldwell Co., Ky., thence to Mo. Have info on descendants of Laffoon, West and Williams to exchange. Who were the 7 children of William and Susannah Laffon, 1800 Census, Pendleton Co., So. Car.? (Mrs. Inez R. Bennett, P. O. Box 124, Magrath, Alberta, Canada.) Feb. 20, 1959.

5428. (C) WHITE(WEIS). Want German anc. of Henry White (Weiss), b. 1780, Va.; d. Henry Co., Mo. (Carey O'Lee Brazil, 1536B Breckenridge Apts., Austin 3, Texas.) March 6, 1959.

5472. (C) CRAVENS. Want dates and par. of John A. Cravens, believed b. 1811, Penna.; rem. to Va., to Mo., to Ark.; m. America ____, b. 1817, Ky. Who was she? Known children: John, b. 1840, Mo.; James; America Elizabeth; Alexander (or Abraham); Brown D.; Margaret Missouri; Arkansas M., b. 1857; Jacob, b. Ark. (Earnest L. Thaxton, Sr., 1917 Eighth St., Lubbock, Texas.) May 8, 1959.

5496. LEWIS-DUFF-HITE-STROTHER-LYNN. Am interested in the anc. of my gr.father, Daniel W. Lewis, son of Gen. George Washington Lewis, who was b. in Va.; m. 10 Nov., 1825, Harriet Duff; came to Grand Pass, Saline Co., Mo., in the fall of 1830; d. 10 Sept., 1856, bur. on farm of bro., William Lewis. Gen. Lewis was in command at the out-break of the Mexican War but was not called into the field. Want data on the Duff family. Believe Gen. Lewis was the son of William Benjamin Lewis who m. 1800, Margaret Hite. He had a bro., Edward. They were sons of Thomas and Jane (Strother) Lewis. Thomas was the eldest son of John and Margaret (Lynn) Lewis, who settled near Staunton, Va., in 1732. Want dates and proof on these Lewises. (Mrs. Chas. Symns, Rte. 3, St. John, Kansas.) June 5, 1959.

5505. (A) EDWARDS. Want par. of William Edwards, b. 1792, Va.; rem. to Ky., thence to Boone Co., Mo. Want res. of his parents. (Capt. O. T. Wills, Finance Corps, U. S. Army, 374 Benjamin Harrison Village, Indianapolis 16, Ind.) June 19, 1959. 1963 address: Maj. O. T. Wills,

CDNT and PROC DIV., FOUSA, Indianapolis 49, Ind.

5682. (A) HOLBROOK-DAVIDSON. Parents, ancestry, dates and locations wanted of Granville Henderson, b. Va., May, 1823; had two known brothers, Nelson and Haywood, and sister, Tennessee Canady (Canaday, Canada) another cousin? Migrated westward to Andrew Co., Mo.; m. 1856, Iowa, Susan Davidson. Was she his 1st wife? If not, want data on other marriages. Connected with Holbrook of New England? Any Rev. War service in this line? (Mrs. Claude E. Apple, Box 33, Braddyville, Iowa.) Feb. 26, 1960.

5691. (B) WITCHER. Want full data on Mary Jane (or Martha Jane) Witcher, b. 18 March, 1834, Pittsylvania Co., Va.; m. 27 July, 1854, Montgomery Co., Mo., Daniel A. Kemp. Will exchange info. (Mrs. Lavonnie Farmer Brimhall, 406 State St., North Bend, Ore.) March 4, 1960.

5698. SEAVER. Want par. of Henry and Elizabeth (___) Seaver of Scott Co., Va., and of their grandson, Jeremia Seaver, b. 10 Nov., 1801, Scott Co., Va.; m. Nancy ___; rem. to Mo. where he died. One son, James Seaver, was a physician. (Mrs. Violetta T. Seaver, Rt. 1, Box 58, Elfrida, Ariz.) March 4, 1960.

5753. (C) ANDERSON-CHANEY. Want par. of Andrew Anderson, b. 9 Jan., 1780, Va.; m. 25 Jan., 1804, Halifax Co., Va., Orpha Anderson; attested by Richard Anderson. Andrew d. in Va., 19 April, 1839. Dau. Eliza m. 21 July, 1829, Halifax Co., Parkes J. Chaney and later rem. to Missouri. (Miss Mamie J. McCormick, P. O. Box 386, Sedalia, Mo.) May 20, 1960.

5783. WILLIAMS-BROWN. Would like to have info re mar. of David Williams who had two sons, David and Miles. He d. by 1790 when land was deeded to the two sons. Miles lived in Brunswick Co., Va., and David in Dinwiddie Co., Va. Would also like mar. of David (the son) to Frances ___, bef. 1806, dau. b. 1 Jan., 1806. Also want mar. of Edward S. Williams bef. 1831, had dau., Mary, b. in Va., 1831, who was living with an aunt, Louisa Brown, 1850 Census of Missouri. (Miss Ethel M. Roseberry, 1701 E. Normal Ave., Rd. 4, Kirksville, Mo.) July 29, 1960.

5860. (B) MAUZEY-SOMMERVILLE. Want mar. record of Elizabeth Mauzey, b. 1792; d. 1872; m. James Sommerville (Summerville), b. 27 Feb., 1793, Winchester, Va.; d. 23 Oct., 1876, Lexington, Mo. No record of this marriage in the Hampshire Co., W. Va., marriage bonds. Family records state marriage in Bloomery, W. Va., 3 April, 1817. (Vera Lee Francis, 1708 Howard Ave., Las Vegas, Nev.) Oct. 14, 1960.

HAWKINS FAMILY. The following information was received from Mrs. R. F. McCarron, 1101 Summer Ave., Hot Springs, Ark. Feb. 10, 1961. Gregory Farmer Hawkins, b. 26 March, 1789; d. 15 Dec., 1859; m. 5 Jan., 1815, Sarah Cannon, b. 4 Feb., 1795; d. April, 1872; dau. of Newbold and Unicy (Bounds) Cannon. Tombstones in Wyaconda Cemetery in Lewis Co., Mo., near Canton, Mo. Sarah Cannon Hawkins' parents are buried in the same cemetery. According to their tombstones, Newbold Cannon was b. 18 March,

1767, and d. 8 Jan., 1850. Unicy Bounds Cannon was b. 1779, and d. 23 Sept., 1831. Also nearby is this pair of stones: Newbould J. Cannon died Sept. 28, 1866, age 57 years, 3 months, 15 days, and Elizabeth A., wife of Newbould J. Cannon, died 17 Sept., 1870, age 59 years, 2 months, 28 days.

Gregory Farmer Hawkins' tombstone is quite large. On the front it is inscribed that he is the son of T. & M. Hawkins, formerly Mary Hargis. On the right-hand side of the stone: Mary Laure, daughter of G. F. and S. Hawkins, formerly Sarah Cannon, born on 22 Feb., 1824, died 17 May, 1840. On the left-hand side of the stone the following is inscribed: Sarah Hawkins, daughter of Newbold and Unicy Cannon, formerly Unicy Bounds, was born in Ky., 4 Feb., 1794. There is no death date on the stone.

Several of Gregory Farmer Hawkins' children are buried in this ceme- tery. His 4th child, Unicy Hawkins, b. 16 June, 1822; d. 28 Dec., 1902; m. 25 Oct., 1838, John Henry Bayne, b. 8 May, 1812, Nelson Co., Ky.; d. 11 A- pril, 1866.

According to information on file in the Lewis Co., Mo., Courthouse, Gregory Farmer Hawkins' estate was probated 27 Feb., 1860. Administrators were John W. Hawkins and Madison C. Hawkins, two of his sons. The children named were: Caroline J., wife of Roswell Durkee; Dr. Madison Cannon Haw- kins, Felix A. Hawkins, Unicy Anne Hawkins, wife of John Henry Bayne; Ros- well, Milton, Nancy Adaline, Irene Force, wife of John L. Long; Lorinda Jane, wife of Marcus D. Bourne. There were 11 children. Mary Larue was dead and for some reason his son, Dr. John W. Hawkins, was not named.

Sarah Hawkins Bayne, gr.dau. of Gregory Farmer Hawkins, and a college professor, wrote the following lineage, believed to be carefully proven al- though the documentation is not given.

John Hawkins was born in London, March 22, 1640; came to America in 1652 with his parents and brothers, Thomas and William. He lived on the James River in Virginia. At the age of 21, he m. Elizabeth Farmer, b. in Bristol, England, 15 Sept., 1643. She came to America with her parents in 1656. "My great, great grandfather, Thomas Hawkins, was born January 20, 1760. He married Mary Hargis Steele, widow, and my grandfather, Gregory Farmer Hawkins, was their eldest son . . . He lived near Greenbriar, Vir- ginia, but afterwards moved to Bath Co., Ky., where the first 8 children were born. They had 11 in all . . . In 1830, my grandparents and family and slaves went to Maysville, Ky., and took a boat on the Ohio river . . ."

5951. DUNCAN-STRATTON-MADDOX-McMAHAN-GIBSON-BROADWATER-GEORGE-COATS- BASKETT. Wish names and birthplaces of par. of Joseph C. Duncan, b. 17 Aug., 1789, Buckingham Co., Va.; d. on a farm near Reform, in Calloway Co., Mo., 22 Jan., 1868; m. (1) Ann Stratton, 2 June, 1809, Powhatan Co., Va.; m. (2) Nancy Maddox, Buckingham Co., Va. Known children: 1. Elizabeth (said to have been named from the grandmother) m. John McMahan in Calloway Co., Mo., and was a widow in 1868. 2. Frederick W. Duncan, b. Buckingham Co., Va., 1816; m. 24 Jan., 1839, Calloway Co., Mo., Elizabeth Gibson; la- ter rem. to Oregon. 3. Onslow (Ouslow) Duncan m. 14 Sept., 1843, Callo- way Co., Mo., Julia Broadwater, and rem. to Audrain Co., Mo. 4. Jerome Duncan, b. 1818, Ky.; m. 24 July, 1851, Mary George, Calloway Co., Mo. 5. Artinicia Duncan m. 16 Oct., 1844, Col. Marshall S. Coats of Coats Prairie, Calloway Co., Mo. 6. Merrett Duncan, b. 1830, Calloway Co., Mo.; m. 25 Oct., 1854, Mary E. Baskett, and rem. or res. Mexico, Mo. 7. Dr.

Edward Duncan, b. 1834, Calloway Co.; m. 10 May, 1866, Martha C. McMahan.
8. Joel Duncan, d. young. 9. Richard Duncan, d. young. (Mrs. Annie J.
Oates, 506 Jackson-Keller Rd., San Antonio 12, Tex.) April 17, 1961.

6011. (A) YANCY-FIELD-WEAR. Want par. and birthplaces of David
Yancey and his wife, Mildred Field. 1830 Census of Barren Co., Ky., shows
a David Yancey family: 3 children in under-ten age group, one male in 18-
25 age group, and one female in 16-25 age group. David may have been from
Culpeper or Albemarle Co., Va. The family was in Cooper Co., Mo., in early
1830's. A dau., Sarah Amanda, m. William G. Wear, 2 Nov., 1837, in Cooper
Co., Mo. (Miss Mamie J. McCormick, P. O. Box 386, Sedalia, Mo.) June 9,
1961.

6059. WILSON. Want par. of Leander Wilson, b. 1798, Va., and proof
of mar. ca 1818-1819 to Mary ___ (who?). 1820 and 1830 Census lists show
them in Lee Co.; 1840 in Polk Co., Mo. Mary d. 1839/40, on the way to Mo.
or after arrival. Leander m. 1840/41, Martha ___ (who?). Could 1st wife
have been Mary Fleming? Samuel Wilson, 1820 Census, b. ca 1770-1775, Lee
Co., Va. Was he father of Leander? Leander had son, Fleming S. Could
this be Fleming Samuel Wilson? (Jessie Baldwin Whitaker, Rancho Grande,
Elko, Nev.) July 28, 1961.

6075. CLAY. My great-grandmother was a Clay. It is family trad.
that she was related to Henry. She was one of 4 full sisters, 3 half- sisters, and one bro., Henry, who d. young. As Rev. John had only one bro.,
Edward, b. 1746, it would sound likely that she was desc. of one of his
sons or grandsons. She m. ___ Stratton; a sister m. ___ Bland, two sisters m. Normans, and Caroline Matilda m. James S. Sadler of Petersburg,
Va. The sisters came to Missouri from Tenn. in 1834. My grandmother,
Martha Stratton, was b. in Tenn., 1834. Would like more data on this
family. (Mrs. W. W. Whitaker, Rancho Grande, Elko, Nev.) Aug. 11, 1961.

6156. (A) WILSON-HARRISON-PROCTOR. Want par. and dates for William
Wilson and wife, Polly Harrison; res. Virginia, Kentucky, Washington and
Franklin Cos., Mo. They had son, James L. Wilson, b. 1830; d. in Kansas;
m. Marilla Proctor. (Mrs. Florence Eva Graybill Wilson, 2441 Himebaugh
Ave., Omaha 11, Neb.) Nov. 10, 1961.

6265. (A) POLSON-LOGSDON. Any additional data wanted for: Greenberry Polson, b. 1812, Penna., and Ansel (or Asel) Polson, b. 1820, Md.,
were prob. brothers. Mother and father were b. in Maryland. They lived
in Virginia until about 1856, rem. to Ill., and, about 1870, rem. to Benton Co., Mo. Greenberry m. Belinda ___ (who was she?), b. 1826, Penna.
Known children: Josephine, William H., Seely A., Asel M., Samuel and
James D.
     Asel Polson, b. 1820, m. Dianah ___ (who was she?), b. 1823, Va.
Known children: Albert G., Provia, Martha C., Charley M., Greenberry,
Asel W., Rebecca A. m. John J. A. Logsdon. (Lt. Col. Kenneth P. Darling,
5704 Nebraska Ave., N. W., Washington, D. C.) Jan. 26, 1962. 1964 ad-
dress: 54 Outer Octagon, Randolph AFB, Texas.

MY FIRST THREE GENERATIONS, WILLS FAMILY. Compiled by Capt. O. T. Wills, Finance Corps, U.S.Army Security Agency, Pacific APO 343, San Francisco, Calif. March 2, 1962. 1964 address: Maj. O. T. Wills, CDNT and PROC DIV., FCUSA, Indianapolis 49, Ind. Richard Wills, son of Frederick William and Frances (Durrett) Wills, b. ca 1769, Albemarle Co., Va.; d. bef. 29 May, 1850, Boone Co., Mo.; m. (1) Clark Co., Ky., 18 Oct., 1796, Eleanor Patton; m. (2) 27 Nov., 1838, in Boone Co., Mo., Lydia Cox. All children by 1st marriage. It is believed that he left Clark Co., Ky., for Boone Co., Mo., about 7 Aug., 1829, as on that date he executed a power of attorney to John Flynn to settle his interest in a slave named Andrew left to the widow of Frederick W. Wills in his will. At this time Richard Wills owned 9½ of the 11 shares by having purchased from the other brothers and sisters. This transaction also establishes beyond doubt that Frances (Durrett) Wills Young was still living at this time. Children:

1. Rev. Marcus P. Wills, son of Richard and Eleanor (Patton), b. ca 1801, Clark Co., Ky.; m. Sarah G. Smith, b. ca 1800, Ky. Rev. Wills was a Christian Church Preacher and quite prominent in pioneer Missouri religious circles. Children:
    1. Elijah Allen Wills, b. ca 1826, Ky.; a physician; m. Eliza Ann Ridgeway, dau. of John D. Ridgeway of Callaway Co., Mo.
    2. Ann M. Wills m. (1) 19 Sept., 1850, Boone Co., Mo., George G. Keith; m. (2) 13 Jan., 1871, as his 2nd wife, Samuel Brown Spence.
    3. S. B. Wills, female, b. ca 1830, Mo.
    4. C. M. Wills, male, b. 1831, Mo.
    5. C. L. Wills, female, b. ca 1833, Mo.
    6. E. J. Wills, female, b. ca 1835, Mo.
    7. W. S. Wills, male, b. ca 1838, Mo.
    8. E. R. Wills, female, b. ca 1842, Mo.
    9. James M. Wills, b. ca 1843, Mo.

2. James Wills, son of Richard and Eleanor (Patton), b. ca 1798, Clark Co., Ky.; m. 14 Feb., 1821, Clark Co., Ky., Constant W. Hampton, b. ca 1798, dau. of John and Judith (____); rem. prior to 183- to Ala., and was res. in Green Co., Ala., when 1850 Census was taken. Would like to contact some of this line. Children (b. Ala.):
    1. Willis Wills, b. ca 1824.
    2. John H. Wills, b. ca 1829.
    3. Nancy Jane Wills, b. ca 1831.
    4. Ellen Wills, b. ca 1833.
    5. Mary Wills, b. ca 1837.
    6. Richard Wills, b. ca 1838.
    7. James Wills, b. ca 1840.

3. Maria Wills, dau. of Richard and Eleanor (Patton), m. 9 Jan., 1821, Clark Co., Ky., Thomas C. Reynolds; rem. ca 1829 to Boone Co., Mo. Children:
    1. Eleanor Reynolds m. ____ Lesley.
    2. Thomas P. Reynolds.
    3. Richard L. Reynolds.
    4. John M. Reynolds.

4. Nancy Wills, dau. of Richard and Eleanor (Patton), m. (1) 29 May,

1822, Clark Co., Ky., Squire J. Redman, d. ca 1836, Boone Co., Mo.,
son of William and Patsy (____); m. (2) 19 July, 1841, Boone Co.,
Mo., Abraham Barger. Squire J. Redman was living in Boone Co.,
Mo., as early as 1826. Probable children of 1st mar.:
  1. Washington Wills Redman.
  2. William T. Redman m. 19 Nov., 1856, Boone Co., Mo.; Nancy
     E. Copher.
  3. Martha Redman.
  4. Richard Redman.
  5. Ellen Redman.
  6. Doshia Redman.
5. George Washington Wills, son of Richard and Eleanor (Patton), b.
   ca 1800, Clark Co., Ky.; d. 8 May, 1851, Boone Co., Mo.; m. (1)
   18 May, 1828, Boone Co., Mo., Theodosia (Winn) Hicks, dau. of Elijah, who d. ca 1853, and Mary (____). Children:
     1. Marcus P. Wills, b. ca 1829, Mo.
   He m. (2) 24 Nov., 1836, Boone Co., Mo., Mary Jane Nelson, b. ca
   1815, Mo., dau. of Robert. Children (all b. in Mo.):
     2. Martha W. (or E.) Wills, b. ca 1837; m. 11 Dec., 1856,
        C. V. Bicknell.
     3. Oliver P. Wills, b. ca 1841.
     4. Isabella Wills, b. ca 1843.
     5. Mary Ann T. Wills, b. ca 1845.
     6. Sarah E. Wills, b. ca 1848.

6329. (A) HEAD-HENSLEY. Want par. of Gavin (Gaven) Head, b. 1770-
1780, Va., and his wife, Catherine "Caty" Hensley, b. 1770-1780, Va. Head
family was in Boone Co., Mo., by 1820. Appear in 1830 Boone Co. Census.
Two of their children were b. in Va.: William H. in 1804 and Alfred in
1812; other known children were Simon Peter and Elizabeth.

(B) CLOPTON. Abner Clopton, b. 16 April, 1778, Va.; d. 1 Aug.,
1863, Pettis Co., Mo.; m. in Va., Rebecca G. ____, d. 2 April, 1852, Pettis Co., Mo. Their son, Abner Clopton, b. New Kent Co., Va., 4 July, 1808.
Father of Abner Clopton, Sr., was William Clopton, Rev. soldier. One
source gives his death as 1 Jan., 1781. Desire data of marriage, name of
wife and children, and service record. (Miss Mamie J. McCormick, P. O.
Box 386, Sedalia, Mo.) April 27, 1962.

6335. (B) WOODS-PAINTER. Who were the parents of Mary Woods, b.
23 Sept., 1798, who is shown in family Bible to have m. Christian Painter
of Botetourt Co., 23 Nov., 1823? Where were they married? They lived
near Troutville, where 14 children were born, until 1857, when they moved
to Cedar Co., Mo. (Mrs. George D. Deck, 924 E. Elm St., Springfield 4,
Mo.) May 11, 1962.

6353. HESTER-BAYNHAM-DULIN. Want family Bible record of Thomas Hes-
ter, b. 21 Oct., 1782, Mecklenburg Co., Va.; d. 21 March, 1842, St. Clair
Co., Mo.; m. 26 Dec., 1810, Halifax Co., Va., Mary Eggleston Baynham, b.
15 Sept., 1791, prob. Halifax Co., Va.; d. 1863, Crittenden Co., Ky.
Thomas Hester was soldier in War of 1812. Their children were: Henry,
Robert, Mary, Martha, Virginia Tabitha who m. Robert Dulin, and Frances.

102

(Mrs. Frank M. (Roberta D.) Stewart, 908 Malcolm Ave., Los Angeles 24, Calif.) May 25, 1962.

6390. GREEN. Want parents, dates and places for James Green and his wife, Margaret ____; res. in Va. in 1786; res. St. Charles Co., Mo., 1797. Children: Robert, John, James, Jr., Squire, Sarah E. (Mrs. James L. Bass, Box 8, Smithton, Mo.) July 13, 1962.

6498. PALMER-BURRIS(BURRUS). Want data on parents, dates and places for Elihu H. Palmer, b. 1780-1790, prob. in Va., and for his wife, Dorothy Ann Burris (Burrus), b. 1795, Va. At least one child, Lucian, was b. in Va., ca 1817. When and where did they marry? Res. Christian Co., Ky., 1827; rem. to Morgan Co., Mo., bef. 1840. Data to exchange. (Mrs. George R. Hickok, 114 N. Aurora, Eldon, Mo.) Nov. 2, 1962.

6461. (B) ASHLEY-EWING(EUING)-EAGEN. Want par. of Thomas Ashley, b. 1799, Va.; d. ca 1850-60, Bates Co., Mo., and of his wife, Mary Ewing, b.1805, Ky. Their first child, b. 1828. Three boys, b. in Mo., were Benjamin Franklin who m. 1849, Priscilla Eagen; William and Peter Ashley. (C. T. Chambers, 3659 6th Ave., San Diego 3, Calif.) Nov. 9, 1962.

6551. LEAKE-DODD. Info desired on par. of William Leake, b. 11 May, 1787, Albemarle Co., Va.; d. 12 March, 1875, Pulaski Co., Mo.; m. May, 1812, Sarah A. Dodd, b. 14 July, 1796, Amherst Co., Va.; d. 3 Dec., 1850, Phelps Co., Mo. Children: Nancy, b. 1812; Polly, b. 1814; John, b. 1817; Hannah, b. 1820; Josiah, b. 1822; James, b. 1826; Polly, b. 1829; Cynthia, b. 1832. (Mrs. Hale Houts, 230 W. 61st St., Kansas City 13, Mo.) Dec. 14, 1962.

6621. (B) ADAMS-POWELL-WOODS. John Adams, b. 1732; d. 1782, Halifax Co., Va.; m. Susan Wood(s). Want her dates and date and proof of their marriage. Their son, Philip Adams, b. 1779; d. 1845, Callaway Co., Mo.; m. (1) Fanny Powell, d. bef. 1816; m. (2) 1816, Amelia Co., Va., Martha Matilda Foster, dau. of Booker. Need Powell data. (Mrs. Merlyn Houck, Rte. 3, Stillwater, Okla.) Feb. 1, 1963.

6633. (B) McCULLOCH(McCULLY)-FARRIS-WHITE. Want proof and additions and corrections to following data: John A. McCulloch, b. ca 1777 (where?); m. Jane Farris; had seven children; estate probated 1 Nov., 1840, Randolph Co., Mo. A son, John McCully, b. 8 April, 1800, Va.; m. (1) Sarah White, near Edwardsville, Ill.; had nine children.
Trad. is that "the McCully or McCulloch family came from Scotland to Ireland, then to America, and settled near Ashville, No. Car." (Mrs. Lillian B. Harmon, 1030 N. E. 31st Ave., Apt. 10, Portland 12, Ore.) Feb. 8, 1963.

6643. (B) CRAVENS-CARLYLE. Want anc. of John Cravens and his wife, Mary Carlyle, b. 20 June, 1773, Va.; d. 17 Aug., 1866, Memphis, Mo. (Mrs. Gladys Jenkins Hazelmire, 1380 So. Clayton, Denver 10, Colo.) Feb. 15, 1963.

6680. MONTGOMERY-CROCKETT-JONES. John Montgomery served in Rev. War, d. 1804, Wythe Co., Va.; m. Ann Agnes Crockett and had a dau., Esther Montgomery, b. ca 1755. Did she m. Robert Montgomery who d. 1807, Garrard Co., Ky.? Some of his children were named in a deed, but need complete list. Want anc. of Robert Montgomery. Were Robert and Esther parents of Easter Ann (Esther?) Montgomery, b. ca 1780; m. ca 1808, George Washington Jones; rem. to Mo.? Want anc. of George Washington Jones. (Mrs. Merlyn Houck, Rte. 3, Stillwater, Okla.) March 22, 1963.

6703. (B) WELCH-MAITHE. Want mar. rec. of Sylvester Asby Welch and Luranna Maithe, whose children, b. in Va., were: Samuel, 1826; Hannah; Martha Ann; and, b. in Mo., were: Isaac, b. 1838; Francis; Elizabeth; William; Caroline. (Mrs. Phillip Huff, 308 E. Benton, Carrollton, Mo.) April 12, 1963.

6772. ASHBROOK-CUNDIFF. Want par. and data re Bowling R. Ashbrook, b. 1807, Chesterfield Co., Va.; had bro., Jordan M.; m. ca 1830, ____ (____), who d. at birth of dau., Lucy Bowling, 1832; m. (2) Elizabeth (____), and moved to Linn Co., Mo., ca 1835, leaving Lucy with his four maiden sisters, Mary, Martha, Jane and Sarah Ashbrook of Manchester, Va. Also need names of parents of Charley Jeremiah Cundiff, b. 1828, Bedford Co., Va.; m. 1855, Lucy Bowling Ashbrook; rem. to Linn Co. (Mrs. Dan Hemphill, 1007 W. 15th St., Odessa, Tex.) June 21, 1963.

6778. QUARLES. Want par., dates and places for William G. (Green or Greenleaf) Quarles from Va., d. 1865, Warrensburg, Mo.; m. Sarah A. (____), b. 1825; d. 1857. Who was she? Believed to have lived in Ky. when son, James Winfield Quarles, was born. William's daus., Amanda and Susan, m. in Mercer Co., Ky., 1848 and 1846, later moved to Warrensburg, Mo. (Mrs. Alfred Wallace, 1255 Stratford Rd., Kansas City, Mo.) June 21, 1963.

6818. (B) APPERSON. Proof asked that Francis Apperson, d. Sept., 1806, Culpeper Co., Va., was father of Dr. John Apperson, d. 1834, Franklin Co., Mo. (Mrs. Philip C. Usinger, 521 Los Palmos Dr., San Francisco, Calif.) Aug. 2, 1963.

6819. (A) SINCLAIR. Want par., wife and children of Robert Sinclair, b. 1758, No. Car.; served in Rev. War from Washington Co., Va.; rem. to Madison Co., Mo., by 1820. (Mrs. Gordon T. Hampton, 6835 Perkins Rd., Baton Rouge 8, La.) Aug. 2, 1963.

6855. GREY-SAUNDERS-CHAPMAN. Want par., dates and places for Louisa M. Grey Saunders, b. 1812, Va. (mother was ____ Grey); d. after 1880, Crawford Co., Mo.; m. Feb., 1837, Va., Anderson Chapman, b. Va.; rem. to St. Louis Co., Mo. Children: Mary Frances, Frank, Alexander Campbell, Reuben, John, Anderson, Julius and Margaret Chapman. (Miss Jennie Stovall, Dallas Hwy., Waxahachie, Tex.) Sept. 6, 1963.

6880. FARIS-LYNCH. Want anc., dates and places for Sarah Faris, b. 1858, Macon Co., Mo.; m. 22 Sept., 1789, Henry Lynch, in Cumberland

Co., Va. Henry and his bro., David Lynch, served in Rev. War. Who were their parents? Henry and Sarah res. in Henrico Co., Va.; rem. ca 1819, to Madison Co., Ky.; rem. 1829, to Mo., where Henry d. 19 July, 1849, Macon Co. (Roy A. Ockert, 1450 Hartford Ave., Akron 20, Ohio) Sept. 27, 1963.

6882. COLE-BOUNDES-ALLISON-STEPHENS. Want par., dates and places for William Temple Cole and his wife, Nellie Boundes. Three of their children have been identified: William Temple Cole, m. Hannah Allison, b. 1764, d. 1843; Stephen Cole, m. Phoebe Allison, sis. of Hannah; and Rhoda Cole, b. ca 1770, d. 1882, m. 1796, Wythe Co., Va., Joseph Stephens, b. 1763. Hannah (Allison) Cole, as a widow with children, and her bro.-in-law, Stephen Cole, moved from Wythe Co., Va., through Ky. to Mo. by 1807, arriving at the site of Boonville, Mo., by 1810. (Mrs. Ira A. Leiter, 637 E. 16th St., Sedalia, Mo.) Sept. 27, 1963.

6885. WALTON-LOVERCHECK-JOHNSON-CREWS-COOPER-THURMOND. Wish anc. of the Walton couple who moved from Va. in 1800's and settled on the Merrimac River in Mo., south of St. Louis. Children: Jane Walton, b. 1822, m. Lovercheck, rem. to Ill.; Joe, m. (1) ____ Johnson, m. (2) Littie Crews, rem. Ark.; Nancy, m. William Crews; Amelia, m. (1) ____ Cooper, m. (2) ____ Fryer; Melissa, m. Pete Thurmond; Mary, m. Harvey Thurmond, rem. Ark. (Miss Winifred Crowe, 1009 E. Fremont, Riverton, Wyo.) Oct. 4, 1963.

6921. CRAWLEY(CRALEY)-MUNKRESS-DAYLEY-ALLEN-BURTON-MORGAN-HORNER. Would like to know if William Crawley, b. Va., ca 1775, was father of: Daniel, b. ca 1805; Littleberry, b.ca 1805; Polly, m. ca 1818, Howard Co., Mo., Ben Munkress; Dactus, m. James Dayley; Huldah, m. John Allen; Elizabeth, b. ca 1806, Dyer, Tenn., m. Joseph Burton; perhaps others. Early people in Howard Co. were Judge Jonathan Crawley who m. Elizabeth Morgan, sis. of Keturah (Morgan) Horner, wife of Col. Horner. They had son, John Chappell Crawley. How were the Crawley-Chappell-Burton families allied in Va., and where did they live? (A. Maxim Coppage III, 4284 Hillview Dr., Pittsburg, Calif.) Oct. 25, 1963.

7141. CHAPMAN-SAUNDERS. Want parents of Anderson Chapman, b. ca 1810, Green Co., Va.; d. ca 1877, Crawford Co., Mo.; m. ca 1836, Green Co., Louisa M. Gray Saunders, b. 1812, Greene Co., dau. of ____ Saunders and ____ (Gray). They and their children rem. to Mo. and settled in Crawford Co. Children were Mary Frances, Walter Frank and Alexander Campbell Chapman. (Miss Jennie Chapman Stovall, Dallas Hwy., Waxahachie, Tex.) May 22, 1964.

7253. MOSS-LAIR-MACKEY. Want parents, dates and places for William Moss who rem. 1816 from Bourbon Co., Ky., to Mo., where he stayed for about two years near what is now Clarkesville, Pike Co., then moved north to what is now Marion Co., where he spent his remaining years. His children: John Moss, m. Mary Lair; Carroll Moss, m. 1818, Mary Mackey; Luke Moss, m. 1819, Hannah Mackey; William Moss, m. Eliza Mackey; Mathew Moss, m.Mary Jane Mackey; America Moss, m. Resin Mackey. (Mrs. Irma F. Miller, 1017 Sunset Dr., Macon, Mo.) Aug. 14, 1964.

PART VI

FAMILY LINEAGES

These brief lineages and miscellaneous notes have been taken from
three sources: 1. Contributions from readers of "The Virginia Gazette,"
Williamsburg, Va., on the Genealogy Page of which a request appeared asking
that such information be sent to A. Maxim Coppage III; 2. the files of
Mr. Coppage, professional genealogist; 3. the files and Rental Library
of Dorothy Ford Wulfeck.

It is to be regretted that many of the contributed lineages are not
completely documented but it is believed that they are correct and that
the necessary proof could be secured by those who are interested, as names
and addresses of contributors appear in this section.

ASHLEY FAMILY

Gen. Wm. Henry Ashley, b. Powhatan Co., Va., pioneer to Missouri;
settled St. Louis, Mo., 1808, and, in 1820, became the first Lieut.-Gov-
ernor of Missouri. In 1823, he fitted out a trapping expedition over the
Rocky Mountains, discovering and using for the first time, South Pass, a
way to California and Oregon. His extensive dealings in furs netted him
over $180,000 per year and in the last years of life he purchased 30,000
arpens of land from Pierre Chouteau in the valley of the Lamine River,
Cooper Co., Mo.
    Old Tavern at Arrow Rock was the scene of a dedication of a memorial
stone (3,000 pound boulder) set in a one and one-half acre plot of ground
at the site of the grave of the general of the Revolutionary War, which
lies three miles north of Lamine, Mo.

From "The Daily Democrat-News," Marshall, Mo. Oct. 10, 1939.

BAILEY FAMILY

Dr. John T. Bailey, aged 73, died at home of Mrs. W. N. Wine, his
daughter, in Fayette, Mo., on 19 Feb., 1897. He was born in Campbell Co.,
Va., 1 Jan., 1824; rem. to Boone Co., Mo., 1837; to Howard Co., Mo., 1854.

BALL FAMILY

John Ball, b. 19 Oct., 1779, in Va., was a son of James Ball, who,
tradition says, was born in Dublin, Ireland; served in the American Revolution; married Margaret Bray. He lived in Owen, Nelson and Fayette Cos.,
Ky., before he rem. to St. Louis Co., Mo., in 1798, and m. Mary Eoff, b.
ca 1789, in So. Car. He d. 31 Aug., 1859, in Ballwin, Mo., the town he
founded. The children of John and Mary (Eoff) Ball were:
    1. Sarah "Sally" Ball m. Joshua H. Ball, b. Ireland.
    2. Susannah m. (1) Frederick Canik; m. (2) after death of 1st hus-
        band, _____ Herzig.
    3. Catherine, b. 1817; m. John Johnson.

4. Margaret m. _____ McCortney.
5. Nancy m. James McCortney.
6. Lucy, died young.
7. Pamelia, died young.
8. George S., died young.
9. Mary, b. 1831; m. Frederick Eikerman.
10. Martha, b. ca 1834; m. James Robert Etherton.

Information from Mrs. Nellie C. Hiday, 1210 16th St., N. E., Salem, Oregon, and Louis E. Pondrom, 1475 S. Florissant Rd., Florissant, Mo.

BALL FAMILY

William Ball, b. ca 1720, Loudoun Co., Va.; served in Rev. War. His son, James Ball, b. ca 1744, Loudoun or Fairfax Co., Va.; left a will in Fauquier Co., Va., 1794; m. Anna Chloe Smith. Their son, Talia- ferro Ball, b. 1782; d. prob. 1846; m. Mildred Foley; rem. to St. Louis, Mo., 1836; returned to Virginia, 1839. Another son of James and Ann Chloe Ball, James, b. 1787; d. 1852; rem. to Ky., 1820; m. Margaret Smith. A son, Capt. John Edmund Ball, b. 1829, Henry Co., Va.; d. 1912, Montgomery Co., Mo.
Nancy, dau. of James and Anna Chloe Ball, m. William Ellis; rem. 1834/ 5, to St. Charles Co., Mo.

Submitted by Louis E. Pondrom, 1475 S. Florissant Rd., Florissant, Mo.

BARBOUR FAMILY

Thomas Barbour was son of Hon. Philip P. Barbour, Speaker of Congress, and of the Convention of 1829-30, and Justice of the Supreme Court of the United States, and his wife, Frances Todd, dau. of Benjamin Johnson of O- range Co., Va. Thomas Barbour m. Catherine Strother of Rappahannock Co., Va., and d. in St. Louis of cholera in 1849.
His brother, Sextus Barbour, d. in St. Louis, Mo.

"Genealogical and Historical Notes on Culpeper Co., Va.," by Raleigh Travers Green, Part I, p. 54.

BATES FAMILY

William S. Bates m. 10 Dec., 1810, Huldah B. Parrish. (Douglas Reg., p. 10) They lived in Goochland Co., Va., although his name appears on the Personal Property Tax List in both Goochland and Fluvanna Cos., Va., the last time being in 1823. The 1830 Census, Marion Co., Mo., shows his name. In 1833, they lived in Lewis Co., Mo., when they appointed their son, James Booker Bates, to return to Virginia and sell certain slaves. (Louisa Co., Va., Deed Book U, p. 495)

Contributed by Mrs. Phyllis Bates Wright, P. O. Box 3515, Richmond, Va. 23234, Professional Genealogist.

BAXTER FAMILY

John Baxter m. ca 1768-70, Elizabeth Sappington, dau. of John who was born 14 July, 1723, Md., and his wife, Margaret ____. John Baxter and family moved to Madison Co., Ky.

Greenberry Baxter, son of John and Elizabeth (Sappington), m. 12 April, 1803, Elizabeth Jones, dau. of Foster and Mourning (Harris), and gr.dau. of Mosais Jones and Christopher and Mary (Dabney) Harris; rem. 1817, to Missouri Territory.

Contributed by Mrs. Berry Boswell Brooks, 3661 James Rd., Memphis 8, Tenn.

BLACKWELL FAMILY

Information on various members of the Blackwell Family may be found in histories of the following Missouri counties: Randolph and Macon, pp. 704, 1199, 789; Carroll, p. 581; Jasper, Vol. II, pp. 764, 749; Franklin, etc., p. 858; Northeast Missouri, p. 1190; Hickory, p. 109; Henry and St. Clair, pp. 630, 632; Jackson, pp. 815, 641, 814; Laclede, etc., p. 1033; Saline, p. 553; Lafayette, Vol. I, p. 282, Vol. II, p. 475; Boone, p. 841; Marion, etc., p. 357; Nodaway, Vol. II, p. 357; Buchanan, p. 672; St. Louis, p. 30; Lewis, etc., p. 714; Kansas City and Jackson, p. 420; Hickory and Polk, etc., p. 831; Greene, p. 649. Also, "Missouri Democrat," Vol. 2, p. 438, Vol. III, pp. 559, 571; "History of Pioneer Families of Missouri," Rose and Bryan, p. 309.

BOTTS FAMILY

Dr. Joshua Botts, b. 8 Sept., 1778, Stafford Co., Va.; d. 21 March, 1863, Jackson Co., Mo., son of Joseph and Catherine (Butler); m. Malinda Holliday, d. 27 Oct., 1873, Jackson Co., Mo.

James Ford Botts, b. 10 Dec., 1801, Culpeper Co., Va.; d. 25 Aug., 1853, Monroe Co., Mo., son of Joseph and Jane (Ford); m. Margaret P. Kinsey.

Peyton Botts, b. 8 Dec., 1805, Culpeper Co., Va.; d. 1 Aug., 1885, Monroe Co., Mo., son of Joseph and Jane (Ford); m. Elizabeth Lewis.

Armistead T. Botts, b. 10 Aug., 1814, Culpeper Co., Va.; d. 5 Sept., 1874, Audrain Co., Mo.; m. Martha E. Spiller.

Ref.: "The Rhodes Family in America," Howard J. Rhodes.

BOWEN FAMILY

Elizabeth Bowen, d. 1845, age 80 years; tombstone at Colony, Knox Co., Mo.; m. ca 1765, in Va., John McMurry, b. 27 Oct., 1752; d. 7 Nov., 1832, Washington Co., Ky.

"The Pettus Family," by A. Bohmer Rudd, p. 12.

BROCK FAMILY

Brock, Uriah, on Pension Roll of 1818, residing in Missouri. Served as Private in Virginia Line.

BURTON FAMILY

William Burton, Pension No. W7960, b. ca 1755, Va.; d. after 1833, Chariton Co., Mo.; aged 78 in Nov. 1833. He enlisted in 1775 as a sergeant under Capt. Joseph Spencer, Orange Co., Va., (see Culpeper Co. Minute Book) and served for seven months.

CHRISTIAN FAMILY

John Christian was married to his wife, Judith, the 23rd day of January, 1772. (Died January 20, 1792)

Mathew Pate, father of Judith Christian, departed this life the 1st day of June, 1780. Ann Pate, daughter of Mathew Pate and Jean, his wife, departed this life the 12th day of August, 1782.

Children of John and Judith Christian:

I. Paul Christian, son of John Christian and Judith, his wife, was born the morning of October 16, 1772. (Died July 22, 1851)

II. Betsey Christian, daughter of John Christian and Judith, his wife, was born January 11, 1775.

III. Ann Christian, daughter of John Christian and Judith, his wife, was born May 7, 1777.

IV. Martha Christian, daughter of John Christian and Judith, his wife, was born the 6th day of January, 1780.

V. Mary Christian, daughter of John Christian and Judith, his wife, was born the 19th day of August, 1782.

VI. Sarah Christian, daughter of John Christian and Judith, his wife, was born the 23rd of April, 1785.

VII. Hugh C. Christian, son of John Christian and Judith, his wife, was born at Redstone, old fort in the state of Pennsylvania, on the 23rd day of January, 1788 — died young.

VIII. Jane Christian, daughter of John and Judith Christian, was born the 1st day of March, 1791.

Marriages of John and Judith Christian's children:

Paul Christian ————— Mary King Sutton
Betsy Christian ————— Wm. Bacon
Anne Christian ————— _____ Longdon
Martha Christian ————— Gilbert Shores
Mary Christian ————— James Collins
Sarah Christian ————— Col. Jesse Jones
Hugh Christian ————— Died young
Jane Christian ————— Presley Oliver

John Christian Bacon, son of William and Betsey Bacon, was born the —-th of September, 1791.

The above copied April, 1960, from an old day book of John Christian's belonging to Richard Christian of Jacksboro, Tex. The book dates back to 1770 -- has family record of three generations in the back as well as birth dates of slaves' children. In the front are accounts, evident that John Christian ran a general Merchandise store. We are also led to believe that John owned an estate called "Merry Oaks," because of house and fence repairs charged to "merry Oaks," Hanover Co., Va.

The following is taken from "Descendants of John Sutton and His Wife Temperance Lane," compiled by Goldsborough and Fisher.

"John Christian was a resident of Hanover Co., Va., for many years prior to the Revolution. He married Judith Pate, daughter of Jeremiah Pate and granddaughter of Matthew Pate. John Christian served as a sergeant in a Virginia regiment, and his name appears in a list of soldiers who received certificates for the balance of their full pay agreeable to an act of the Assembly passed in the November session of 1792. He was one of the Revolutionary soldiers to whose memory a tablet was dedicated in Lexington, June 1940."

Paul Christian was born the 16th of October, 1772, in St. Paul's Parish, in the county of Hanover, state of Virginia -- and moved with his father for Kentucky in the fall of 1787 - he lived in Lexington in March, 1788, resided there until the fall of 1831. September 27th he moved to Missouri and settled in Randolph County.

I. Paul Christian, son of John Christian, married Polley Sutton the 2nd day of May, 1799. (Died July 22, 1851) Polley K. Sutton was born July 6, 1784, daughter of Robert and Caroline Sutton. Polly King Sutton Christian died March 23, 1877. Polly and Paul both died in Randolph Co., Mo. Children of Paul and Mary "Polly" King Christian:
    i.   Virginia Christian, daughter of Paul and Polley Christian, was born the 22nd day of May, 1800.
    ii. John B. Christian, son of Paul and Polley Christian, was born the 29th of April, 1802, and departed this life on Saturday, 12 o'clock at night, February the 19th, 1803.
    iii. Napolean Bonaparte Christian, son of Paul and Polley Christian, was born the 28th of April, 1804.
    iv. Robert Sutton Christian, son of Paul and Polley Christian, was born the 30th of November, 1806.
    v.   Caroline Coleman Christian, daughter of Paul and Polley Christian, was born the 23th of June, 1809.
    vi. Thomas Coleman Christian, son of Paul and Polley Christian, was born the 27th of March at 3 o'clock in the morning, 1812.
    vii. Sarah Tinsley Christian, daughter of Paul and Polley Christian, was born the 27th of October, 1804.
    viii. William Sutton, son of Paul and Polley Christian, was born the 2nd day of February, 1817.
    ix. Mary King Christian, daughter of Paul and Polley Christian, was born October 27, 1820.

x. Paul Jones Christian, son of Paul and Polly Christian, was born the First day of January, 1823.

xi. Gusteavers Bower Christian, son of Paul and Polly Christian, was born the 2nd of July, 1824, and departed this life the same month.

xii. George Richard Christian, son of Paul and Polley Christian, was born the 20th of June, 1828. (Died Jan. 7, 1909) Born in Scott Co., Ky.

1787 — was a 'locus' year
1804 — was a 'locus' year
1821 — was a 'locus' year
You may look for locus in the year 1838 — so says Paul Christian.

COPPAGE FAMILY

George Helm Coppage, b. 20 Sept., 1805; m. Margaret "Peggy" Thornton, dau. of Thomas III and ____ (Kitchen) of Loudoun Co., Va.; rem. to Phelps Co., Mo. Thomas Thornton's 2nd wife was Mary "Polly" Coppage, sis. of George Helm Coppage.

"The Coppege-Coppedge Family, 1542-1955," by A. Maxim Coppage III and John E. Manahan, p. 81.

COPPAGE FAMILY

William Coppage, son of Wm. and Judith (Scott) Coppage, was born in Culpeper Co., Va., and moved to Leeton, Mo., m. Nancy Jennings; the old Coppage Bible burned in his fire in 1876. He bought land in Henry Co., Mo., for 15¢ an acre. The children of Wm. and Nancy were:
1. Theresa Jane Coppage, 1st white child born in Clinton, Mo., in 1839.
2. John W. Coppage, b. 1844; d. 1930; m. Lenora Avery, dau. of Judge Avery. They were the parents of 10 children, one of whom was Rev. John Oscar Coppage, minister, athlete, contractor and mountain climber, b. 1874, and who lived in Shasta, Calif., and San Antonio, Tex.

"The Coppage-Coppedge Family, 1542-1955," by A. Maxim Coppage, III, and John E. Manahan, pp. 63-64.

COPPEDGE FAMILY

James W. Coppedge, son of Charles Lunsford Coppedge of Amherst Co., Va., and Lydia (Wyatt) Coppedge of Orange Co., Va., and grandson of Thomas Coppedge, b. 1752, Northumberland Co., Va., and who d. 1843, (Thomas, the grandfather, was a poet, song-writer and soldier of the Revolutionary War,) m. Dorothy Ann Eliza Tiller and moved to Potosi, Mo., in a covered wagon in 1842.

Houston Harrison Coppedge, brother of James, came to Missouri, and then to Grove, Okla., and was father of Judge Adam Vencil Coppedge of Grove,

Okla.

Other children of Charles Lunsford Coppedge were: Wm.; Sophiana; Charles; Adam Clark Coppedge, a Confederate Soldier; James who may have been the James A. Coppedge, St. Louis, Mo., policeman, who disappeared in 1886; Isaac; Lydia F., who m. J. W. Key; Emma; Richard.

"The Coppage-Coppedge Family, 1542-1955," by A. Maxim Coppage, III, and John E. Manahan.

COWHERD FAMILY

Francis Cowherd, Jr., "Frank," b. Orange Co., Va.; rem. to Independence, Jackson Co., Mo., where he is said to have died in 1864 or 1865; m. in Va., Sally Henshaw, b. 1799; d. 1849, dau. of John. He was son of Maj. Francis Cowherd (1753-1833) of "Oak Hill," Orange Co., Va., and his wife, Lucy Scott (1763-1847).

"Cowherd Genealogy," by Edythe Cowherd Newton, pp. 41-2.

CROSS FAMILY

Agnes Poague Cross, b. 1 Dec., 1830, Buchanan, Botetourt Co., Va.; d. 19 Jan., 1890, Pineville, McDonald Co., Mo., dau. of James Moore Poague and Sarah Boyd Moore; m. 14 March, 1861, Princeton, Mercer Co., Mo., William Warren, b. 16 Dec., 1825, Greenbrier, Robertson Co., Tenn.; d. 4 June, 1890, Pineville, McDonald Co., Mo., son of Sebirt Asher Warren (b. Va.) and Frances Bushrod Swift.

"Southside Virginia Families," Vol. II, by John B. Boddie, p. 370.

CRUMP FAMILY

Richard Crump of Virginia was born in 1772, and was married in 1769, to Sarah Smith, daughter of William and Joice (Humphrey) Smith. They settled in Callaway Co., Mo. Richard Crump died in 1828, and his wife in 1839. Their children were:
1. Lucinda Crump married John B. Bragg and d. at Springfield, Mo.
2. Turner Crump, moved to Oregon.
3. Nancy Crump died prior to 1828.
4. Richard Crump died in Boone Co., Iowa; m. ____ Love; had son, Benjamin Crump, who lived in Centralia, Mo.
5. America Crump drowned in Ky. River, 1819.
6. Thompson Smith Crump, b. 1806; m. Louisa Hays.
7. Henry S. Crump died prior to 1828.
8. Sally Crump m. James Dunlap and d. near Fulton, Mo.
9. Mary F. Crump m. ____ Wyatt.
10. James Crump m. Polly Martin; d. Callaway Co.; had six children.
11. John H. Crump.
12. Benedict Crump d. Tray, Mo.; had a dau., Sarah Crump.
13. Lydia Ann Crump m. Henry Veers and had 3 children.

Ref.: "The Boone Family," by Hazel A. Spraker.

DAMERON FAMILY

George Ball Dameron of Northumberland Co., Va., m. Mary Woosham of Dinwiddie Co., Va.; rem. to Caswell Co., No. Car.; rem. to Randolph Co., Mo. In their calvacade were 150 persons, 40 of whom were related. Their youngest child was Logan Douglas Dameron, father of E. C. Dameron, 5 Lenox Place, St. Louis, Mo.

DUNCAN FAMILY

Henry Duncan, son of Charles, b. 1777, Culpeper Co., Va.; d. 8 Dec., 1852, Cooper Co., Mo. (age 68 in 1850 Census); m. 1803, Bath Co., Ky., Mary "Polly" Combs, b. Shenandoah Co., Va.; d. 3 May, 1842, Lone Elm, Mo., dau. of William Combs.

Ref.: "Descendants of William Duncan, the Elder," by Nancy Reba Roy. San Diego. 1959.

GENTRY FAMILY

The lineage of Reuben Estes Gentry, b. 6 June, 1785, Va.; d. 6 Nov., 1839, Pettis Co., Mo., and of his 18 brothers and sisters, many of whom went to Missouri, may be found in "Gentry Family in America," by Richard Gentry and "The Boone Family," by Hazel A. Spraker.

GILLIAM FAMILY

Charles Gilliam and wife, Elizabeth (Woodson) Gilliam, moved in 1817, from Cumberland Co., Va., to the Chariton Co. area in Missouri. Among their children was Elizabeth Gilliam who was born in Saline Co., Mo.

Contributed by Joida Whitten, 5314 Emerson, Dallas 9, Texas.

GLASSCOCK FAMILY

Charnel Glasscock, b. ca 1770-2, prob. Fauquier Co., Va., son of Peter, Jr., and Elizabeth (Madden); m. Mary Luckey; rem. to Cape Girardeau Co., Mo., and later to Jackson Co., Mo.
Fielding Glasscock, b. ca 1773, prob. Fauquier Co., Va., son of Peter, Jr., and Elizabeth (Madden) of Fauquier Co.; m. Polly ____; rem. bef. 1850, to Cape Girardeau Co., Mo.

"Gillmore-Carter and Allied Families," by Helen Gilmore Smith and Dolly Reed Gilmore Barmann, p. 63.

GRAY FAMILY

Yancy Alexander Gray, b. Oct. or Nov. 2, 1806, Va.; d. 17 Aug., 1887; bur. in the I.O.O.F. Cemetery at The Dalles, Oregon; m. (1) prob. in Missouri; m. (2) 22 April, 1846, Randolph Co., Mo., Martha Barnes Jackson, b. 1826; d. 1913, dau. of Hancock Jackson (1796-1876) and Ursula Oldham, both of Ky. He left Missouri in 1869, buying his farm on 5-mile Creek near The Dalles, Wasco

Co., Oregon. Children: (by 1st mar.) John Will Gray, Fannie Gray and
three others not named in the sketch; (by 2nd mar.) Jack Gray m. Emma ____;
Mildred Gray, "Aunt Mitt," m. George Noble; George Gray m. Lucy ____; Alexander Hamilton Gray m. Lydia ____; Thomas Franklin Gray (1859-1925) m. Margaret Jeffers.

Contributed by Mrs. G. A. Jacob, 201 So. Palouse St., Walla Walla,
Wash. 99362, granddaughter of Thomas Franklin Gray.

GREEN FAMILY

Eliza Green, dau. of Willis and Sarah (Reed), was born in Culpeper,
Va., ca 1788; m. Dr. Ben Edwards, bro. of Gov. Ninian and Judge Cyrus Edwards; lived at Kirkwood, Mo.

"Genealogical and Historical Notes on Culpeper Co., Va.," by Raleigh
Travers Green, Part I, pp. 63, 67.

HALBERT FAMILY

James Halbert, b. 8 Sept., 1778, Va., son of William and Elizabeth
(Hill) Halbert, who moved to So. Car. in 1786; m. Fannie Pepper; rem. ca
1814 to St. Francois Co., Mo., afterwards to Steelville, Crawford Co., Mo.

"Historical Southern Families," by John B. Boddie, Vol. I, pp. 229-30.

William Halbert, b. 17 May, 1784, Va., son of William (b. 1744, Essex
Co., Va.) and Elizabeth (Hill) (b. 1747, Caroline Co., Va.); m. Bettie
Bowen; rem. ca 1844 to Missouri and some descendants now live in Steel-
ville, Mo.

Same reference as above.

HOBBS FAMILY

Ezekiel Hobbs, b. ca 1808, Va.; m. 14 June, 1827, Boone Co., Mo.,
Mariah Ball, dau. of Allen and (1) Betsey (Christeson); res. ca 20 years
in Boone Co., Mo.; rem. to Columbia Co., Wash., where both d. after 1880.
Children: (b. Boone Co., Mo., order not known)
1. Mary Hobbs, b. 1829; m. 6 May, 1847, Boone Co., Mo., David A.
   Williams.
2. Jane Hobbs m. ____ Idol.
3. Rebecca "Becky" Hobbs m. ____ Hensley.
4. Pauline Hobbs m. ____ Hancock.
5. Margaret Hobbs m. ____ May.
6. Elizabeth "Liz" m. ____ Berkley.
7. Emily "Em" m. ____ Ousley.
8. Joseph Hobbs, b. 1844, Mo.
9. Cordelia Hobbs, b. 25 Jan., 1848, Mo.; m. 26 Aug., 1862, Wasco
   Co., Ore., John Stewart.

114

Columbia Co., Wash. Dist. 1, 1880 Census

No. 50.					
Hobbs, Ezekiel	72	farmer	Va.	Va.	Va.
Hobbs, Mariah	72	wife	Ky.	Ky.	Ky.
Williams, Mary	51	dau.	Mo.	Va.	Ky.
Hobbs, Jos. M.	36	son	Mo.	Va.	Ky.
Hobbs, Corali	8	gr.dau.	Wash.	Mo.	Iowa
Muldoon, ____	31	boarder	Mo.	Tenn.	Mo.
Muldoon, Kate	6	gt.gr.dau.	Tex.	Ireland	Mo.
Williams, Thomas E.	13	gr.son	Kans.	Mo.	Tenn.
Hensley, Jas. E.	22	gr.son	Mo.	Mo.	Mo.

Contributed by Mrs. Nellie C. Hiday, 1210 16th St., N. E., Salem, Oregon.

HORD FAMILY

Elizabeth Hord, aged 85; d. Feb. 20, 1897, near Harrisburg, Mo. She was wife of Daniel Hord and came from Virginia in the 1830's. They were parents of T. B. Hord, bur. Harrisburg, Mo.

HORNER FAMILY

Col. Major Horner, b. 19 Dec., 1787 or 1789, Chesterfield Co., Va.; d. 8 March, 1867, Huntsville, Mo.; bur. Sugar Creek, Randolph Co., Mo.; m. 7 Nov., 1812, Keturah Morgan; served in War of 1812; Indian Wars; Morman War and was Curator of the University of Missouri; res. Howard Co. and Randolph Co., Mo. Children: Sarah, Ed, John, Lucy T., Fannie H., Laura R., James S. and Rebecca Horner.

HUME FAMILY

John Hume, b. 6 July, 1771, Madison Co., Va.; d. 18 Sept., 1842; m. Anna Crigler; rem. to Madison Co., Ky., and later to St. Louis, Mo. John Hume was son of George and Jane (Stanton) Hume.

"Early American History: Hume and Allied Families," by W. E. Brockman, pp. 52, 56.

JAMES FAMILY

Elizabeth James, dau. of John and Elizabeth James, b. 9 Dec., 1779, was related through the Strother Family to both Presidents Madison and Taylor. She m. her cousin, Henry Basye, son of Edmond and Nancy (Mauzey) Basye of Fauquier Co., Va., and d. in Rocheport, Boone Co., Mo., in 1852.

"The Basye Family in America," by Otto Basye, pp. 399, 401.

LEWIS FAMILY

John G. Lewis, Sr., b. 1802, Va.; m. Milly Hardin, b. 1796-1800, in Va., dau. of Charles: children: Eliza and Clarissa, b. Ky.; Milley M. and

John G. Lewis, b. Mo. Charles Hardin res. 1860, Ray Co., Mo.

From Franklin M. Gentry, 215 Manhasset Woods Rd., Manhasset, N. Y., 1952.

MOSS FAMILY

Dr. James Winn Moss, son of Dr. Hugh Moss who served in the Rev. War, m. 1801, Mary Woodson, dau. of Maj. Josiah and Elizabeth (Woodson) Woodson. They moved from Albemarle Co., Va., to Boone Co., Mo. Children:
1. Elizabeth Woodson Moss, b. 16 March, 1804, Mason Co., Ky.; d. 8 Feb., 1873, St. Louis, Mo.; m. (1) 18 July, 1822, Dr. Daniel Pinchbeck Wilcox, b. ca 1800, Ky.; d. 10 Feb., 1831, Mo., son of George and Elizabeth (Pinchbeck) of Rowan Co., No. Car. He served in the Missouri State Legislature. She m. (2) 17 Oct., 1832, Boone Co., Mo., Gen. William Ashley, Congressman from Missouri who d. 26 March, 1838. She m. (3) Hon. John J. Crittenden, Senator from Kentucky, former Attorney General under President Fillmore, d. 28 July, 1863, Frankfort, Ky. His widow then went to New York until 1872, when she rem. to St. Louis and lived with her daughter, Mrs. E. Carrington Cabell, until her death on the 8th of Feb., 1873.
Readers who are interested in this family would enjoy "Three Lives of Elizabeth," by Shirley Seifert, Lippincott, 1952, an historical novel portraying in fascinating details the lives and careers of these three well-known men and the social life of Missouri, Kentucky and Washington, D. C., in which Elizabeth enjoyed her special recognition.
Dr. Wilcox is buried in what was then the Dr. James W. Moss family cemetery in Boone Co., Mo. Gen. Ashley is buried in Cooper Co., Mo., on an Indian Mound over-looking the Missouri River. Hon. Crittenden is buried in the Bellefontaine Cemetery in St. Louis, Mo.
Other children of Dr. James Winn Moss and his wife, Mary (Woodson):
2. Woodson Josiah Moss.
3. Olin Perry Moss.
4. Mary Jane Moss.
5. James Hugh Moss, b. Boone Co., Mo.

"Wilcoxson and Allied Families," by Dorothy Ford Wulfeck, p. 75; notes from Mr. E. C. Cabell Gray to A. Maxim Coppage.

McKINNEY FAMILY

John McKinney, b. 3 April, 1798, on the Holston River, Washington Co., Va.; by 1819, he was in Howard Co., Mo.; m. 13 June, 1819, Anna (Austin) Keshler. About 1830 he moved the family to Oak Grove, Jackson Co., Mo., where he was a farmer, postmaster and itinerant Methodist minister.
In 1847 John McKinney moved to Oregon and d. Brownsville, Oregon, 17 June, 1878.

Contributed by great-grandchild, Miss Jessie Brown, 2819, S. E. 61st Ave., Portland Oregon, 97206.

OWEN FAMILY

John Owen, d. ca 1840, in Ky.; m. 10 May, 1807, Clark Co., Ky., Sarah
Gordon, b. 4 March, 1788; d. 27 Dec., 1877, in Missouri, dau. of John Gordon, b. Va.; d. 1839, Clark Co., Ky., and his wife, Mary Rountree. It is
believed that his dau., Sarah Gordon, was born in Va. Children: David
Gordon Owen, Elizabeth, Jackson, Richardson, James, Margaret, Katherine,
Mary, Robert and Sarah Ann Owen.

Compiled and contributed by Mrs. A. L. Tapp, 3219 20th St., Lubbock,
Texas, for "Wilcoxson and Allied Families," by Dorothy Ford Wulfeck.

PETERMAN FAMILY

Francis Marion Peterman moved from Berkeley Co., Va., to Carroll Co.,
Mo., 1852, with the Williamson Family; m. (1) 1853, Sophia Ann Williamson,
dau. of Leonard and Margaret (Cross). Children:
1. Sterling Price Peterman.
2. Jasper O. Peterman.
3. Margaret Peterman m. A. J. Casebolt, Carroll Co., Mo.
4. Emily Peterman m. Rufus Hill.
He m. (2) Virginia Rogers of California, Mo., but they had no children.

Contributed by Joida Whitten, 5314 Emerson, Dallas 9, Texas.

PETERS FAMILY

Samuel Peters, b. 1769, Culpeper Co., Va., m. _____ Byler; rem. to Bedford Co., Tenn., thence to Cooper Co., Mo.; d. 1858. Children:
1. Samuel Peters, Jr.
2. Newton C. Peters.
3. _____ m. _____ McFarland.
4. Elizabeth Peters m. James Hill, one-time Sheriff of Cooper Co., Mo.
5. Priscilla Peters m. Harvey Harper.
6. Katie Peters m. (1) Thomas Patrick; m. (2) Samuel Cole.
7. Sallie Peters m. James Gallagher.

Contributed by Mrs. Hallie Harper Springsteen, 2255 Fairfax St., Denver, Colo.

PETTUS (PETTIS) FAMILY

Dabney Pettus, b. prob. 1780, Fluvanna Co., Va.; d. 1852, Boone Co.,
Mo.; m. (1) and divorced in 1803; m. (2) in Va., Elizabeth Turner.

"The Pettus Family," by A. Bohmer Rudd, p. 16.

Spencer Pettis, b. 1802, Caroline Co., Va.; d. 26 Aug., 1831, son of
John and Martha "Patsy" (Reynolds); first Congressman from Missouri, 1828;
re-elected in 1830.

Ibid., p. 52.

PRICE FAMILY

William Price and his son, Capt. Joseph Price, who was b. Greenbrier
Co., W. Va., near White Sulphur Springs, 1813, came directly to and settled
in Callaway Co., Mo. The father of William, Samuel Price, served in the
Rev. War and moved to Lewisburg, W. Va., 1784.

Capt. Joseph kept an interesting diary of his trip to the gold fields
in 1850, which has been published. He m. Elizabeth Renfro, dau. of Dr.
William Renfro (see sketch). They were parents of Sally W., b. 1842; China
Rothwell, b. 1845; Nancy L. Price, b. 1847.

RENFRO FAMILY

The following gem is taken from an original manuscript, No. 58-0060,
"Journals and Diaries, Stephens Family Genealogy," Vol. XVI, deposited
with the Missouri Historical Society, Jefferson Memorial, St. Louis, Mo.,
and was submitted by Mrs. W. S. Rodman of Columbia, Mo., ca 1914.

"My great-grandfather, Moses Renfro, b. 1728; m. Bedford Co., Va.,
to Elizabeth Turpin (1748-1844), his 2nd wife, and were parents of my
grandfather, Dr. William Renfro, b. 1781, Franklin Co., Va.; m. 1808,
Sally Creal Stephens, dau. of William and Lizzie (Leachman) Stephens.
(The father, Moses, was an eminent Baptist minister of the day and preached
a sermon at the age of 96 in 1824. His ordination papers, now over 200
years old (1964) are still in possession of the Missouri Renfro family
heirs. -- A. M. Coppage)

"Dr. Renfro migrated to Garrard Co., Ky., and was once associated
with the renowned surgeon, Dr. Russell, of Lexington, Ky. The physician
distilled his own herbs, peppermint, lavender, sweet balsam, mountain
sweet and oil of herbs. In a letter to his wife, Columbia, Mo., 1837, he
says: 'I often trod among those lofty pines, whose beautious branches
thickly spread a covering o'er the ground; and, from a distance, showed
their tops, while herbs are found beneath. From them I drew the precious
oil, to annoint the poor, and often travel late at night, in hopes, to
make a cure. I give relief without dispute almost where ere I go. I take
diseases out by root, and strength and health restore.'

"In 1833, Dr. Renfro settled four miles north of Stephens, Callaway
Co., Mo., where he lived until his death, 1864. He took three of his four
sons-in-law into his home and, for two years each, taught them medical
skills without requiring payment. They were Dr. John Rothwell, b. Albemarle Co., Va., 1805, who m. China Renfro; Dr. Wm. E. Stephens, who m.
his cousin, Marianna Renfro; and Sally J. Renfro who m. her cousin, Dr.
Locke Stephens, b. Garrard Co., Ky., 1812. Another daughter, Elizabeth
Renfro, b. 1817, m. Capt. Joseph Price, b. near Lewisburg, Greenbrier Co.,
W. Va.; d. Callaway Co., Mo., 3 Oct., 1870. Capt. Joseph Price was a son
of William and Sallie (Walkup) Price and grandson of Samuel.

"A stranger than fiction story is told in the Renfro family. During
the time in Kentucky forts, Elizabeth (Turpin) Renfro, mother of the doctor, dreamed three times that Indians had attacked their home. This so
impressed her husband that he insisted she take Queen Lett, a Negro woman,
and go to a larger fort for safety. After they had gone the Indians did

118

fall upon the fort, killing her brother and all the people excepting her
husband, their son, James, and one woman and child. The night that Queen
Lett arrived at the larger fort she gave birth to a son. This son came to
Missouri with Dr. Wm. Renfro and was affectionately known to his children
as "Uncle Bob." Queen Lett, his mother, said that her mother, on the Guinea
Coast of Africa was a Queen, and that she, Queen Lett, had been kidnapped
there."

The Renfro family is French and is sometimes spelled Rentfro.

RILEY FAMILY

Thomas Riley, b. 11 Jan., 1793, prob. Culpeper Co., Va.; d. 16 July,
1869, DeKalb Co., Mo.; m. ca 1816, Elizabeth Wyckoff, b. 13 Nov., 1789,
Loudoun Co., Va.; d. 17 July, 1845, sister of Nicholas Wyckoff. Both are
buried (with suitable stone) at the McDaniel Cemetery, near Cameron, Mo.
Children:
1. William W. Riley, b. 1818; d. 1885; m. 11 Aug., Scott Co., Ky.,
   Mary Ann Sharp, dau. of Lindsey Sharp.
2. Jonathan Riley, b. ca 1819; m. 24 June, 1849, DeKalb Co., Mo.,
   Elizabeth Buckingham.
3. Harriett Riley, b. 1825; d. 1843; m. 8 June, 1843, Scott Co., Ky.,
   Thomas F. Butler.
4. Nicholas Riley, d. DeKalb Co., Mo.

Contributed by Raymond Riley, Riley Dental Laboratory, Box 31, Chilli-
cothe, Mo.

RODGERS FAMILY

A Rodgers resident of Halifax Co., Va., removed to Callaway Co., Mo.
Another moved from Virginia to Clermont Co., Ohio, thence to Ripley Co.,
Ind., then to Dade Co., Wisc., and to Lee Co., Iowa, from where he settled
in Northeast Missouri.

A Rodgers family moved from Rockingham Co., Va., to Morgan Co., Mo.,
then to Randolph and Macon Cos., Mo. Another one moved from Ohio Co., Va.,
to Howard and Cooper Cos., Mo.

A Rodgers family went from Greenbrier Co., Va.-W. Va., to Knox Co.,
Ill., and from there to Daviess Co., Mo.

Isaac Rodgers is found in the 1830 Census of Madison Co., Mo., as between 20 and 30 years of age, with wife of same age group and a son under
five years of age. He was a son of Adenston Rodgers.

Adenston Rodgers was living in French Louisiana about 1802, the Cape
Girardeau region of Missouri from which St. Francois and Madison and other
counties were formed. It would appear that he was a son or grandson of
Adaston Rogers, mentioned in Will and Deed books of Goochland Co., Va.,
in 1740's.

Francis Rodgers and Washington Rodgers were sons of Isaac Rodgers.

The 1850 Census, St. Francois Co., Mo., lists William Rogers, age 55,
b. Va., with wife, Christina, age 50, b. Va., and children, b. Tenn.

ROTHWELL FAMILY

Dr. John T. Rothwell, b. 1810, Va.; m. China Renfro, dau. of Dr. William and Sally Creel (Stephens) Renfro; res. 1850, Callaway Co., Mo. Children: William R., b. 1832, Ky.; Thomas Peyton, b. 1834, Mo.; Gideon F., b. 1836; Sally b. 1838; Minerva, b. 1840.

Ref.: Manuscript of "Stephens Family and Stephens College," by A. Maxim Coppage III.

SAGE FAMILY

Charles Sage, b. 1797; d. 1872/3; rem. from Grayson Co., Va., to Jackson Co., Mo., sometime between 1832 and 1843. Samuel Sage, his brother, moved from Grayson Co., Va., to Taney Co., Mo., at the same time.

Ref.: "Historic Spots in Wyandotte," by Grant Harrison of Lawrence, Kans., 1930, and "Red Trails and White," by Bonnie Ball, 1955. (Copy in Harry Truman Library, Independence, Mo.) Taken from documentary records.

Others, mentioned in the same documents as from Grayson Co., Va., were Joseph Briant and Nancy Hackler.

Contributed by Mrs. Bonnie S. Ball, Box 312, Haysi, Va. 24256.

SCOTT FAMILY

Allen Scott, b. 12 April, 1805; d. 3 March, 1876, said to be son of Col. John Scott of Virginia; m. 12 Jan., 1836, Ann C. Edmondson, b. 15 May, 1815; d. 28 Aug., 1885.
Allen Scott left Glade Springs, Washington Co., Va., in 1836, after his marriage, and came to Cole Co., Mo., where he settled near Russelville, moving to Vernon Co., Mo., in 1870. The vital statistics were recorded by his son, William Scott, in his Family Bible, which is in the possession of Miss Leona DeWitt, Box 348, Cottonwood Falls, Kansas 66845.
My grandfather has stated that Allen's father was Col. John Scott, of whom I can find no trace in Washington Co. However, Allen's brothers were named Smith Scott and Hutton Scott, among others, and the will of Thomas Scott (possibly an uncle of Allen Scott), filed 1797, Rockbridge Co., Va., names sons, Andrew, John, Smith, William Harrison (despite Clements, this is only one person) and Thomas Scott, which shows that "Smith" was a family name for this branch of the family.
The sister of Ann C. Edmondson wed a rather prominent Dr. Snead (or Sneed) in Washington Co., Va. The John Scott, named in the will, wed 1795, Esther Houston, dau. of John Houston. My grandfather also recalls that Smith Scott, brother of Allen Scott, moved to Galesburg, Ill., and his brother, Hutton Scott, went to Iowa and died in Nebraska while living with a married daughter.

Contributed by Douglas R. Scott, 1535 S. E. 29th St., Apt. 11, Portland, Ore. 97214.

SCROGGIN—GREENE FAMILY

Rev. John Scroggin, Jr., b. ca 1784, Pennsylvania; d. Sept., 1871, Hempstead Co., Ark.; m. 27 July, 1804, Washington Co., Va., Elizabeth White, b. ca 1786, Va.; d. after 1860, Hempstead Co., Ark., dau. of John and Martha (Phillips) of Virginia and White Co., Tenn.; res. Cooper and Morgan Cos., Mo.

A son, James Walker Scroggin, b. 15 Sept., 1805, Va.; d. 4 Dec., 1864, Hempstead Co., Ark.; m. 12 Jan., 1826, White Co., Tenn., Sarah Griggs Greene, b. 27 Nov., 1806, Ky.; d. 30 April, 1872, Hempstead Co., Ark., dau. of Rev. John and Rachell (Mackey) of Kentucky and Tenn., and granddaughter of Jarvis Green (Rev. soldier and half-brother of Gen. Nathaniel Green) whose wife was Sarah Griggs of No. Car.

The will of Rev. John Green, dated 13 Dec., 1852, White Co., Tenn.; probated 1 Aug., 1853, names wife, Judith Greene (his 2nd wife), dau. Nancy Bell, granddaughter, Eveline, son, William.

A Chancery Suit followed and proves his children and grandchildren and their residences. Oliver T. Schoolfield of Bledsoe Co., Tenn., vs William Green and John W. May, Admrs. of John Green, dec'd.; Judith Green (widow), Nancy Bell, Susan J. May, William Wilson, Sarah Wilson, Mary Green, Nancy Green, all citizens of White Co., Tenn.; Stephen Cope and Elizabeth Cope of Warren Co., Tenn.; James Scroggins and Sarah Scroggins of the State of Arkansas; P. G. Avery, William L. Avery, Roberson L. Avery, Richard Faville, Nancy Faville, Richard Edings, Susan Edings, A. C. Avery and James M. Avery, all citizens of the State of Missouri; John Hasten, David Hasten, James Hasten, Elizabeth Hasten, ?Woodson Hasten, James Chambers, all citizens of the Oregon Territory.

All of the above-named defendants are the children and grandchildren or the husbands of the children and grandchildren of the said John Green. (Taken from old Chancery Files.)

From old Book in Basement Vault, "Receipts, Powers of Attorney, Guardians, Etc."

p. 79. James P. Hastain and John G. Hastain of Maryville, Yuba Co., Calif., appoint Daniel M. C. Hastain of Henry Co., Mo., their Atty. in fact regarding estate of John Green, dec'd., of White Co., Tenn.

p. 81. David M. Hastain of Henry Co., Mo., appoints Daniel M. C. Hastain his Atty. in fact . . . John Green his grandfather. This April 22, 1854.

p. 82. Woodson A. Hastain, Mary Ann Dice, formerly Mary Ann Hastain, now wife of Abner H. Dice, heirs of John Green. (These in Benton Co., Mo.) (Above documents filed in Chancery Court, Dec., 1857.)

Hempstead Co., Ark. Deed Book F, p. 33. Peter Kinsey of Hempstead Co. . . . $1000.00 . . . to James W. Scroggin of Morgan Co., Mo. . . . tract in Hempstead Co. . . . Twp. 9, Sec. 9, R26W, about 160 acres in the District of land subject to Sale at Washington, Ark. Martha A. Kinsey, wife, relinquishes Dower. Feb. 13, 1844. Wit.: Samuel Leslie, P. G. Avery. Teste.: Wm. McDonald, J. P.

On a genealogical trip this past April, I discovered a Scoggin family

Bible, in possession of a cousin, in Nashville, Ark. This Bible had been the property of my ancestor, James Walker Scoggin and his wife, Sarah Griggs Greene (he b. 15 Sept., 1805, Washington Co., Va., first son of Rev. John and Elizabeth (White) Scoggin), and the Bible herein listed James' middle name as "Walker" not "William," as I had previously thought, and also listed the name of their last son, my great-grandfather, as Jacob Walker Scoggin, again, not "William" as I had thought.

My Rev. John Scoggin, Jr., appears to have been a son of John Scoggin, Sr., and his wife, Sarah (?Walker), who appeared in Washington Co., Va., in 1796, when they purchased land from Thomas Johnston and his wife, Fanny (Deed Bk. 1, p. 451). They purchased more land in 1797, from William and John Walker (Deed Bk. 1, p. 541). John Scoggin, Sr., was also listed (in Deed Bk. 3, p. 219, Washington Co., Va.) as a Trustee for the establishment of the (Meherrin) Methodist Church, at time it was organized, in late 1803. Rev. John Scoggin, Jr., was later a Methodist minister, both in White Co., Tenn., and in Hempstead Co., Ark., when he was a very old man.

Although Rev. John Scoggin, Jr., was born in Pennsylvania, I firmly believe that his parents were Virginians, partly because he had an older brother, Jesse Scoggin, who was born in Virginia before he was born in Pennsylvania, and the thought has occurred to me that John, Sr., may have been a circuit-rider minister who was sent to Pennsylvania shortly prior to John, Jr.'s, birth, and later was sent back to Virginia.

James Walker Scoggin and wife, Sarah Griggs (Greene) Scoggin, left their home in White Co., Tenn., in 1830, with two small children, and settled in Cooper or Morgan Co., Mo., where they lived until they moved to Hempstead Co., Ark., in 1846. James Walker Scoggin was a Justice of the Peace in Missouri. They left married children in Missouri.

Compiled and contributed by Mrs. William J. Doliante, 12 Tauxemont Rd., Alexandria, Va. 22308.

SNELL FAMILY

Loudoun Snell, b. April, 1774, Va.; d. 20 Feb., 1839, Boone Co., Mo., son of John, Jr., of Spotsylvania Co. and Orange Co., Va.; m. Judith ____, d. 3 Oct., 1841, age 63. Their children were born and married in Scott Co., Ky., and Loudoun Snell moved to Callaway Co., Mo., ca 1824.

Cumberland Snell, b. 1779, Orange Co., Va.; d. 1 Nov., 1825, Boone Co., Mo.; brother of Loudoun Snell; m. 1806, Elizabeth Emison, b. 9 Feb., 1784; d. 5 Oct., 1844, dau. of Ash and Mary (Mitchell) Emison.

Ref.: "The Emison Families Revised," by James Wade Emison, Vincennes, Ind., p. 115.

STEWART FAMILY

Townsend Stewart, b. 26 April, 1814, Va.; d. 2 Oct., 1860, Boone Co., Mo.; said to have had 8 sons and 2 daus. Will of Townsend Stewart, No. 1765, Boone Co., Mo.; Administration granted 13 Oct., 1860, to Joel Hayden; final sett. 4 April, 1864. Heirs: widow, Sarah M. Stewart, William Wormley Stewart, Hayward F. Stewart, Elizabeth, Virginia, Thomas, Carter,

George, Townsend, Thornton and Silas Stewart.

Sarah M. Carter, b. 17 Jan., 1820, Prince William Co., Va.; m. 6 Oct., 1836, Townsend Stewart. She d. 25 Jan., 1902, Boone Co., Mo.

Other tombstones in the Carter-Hamilton Cemetery, Boone Co., Mo.:

William W. Stewart, son of T. and S. M., d. Jan. 25, 1865, age 27 y. 4 m. 25 da.

Hayward F. Stewart, son of T. and S. M., d. April 15, 1865, age 26 y. 5 m. 14 da.

George J. Stewart, son of T. and S. M., d. Sept. 26, 1876, age 19 y. 5 mo. 14 da.

There are three other Stewart tombstones of later date.

Will of William Stewart, Boone Co., Mo., No. 361. Administration granted, 18 Oct., 1839, to Joannah Stewart; final sett. 18 May, 1846. Heirs: Johannah Stewart, widow; Susan B. Stewart, Townsend Stewart, Silas Stewart, Amanda M. Stewart, Alexander Stewart, Thomas Stewart.

Will of Joanna Stewart, Boone Co., Mo., No. 463. Administration granted, 26 Sept., 1842; final sett. 14 Sept., 1848. Heirs: son, Lawson Stewart; dau. Amanda M. Hill; son, Thornton Stewart; niece, Ann E. Barnett. Extr. Mark A. Chilton. Wit.: James Grady, James McKenzie and John M. Brooks.

Some Boone Co. Marriages:

Silas Stewart m. 24 Jan., 1840, Elizabeth Hill.

Amanda Melvina Stewart m. 23 Jan., 1840, Elias Hill.

Alexander Stewart m. 14 Sept., 1854, Nancy Jane McGrew.

Will of James W. Hill names an heir, Elizabeth Stewart, and Silas Stewart is Admr. of the est. 22 Sept., 1853.

ANOTHER STEWART LINE

George Washington Stewart, b. 1777, Va.; m. Mary Smith, b. ca 1778, Va. (1850 Census, Mo.); res. Washington Co., Va., when son, John Stewart, was born 1799-1800; rem. to Eastern Tenn., thence to Fountain Co., Ind., by 1850, in Holt Co., Mo., where Mary was head of the house. Known children: John, Robert Smith, James H., Burrel, Mary, G. W., and Hugh Smith.

John Stewart, b. ca 1800, Washington Co., Va.; m. (1) _____; m. (2) Mary Scott; farmed in Holt Co., Mo., until about 1845 when he moved to the Oregon Territory.

Donation Land Claim of John Stewart, No. 175, Benton Co., Ore., shows he was b. 1799, Va.; m. 7 Jan., 1843, Holt Co., Mo., Mary; sett. claim 14 Aug., 1846. Affidavits: Joseph C. Avery and Heman C. Lewis. Children: (by 1st wife) (order not known)

1. Archimedes Stewart, b. 1827, Tippecanoe Co., Ind. (from Donation Land Claim No. 176, Oregon); m. 19 Oct., 1848, Benton Co., Ore., Matilda ____.
2. Calvin (or Colvin) N. Stewart; m. and had 5 children.
3. Hugh Stewart.
4. Minerva Stewart m. Mr. Dice.
5. Elizabeth Stewart m. Mr. Ringer.

(by 2nd wife)

6. John Stewart, b. Holt Co., Mo.
7. Cerenda Stewart m. Miner M. Swick.

Contributed by Mrs. N. C. Hiday, 1210 16th St., N. E., Salem, Oregon.

SUTTON FAMILY

Robert Sutton, b. 1761; d. 2 Dec., 1828, son of John, Sr., and Temperance (Lane); m. Caroline Coleman, b. 1762; d. 1827, Caroline Co., Va.

A dau., Mary "Polly" King Sutton, b. 6 July, 1784, Scott Co., Va.; d. 23 March, 1877, Randolph Co., Mo.; m. 2 May, 1799, Paul Christian. See CHRISTIAN FAMILY.

Contributed by Mrs. Forrest B. Doshier, 1501 Rusk St., Amarillo, Tex.

TERRILL FAMILY

Robert Terrill, b. 1777; d. 1827, son of Edmond and Margaret "Peggy" (Willis); m. 1799, Mary "Polly" Lacy, b. 1776; d. 1850.

A son, James Terrill, b. 29 Dec., 1801, Albemarle Co., Va.; d. 9 Sept., 1876, Randolph Co., Mo.; m. 18 May, 1833, Eliza Ann Crisler, b. 6 Sept., 1813; d. 2 Feb., 1905, dau. of Jonas (1785-1858) and Elizabeth (Price), 1788-1880, of Madison Co., Va.

Contributed by Mrs. Forrest B. Doshier, 1501 Rusk St., Amarillo, Tex.

TURNER FAMILY

Boonesboro Cemetery, Boonesboro, Howard Co., Mo., has tombstones for Henry Turner, b. 1792; d. 29 Aug., 1858, and for his wife, Ann K. Turner, b. Aug. 15, 1791; d. Nov. 14, 1866.

Lucretia Turner, dau. of Henry and Ann K. Turner, b. Fauquier Co., Va., Dec. 2, 1833; d. July 25, 1870. Robert H. Turner, her brother, b. Fauquier Co., Va., June 5, 1828; d. March 28, 1879. Amelia H. G. Turner, b. Louisa Co., Va., Aug. 25, 1835; d. Sept. 27, 1886. They are in a fenced-in lot which has a Wythe tombstone, also.

UTTERBACK FAMILY

James Travis Utterback, b. 1825, New Baltimore, Fauquier Co., Va., son of Armistead and Mary "Polly" Price (Crump); m. (1) 1850, Anna Perry of Upper Culpeper Co., Va.; rem. ca 1850 to St. Louis, Mo., where he became a wealthy shoe merchant; m. (2) Abby Turner of Booneville, Mo.; m. (3) Miss Ballard of St. Louis, Mo., who was the mother of his son.

Ref.: "The Utterback Family, 1620-1938," by William I. Utterback. 1937.

WALTON FAMILY

William Walton, b. ca 1778, Henrico Co., Va.; m. 31 Dec., 1802, Louisa Co., Va., Martha "Patsey" Warren, dau. of Rev. Bartholomew Warren, ancestors of Charles Carter Anderson of Richmond, Va., who was born in the Colonial Inn operated by William. They had a son, John William Walton, who m. twice and res. Boone Co., Mo.

Ref.: "Wilcoxson and Allied Families," by Dorothy Ford Wulfeck, p. 417.

WARREN FAMILY

Sebert Asher Warren, b. 2 July„ 1790, Va.; d. 12 Sept., 1853, Bolivar,
Polk Co., Mo.; rem. to Robertson Co., Tenn., bef. 1810; rem. to Mo., 1851;
m. March, 1810, Robertson Co., Tenn., Frances Bushrod Swift, b. 2 June,
1791, No. Car.; d. 13 Sept., 1865, Walnut Hill, Marion Co., Ill., dau. of
Richard and Katherine (Moss) Swift. (Note: Their children with dates of
birth are given in this reference.)

"Southside Virginia Families," Vol. II, by John B. Boddie, p. 369.

WHITTEN FAMILY

I. Thomas Whitten, b. 1749, Bedford Co., Va.; d. 1800, Botetourt Co.,
Va.; m. 1772, Martha Paxon (?Paxton); served as a private from Washington
Co., Va., in the Rev. War, 1776-1783.
II. Joseph Whitten, b. 1794; m. (1) 1817, Elizabeth M. Johnson, b.
1796; d. 1841; m. (2) Jane P. Moon between 1841 and 1844. According to
the Census of Bedford Co., Va., for 1850, she was born about 1820. (There
is a Jane P. Whitten listed in the 1883 Pension Lists of Bedford Co., Va.,
as the widow of a veteran of War of 1812.)
Children, as listed on 1850 Census of Bedford Co., Va.: Jane G., 15;
Martha (?S.), 13, (these two girls should be children of the first marriage,
as are Joseph and Thomas listed later); Jacob M., 6; James P., 4; Lucy B.,
3; Mary T., 2; Zachary T., 10 months old. (For descendants of Jane G. Whitten, above, refer to DAR Lineage Book, Vol. 77, 1909, Elizabeth Snow Black,
No. 76 597.)
III. Thomas J. Whitten, b. 3 May, 1828, Va.; d. 19 July, 1879; m.
Eliza Lee, b. 17 Feb., 1839; d. 4 Dec., 1878, dau. of Atkinson Hill Lee,
and his wife, Susannah (Wilcoxson), of Ky. and Howard Co., Mo.
III. Joseph G. Whitten, b. 10 Aug., 1830, Bedford Co., Va.; d. 1
Jan., 1909, Howard Co., Mo., son of Joseph and Elizabeth M. (Johnson); m.
(2) 1 Jan., 1868, Howard Co., Mo., Sarah (Lee) Chancellor, b. 1837, Howard
Co., Mo.; d. there, 1913, widow of Joseph Chancellor and dau. of Atkinson
Hill Lee and his wife, Susannah (Wilcoxson), of Ky. and Mo., and gr.dau.
of Wilford Lee, son of John Lee who moved from Virginia to Kentucky. Joseph
G. Whitten had m. (1) 1860, in Va., Elizabeth Stanly of Kanawha Co., W. Va.,
who d. 1863, leaving one dau., "Tille," who m. M. C. Daniel and res. in
1909 in Huntington, Va.
Sarah (Lee) Chancellor and Joseph Chancellor were the parents of Bettie,
Ida and Joseph Chancellor and Mrs. Howard Cason (Lillie Chancellor).
III. Jacob M. Whitten, b. 13 Jan., 1844; Bedford Co., Va.; d. 9 June,
1912, Howard Co., Mo., where he rem. in 1869; m. (1) Sallie J.   who d.
leaving 2 daus. and 1 son. He m. (2) Annie Blankenbaker, b. 1857; d. 1914,
sister of Guy Blankenbaker.

Contributed by Joida Whitten, 5314 Emerson, Dallas 9, Texas.

WILLIAMSON FAMILY

Leonard Williamson m. Margaret Cross; rem. 1852, from Berkeley Co.,
Va., to Carroll Co., Mo. Children:

1. Margaret Elizabeth Williamson m. (1) Thomas Davis; m. (2) Isaac Kile.
2. Richard Jack Williamson, bur. Carroll Co., Mo.
3. Mary Ellen "Molly" Williamson m. Benjamin Davis.
4. Sophia Ann Williamson m. Francis Marion Peterman.

WILSON FAMILY

Martha Agnes Wilson, b. Prince Edward Co., Va., dau. of Dr. Goodridge Wilson and his wife, Elizabeth Woodson (Venable) Wilson; m. Judge Robert Bentley Frayser as his 2nd wife; rem. soon after 1851, to St. Charles Co., Mo.

"Historical Southern Families," Vol. III, by John B. Boddie, p. 66.

WINSTON FAMILY

James Winston, son of George and Dorothea (Henry), dau. of Gov. Patrick Henry of Virginia, was a distinguished lawyer and politician of Missouri.

"Genealogical and Historical Notes on Culpeper County, Virginia," by Raleigh Travers Green. Part I, p. 76.

WISE FAMILY

Richard Wise, b. 10 Nov., 1799, Culpeper Co., Va.; rem. to Montgomery Co., Ky., ca 1811, with his parents; m. 29 March, 1821, Martha "Patsy" Gillmore, b. 20 Jan., 1805, Montgomery Co., Ky., dau. of Mrs. Martha Gillmore (1786-1867); rem. to Callaway Co., Mo., after the birth of their 9th child in 1837.

"Gillmore-Carter and Allied Families," by Smith and Barmann, p. 41.

WITHERS FAMILY

John Withers, b. 22 May, 1768; d. Dec., 1838, son of John and Hannah (Routt) Withers of Stafford Co., Va., and Jessamine Co., Ky.; m. 1797, Mary Emison, b. 11 March, 1775, near Chambersburg, Penna.; d. 11 April, 1870, dau. of Hugh and Mary (Baird) Emison; res. 1802, Scott Co., Ky.; rem. to Withers Mills, Marion Co., Mo.

Ref.: "The Emison Families Revised," by James Wade Emison, Vincennes, Ind.

WOODSON FAMILY

Charles Friend Woodson, b. 20 Nov., 1794, at "Neck of Land," Four Mile Creek, Chesterfield Co., Va.; d. 9 June, 1887, at "Mt. Airy," Upper Dardenne, St. Charles Co., Mo., son of Capt. George Woodson; m. 15 April, 1830, at "Millwood," Prince Edward Co., Va., Anne Thomas Wilson, b. 7 Dec., 1806, Prince Edward Co., Va.; d. 28 Feb., 1887, at "Mt. Airy," dau. of Dr.

126

Goodridge Wilson and Elizabeth Woodson (Venable) of Prince Edward Co., Va.
They moved to St. Charles Co., Mo., between 1840 and 1842.

"Historical Southern Families," by John B. Boddie. Vol. III, p. 66.

Elizabeth Woodson m. Charles Gilliam; rem. from Cumberland Co., Va.,
to Chariton Co., Mo., 1817; later rem. to Saline Co., Mo. One of their
children was Elizabeth Gilliam.
Mary Woodson. See MOSS FAMILY.
Richard Goodridge Woodson, b. Sept., 1833, at "Millwood," Prince Edward Co., Va.; d. 8 March, 1911, at Dardenne, Mo., son of Charles Friend
Woodson, and his wife, Anne Thomas Wilson; m. 15 July, 1868, at "Belle-
meade," Upper Dardenne, Mo., Grace Lee, b. 7 Aug., 1850, Port Jervis, Orange
Co., N. Y.; d. 22 Feb., 1936, Dardenne, Mo., dau. of Philip and Nancy Jane
(Cunion).

Ibid., p. 67.

Richard Woodson and wife, Rachel (Robertson) Woodson, moved from Prince
Edward Co., Va., to Chariton Co., Mo., with their cousins, the Gilliams, in
1817. Children:
1. William Cowper Woodson m. (1) Elizabeth Daniel Lewis; m. (2)
    Mrs. Juliet Colson Cowle (nee Howard).
2. James Edward Woodson m. Elizabeth Gilliam, dau. of Charles
    and Elizabeth (Woodson). She m. (2) William E. Goode, who
    had been married twice, 1st to Elizabeth's sister, Judith A.
    Gilliam of Va.; rem. to Cambridge, Saline Co., Mo. They had
    William P., George and Mary A. Goode. He m. (2) Lucy C. Jones
    of Kentucky and had Lizzie Parish Goode.
3. Elizabeth Morton Woodson m. John Fontaine Nicolds.
4. Martha Woodson m. James J. Miller, son of ex-Gov. Miller of
    Missouri.
5. Richard Woodson, Jr., m. (1) Roanna Ewing; m. (2) Frances
    Ann Adie.
Rachel (Robertson) Woodson m. (2) Col. John Bell, Judge of the Supreme
Court of Missouri, and had Mary Bell who d. young, and John P. Bell who m.
Piney Wilson of Saline Co., Mo.

Contributed by Joida Whitten, 5314 Emerson, Dallas 9, Texas.

EDWARDS FAMILY

William Edwards, b. ca 1765, Va.; m. ca 1790, near Fairfax, Va., Sallie
Leachman, dau. of John and Sarah (Creal). Children: Sallie who m. Dr. Thomas Peyton Stephens, Rockingham Co., No. Car., Garrard Co., Ky., and Callaway Co., Mo., in 1817; Virgil, unmd., lived in Callaway Co., Mo., in 1850;
Mathew H. who m. Nancy Stephens, 18 Aug., 1819, and Nancy Edwards who m.
John Williamson, 3 Aug., 1812. Some think Wm. had a bro., Ambrose, and
possibly a bro., David.

From: "Genealogical Data from Margurite Stephens Anderson," mss., Bk.
1, p. 35. Deposited in Missouri Historical Society, Jefferson Memorial, St.

Louis, Mo.

Henry Edwards, son of Ambrose, m. Sarah Dabney of Hanover Co., Va.,
and came to St. Charles Co., Mo. They had a son, Henry, b. Henry Co., Va.,
13 Sept., 1836, who came with his parents to Missouri.

"St. Charles, Warren and Montgomery Cos., Mo.," p. 472.

"The Old Free State," by Landon C. Bell, 1927. Vol. II.

p. 101. Benjamin Howard, born in Virginia, was Governor of the
Missouri Territory, 1810-12.
p. 103. David Patterson Dyer, a Representative from Missouri, was
born in Henry Co., Va., 12 Feb., 1838.
Joseph J. Gravely, a Representative from Missouri, was born
in Henry Co., Va., in 1828.
John William Noell, a Representative from Missouri, was born
in Bedford Co., Va., 22 Feb., 1816.
Thomas Lawson Price, a Representative from Missouri, was
born in Pittsylvania Co., Va., 19 Jan., 1809.

Other native Virginians who moved to Missouri are mentioned, as follows:
p. 145-6. Caspar Wistar Bell.
p. 221. Sarah Hardy, Alexander McCluer and Joseph Hardy.

PART VII

MISCELLANEOUS RECORDS

1850 Census, Boone Co., Mo. (Incomplete)

1912	Samuel Austin	65	Va.
	Susan Austin	67	Va.
65	Washington Bailey	64	Va.
	Hanna? Bailey	60	Va.
	Sarah A. Bailey	19	Va.
	George W. Bailey	16	Va.
	Eliza A. Bailey	12	Va.
1834	Robert V. Bailey	50	Va.
	John T. Bailey	25	Va.
	Robert Bailey	22	Va.
	Joseph Bailey	16	Va.
	William H. Bailey	12	Mo.
	Josiah L. Buster	40	Va.
533	Moses Baker	53	Ky.
	Mary B. Baker	35	Va.
	Martha J. Baker	15	Mo.
	James M. Baker	11	Mo.
	Margaret S. Baker	2	Mo.
1440	James Beal	37	Va.
	Mary A. Beal	34	Va.
	James W. Beal	9	Va.
	Elijah B. Beal	7	Va.
	Lydia M. Beal	3	Mo.
	Rebecca A. Beal	1	Mo.
972	James Beasley	62	Va.
	Julia Beasley	44	Va.
	James Beasley	21	Mo.
	William Beasley	19	Mo.
1096	James C. Beattie	39	Va.
	Ann Beattie	32	Va.
	Nancy E. Beattie	13	Va.
	Joseph Beattie	11	Va.
	David C. Beattie	8	Va.
947	Stephen Bedford	59	Va.
	Elizabeth M. Bedford	50	S.C.
	Susan Bedford	22	Ky.
	Sarah Bedford	17	Mo.
	Ellen Bedford	15	Mo.
	Robert Bedford	19	Mo.

947	(cont.)		
	Richard Bedford	8	Mo.
	Wm. Bedford	12	Mo.
1458	Almond Behart	29	Va.
	Louisa C. Behart	24	Va.
	Augustus Behart	16	Va.
	William Behart	5	Va.
	Almond Behart	4	Mo.
	Luther D. Behart	2	Mo.
	Marcellus Behart	1	Mo.
916	Henry Berry	55	Va.
	Nancy Berry	42	Ky.
	Bloomfield Berry	19	Ky.
	Erastus Berry	17	Ky.
	John H. Berry	13	Ky.
	D. F. (female)	11	Ky.
	Jasper Berry	7	Ky.
	Harrison Berry	5	Mo.
	William Berry	3	Mo.
940	William Berry	84	S.C.
	Ezekiel E. Hickman	45	Va.
	Nancy Hickman	42	Ky.
	Lycugus Hickman	20	Mo.
	Lycander Hickman	17	Mo.
	Cornelia Hickman	14	Mo.
	Marrium Hickman	10	Mo.
1542	Thomas Berry	57	Va.
	Maria Berry	65	Va.
	Elizabeth J. Berry	31	Ky.
	Joseph Berry	26	Ky.
	John T. Berry	24	Ky.
	James Berry	21	Ky.
	Ann R. Jones	29	Ky.
	William Jones	10	Mo.
	Elizabeth Jones	7	Mo.
	Alfred Jones	5	Mo.
657	Reubin Biooker?	30	Ky.
	Martha J. Biooker	27	Va.
	Benjamin F. Biooker	4	Mo.
	Daniel B. Biooker	2	Mo.

914	Joseph Birch	38	Va.
	Elizabeth H. Birch	38	Ky.
	Mary C. Birch	14	Mo.
	H. F. (female)	13	Mo.
	C. C. Birch	12	Mo.
	Susan E. Birch	9	Mo.
	W. T. Birch	7	Mo.
	James H. Birch	6	Mo.
	Margaret J. Birch	3	Mo.
	Ann Birch	9/12	Mo.
	Margaret Chaney	75	Va.
91	Levin Bishop	60	Md.
	Judith Virginia	57	Va.
	Elijah J. Bishop	20	Mo.
	James Bishop	16	Mo.
	Moses G. Bishop	14	Mo.
	Mildred A. Bishop	11	Mo.
1859	Alexander Bishop	32	Va.
	Mary Bishop	33	Ky.
	Clayetta Bishop	5	Mo.
	Mariah L. Bishop	3	Mo.
	Robert Bishop	½	Mo.
	Mary Bishop	16	Ky.
1864	Nimrod Bishop	60	Va.
	Lucy Bishop	42	Va.
	Nimrod Bishop	14	Ky.
	Jane Morrison	40	Ky.
489	James Black	46	Va.
	Elizabeth Black	38	Ky.
	William Black	16	Ind.
	John Black	7	Mo.
	Thomas Black	5	Mo.
	Charles Black	10/1	Mo.
	Enoch Gallop	35	Ky.
1252	William Blackburn?	63	Va.
	Emily Blackburn	33	Va.
	John Blackburn	11	Mo.
	William Blackburn	10	Mo.
	Robert Blackburn	8	Mo.
	Elijah Blackburn	6	Mo.
	Rhoda J. Blackburn	4	Mo.
	David Blackburn	1	Mo.
608	Burdette A. Blanton	52	Ky.
	Mary J. Blanton	47	Va.
	Robert W. Blanton	21	Ky.
	Burdette C. Blanton	16	Ky.

608 (cont.)			
	Thomas H. Blanton	14	Ill.
	Mary G. C. H. Blanton	12	Ill.
	James W. Daniel	4	Mo.
974	Granville Bledsoe	38	Va.
982	Edley Bledsoe	46	Va.
	Cynthia Bledsoe	43	Ky.
	Jane Bledsoe	18	Ky.
	Valentine Bledsoe	16	Ky.
	Lucinda Bledsoe	13	Mo.
	Martha Bledsoe	11	Mo.
	Stephen Bledsoe	8	Mo.
	Sarah F. Bledsoe	2	Mo.
	Edsley Bledsoe	16	Mo.
	John Bledsoe	13	Mo.
1449	John Bledsoe	45	Va.
	Mary Bledsoe	40	Ga.
	Mary J. Bledsoe	17	Mo.
	Lucinda Bledsoe	15	Mo.
	Abraham Bledsoe	10	Mo.
	Martha Bledsoe	9	Mo.
	Barthena Bledsoe	7	Mo.
	Thomas Staples	9	Mo.
	Aaron Bledsoe	4	Mo.
	Nancy Bledsoe	8/12	Mo.
1451	Loving Bledsoe	38	Va.
	Margaret Bledsoe	39	Tenn.
	Leroy Bledsoe	15	Mo.
	Elizabeth Bledsoe	14	Mo.
	William Bledsoe	12	Mo.
	Louisa Bledsoe	11	Mo.
	Sarah Bledsoe	7	Mo.
	Mary Bledsoe	4	Mo.
	Martha Bledsoe	3	Mo.
1453	William Bledsoe	29	Ky.
	Nancy Bledsoe	29	Ky.
	Austin Bledsoe	9	Mo.
	Adaline Bledsoe	5	Mo.
	Valentine Bledsoe	64	Va.
92	John M. Boothe	30	Va.
	Selfa? Boothe	24	Ky.
	Milton Boothe	8	Mo.
	Peter Boothe	6	Mo.
	Arthur Boothe	1	Mo.

94	Peter J. Boothe	33	Va.
	Mary Boothe	32	Ky.
	Ann E. Boothe	10	Mo.
	John M. Boothe	8	Mo.
	Eliza T. Boothe	5	Mo.
	Nathaniel Boothe	3	Mo.
	Silas Boothe	9/12	Mo.
809	Richard A. Bondurant	41	Ky.
	Susan Bondurant	35	Va.
	Lucy D. Bondurant	10	Mo.
	Sarah F. Bondurant	9	Mo.
	Susan F. J. Bondurant	6	Mo.
	Margaret Bondurant	4/12	Mo.
725	Elsie A. Bosh? (Bash)	23	Ky.
	William H. Bosh	33	Ky.
	Mary M. Bosh	3	Mo.
	Abner Bosh	1	Mo.
	Judith McGhee	49	Va.
	Harriett	25	Va.
886	James Bowling	52	Va.
	Margaret Bowling	50	Va.
	Martha A. Wills	30	Va.
	Robert M. Wills	33	Va.
	James Bowling	20	Va.
	Frances Bowling	16	Mo.
	Roderick Bowling	10	Mo.
	Margaret Wills	9	Mo.
1072	Enoch Bowling (Bowlding)	25	Va.
	Sarah A. Bowling	26	Mo.
	Christopher Bowling	3	Mo.
1002	Samuel Bowling (Bowlding)	45	Va.
	Elizabeth Bowling	40	Va.
	Eugenus Bowling	17	Ind.
	Amos Bowling	15	Ind.
	Melinda Bowling	13	Mo.
	Lavina J. Bowling	10	Mo.
1098	John Bowman	42	Va.
	Sarah E. Bowman	37	Va.
	Mary F. Bowman	11	Va.
	Jeannetta W. Bowman	5	Mo.
	William F. Bowman	3	Mo.
	Nancy McDonald	28	Va.

758	Louisa W. Booker	42	Va.
	William Booker	24	Va.
	Louisa Booker	18	Va.
	Martha Booker	16	Va.
	James T. Booker	3	Mo.
1555	Austin Bradford	57	Va.
	Lavena Bradford	40	Va.
	George A. Bradford	20	Ky.
	Catherine Bradford	19	Ky.
	Margaret A. Bradford	16	Ky.
	Fulton H. Bradford	14	Ky.
	Minerva Bradford	12	Ky.
	Narcissa Bradford	10	Mo.
	Alexander Bradford	6	Mo.
	Virginia Bradford	4	Mo.
736	Richard C. Branham	42	Ky.
	Emily E. Branham	30	Ky.
	William H. Branham	14	Mo.
	Laura H. Branham	9	Mo.
	Julia L. Branham	7	Mo.
	John S. Branham	4	Mo.
	Elizabeth Patterson	29	Va.
	Wilson H. Smith	18	Mo.
1053	Hamilton Brewer	41	Va.
	Martha J. Brewer	41	Va.
	William T. Brewer	9	Mo.
	Nancy W. Brewer	7	Mo.
	Sarah E. Brewer	1/12	Mo.
1301	Martha Briant (Bryant?)	59	Va.
	Jeremiah M. Briant	25	Va.
	Jeremiah Jones	11	Mo.
	Cornelia Coons	27	Ky.
	Martha A. Coons	3	Ky.
448	N. B. Brink	25	Ala.
	Elisa Brink	19	Ky.
	Charles F. H. Brink	2	Mo.
	Sarah A. Brink	2/12	Mo.
	Ann Brink	62	Va.
	William Furnish	11	Mo.
1441	Mary M. Britt	64	N.C.
	Bowlin B. Britt	28	Va.
	Thomas N. Britt	24	Va.

1446	James W. Britt	30	Va.	973	C. R. F. Brushwood	33	Va.
	Nancy Britt	30	Va.		Catharine A. Brushwood	30	Ky.
	Richmond A. Britt	6	Va.		Mary E. Brushwood	9	Mo.
	Lewis B. Britt	4	Mo.		David Stephen	16	Mo.
	Eliza J. Britt	3	Mo.				
	George A. Britt	1/12	Mo.	977	John Brushwood	50	Va.
					Richard Brushwood	25	Va.
473	John M. Brooks	31	Ky.		Mahala Brushwood	20	Ind.
	Julia A. Brooks	32	Va.		John Brushwood	2	Mo.
	Edward C. Brooks	1/12	Mo.		Samuel Brushwood	1	Mo.
1705	John Broughton	44	Va.	995	John Brushwood	34	Va.
	Milly Broughton	38	Tenn.		Sarah Brushwood	26	Ky.
	Henry Broughton	18	Mo.		Martha A. Brushwood	12	Mo.
	Adelia Broughton	17	Mo.		Richard Brushwood	9	Mo.
	Harriett Broughton	10	Mo.		Mary C. Brushwood	7	Mo.
	Mary Broughton	8	Mo.		Eliza J. Brushwood	5	Mo.
	Zerelda Broughton	5	Mo.		John M. Brushwood	2	Mo.
	Sarah Broughton	3	Mo.				
	John Broughton	12	Mo.	545	Thomas Budkley	50	Va.
					Elizabeth Buckley	44	Va.
1156	William M. Brown	23	Md.				
	Ellen J. Brown	15	Va.	617	John B. Bugg	25	Va.
	Mary E. Brown	9/12	Mo.		Amanda M. Bugg	17	Mo.
1664	Hiram Brown	52	Va.	912	Wilson Bugg	60	Va.
	Mary Brown	39	Va.		Elizabeth Bugg	18	Va.
	Hezekiah Brown	24	Va.		Samuel S. Bugg	16	Mo.
	Minerva Brown	20	Mo.		Cyrus Bugg	16	Mo.
	John W. Brown	16	Mo.		Jesse Bugg	23	Va.
	Phoeba A. Brown	14	Mo.				
	Elizabeth Brown	12	Mo.	911	Leonard Bugg	37	Va.
	Sophia Brown	10	Mo.		Mary A. Bugg	22	Va.
	Martha Brown	4	Mo.		Sarah E. Bugg	11/12	Mo.
1671	Thomas Brown	57	Ky.	17	John Bundridge	52	Ky.
	Elizabeth Brown	50	Va.		Sarah Bundridge	61	Va.
	Milton Brown	15	Mo.		Sarah J. Bundridge	17	Mo.
					Angeline? Bundridge	15	Mo.
1799	Joseph Brown	60	Va.		George Bundridge	12	Mo.
	Jemima Brown	55	Ky.		David Bundridge	10	Mo.
	Haden Brown	32	Ky.				
	William Brown	24	Mo.	1309	David M. Burnham	25	Mo.
	Waller Brown	19	Mo.		Ann C. Burnham	22	Va.
	Henry Brown	13	Mo.		Mary T. Burnham	8/12	Mo.
	Harrison Brown	11	Mo.				
				1628	John D. Burnett	65	Va.
397	James? Bryson	24	Ky.		Sarah A. Burnett	50	Md.
	Nancy Bryson	24	Va.		Mary E. Burnett	22	Mo.
	John Bryson	2	Mo.		Allen Burnett	15	Mo.
	Solomon Bryson	1	Mo.		Sarah J. Burnett	12	Mo.

1013	Travis Buroughs	42	Va.

1119	John Buswright (Bunwright)	67	Va.
	Sarah P. Buswright	58	Va.
	John P. Buswright	18	Mo.

812	Elijah Byers	52	Va.
	Martha F. Byers	30	Va.
	William J. Byers	22	Va.
	Susan E. Byers	23	Va.
	Mary J. Byers	21	Va.
	Elijah G. Byers	17	Mo.
	John Byers	10	Mo.
	Lucy Byers	13	Mo.
	Robert Byers	4	Mo.
	Henrietta Byers	1	Mo.
	Richard Reid	21	Ky.

354	Davidson Callihan	29	Mo.
	Elizabeth Callihan	19	Mo.
	Nancy Pendergast	55	Va.
	Nancy Pendergast	15	Mo.
	Louisa Pendergast	13	Mo.
	Bill Pendergast	13	Mo.
	Sagnata Callahan	5	Mo.

324	Joseph Camden	43	Va.
	Rebecca H. Camden	43	Va.
	Granville Camden	19	Va.
	Montgomery Camden	18	Va.
	Calvin Camden	16	Va.
	Elizabeth A. Camden	13	Va.
	Mary J. Camden	11	Va.
	Tabitha Camden	11	Va.
	Hiram Camden	5	Va.
	Mariah Camden	6	Va.
	G. M. D. L. Camden	4	Ind.
	Leander Camden	2	Mo.

331	Addison Camden	39	Va.
	Catherine Camden	39	Va.
	Hiram Camden	18	Va.
	Mary Camden	16	Ill.
	Alfred Camden	8	Mo.
	Margaret Camden	6	Mo.
	Albert Camden	4	Mo.
	Allen Camden	1	Mo.

329	H. R. C. Camden	44	Va.
	Milinda Camden	45	Va.
	Jane Camden	21	Va.
	Campbell Camden	18	Va.

824	Joseph Carpenter	50	Va.
	Arabella Carpenter	38	Ky.
	Mary F. Carpenter	16	Mo.
	William Carpenter	14	Mo.
	Sarah C. Carpenter	11	Mo.
	James Carpenter	4	Mo.

1742	Peter F. Carter	28	Va.
	Sarah E. Carter	6	Mo.
	James J. Carter	2	Mo.

1150	John Carruthers	57	Va.
	Ann Carruthers	44	Va.
	Thomas H. Carruthers	21	Va.
	Margaret Carruthers	18	Va.
	Martin V. Carruthers	14	Mo.
	James F. Carruthers	13	Mo.
	Elizabeth V. Carruthers	10	Mo.
	Lucy F. Carruthers	8	Mo.
	William Carruthers	6	Mo.
	Julius F. Carruthers	4	Mo.
	David Carruthers	24	Va.
	Martha E. Carruthers	22	Va.
	Mary J. Carruthers	25	Va.

Samuel Crockett	76	Va.
Elizabeth Crockett	55	Va.
Walter Crockett	36	Tenn.

Thomas Coons	68	Va.
Nancy Coons	65	Va.
Rebecca Coons	36	Ky.

1850 Census, Bates Co., Mo.

326 Abraham Wilcox   45 Va.
    Nancy Wilcox   21 Va.
    Margaret Wilcox   19 Va.
    George Wilcox   17 Mo.
    James A. Wilcox   11 Mo.
    Manerva Wilcox   8 Mo.

1850 Census, Calloway Co., Mo.

950 Parthena F. Dearing 34 Va.   375 Amos Wilcox   58 N.C.
    Edwin H. Dearing   12 Va.   Lavinia Wilcox   59 Va.
    Joseph A. Dearing   11 Va.   Lydia J. Wilcox   25 Ky.
    Virginia A. Dearing   9 Mo.
    John D. Dearing   7 Mo. 1162 John Yates (family) 55 Va.
    Sarah F. Dearing   4 Mo.

1850 Census, Howard Co., Mo.

Paschal Twyman   47 Va.   Caleb Wilcoxon   28 Ky.
Elizabeth Twyman 47 Va.   Julia A. Wilcoxon   23 Va.
Elizabeth Twyman 19   Ann J. Wilcoxon   3 Va.
Martha Twyman   16   Susan C. Wilcoxon 6/12 Va.
Nancy Twyman   14   Nancy A. Ashbrook 37 Va.
Malinda Twyman   10   Oscar Ware   17 Mo.
Alice Twyman   8   Jas. L. Simmonds   9 Mo.
Arlena Twyman   6

1850 Census, Livingston Co., Mo.

587 John Hagens   63 Va.
    John Hagens   24 Ky.
    James Hagens   20 Ky.
    Humphrey Hagens   18 Ky.

Soldiers of the War of 1812 who were living in Boone Co., Mo., in 1857. From Vol. 8, p. 102, "Missouri Historical Review." (Those born in Virginia are shown below.)

     John Caruthers, aged 64
     Abe Davenport, aged 64
     Berkley Estes, aged 60
     Thompson Hardin, aged 72
     Fleetwood Herndon, aged 67
     Greenbury Jacobs, aged 73
     Hiram Phillips, aged 66
     Norborne B. Spottswood, aged 67
     Cornelius Vanansdal, aged 63
     James Miller, aged 67

VIRGINIA PIONEERS TO BOONE CO., MO., LIVING IN 1897, from The Columbia Herald, Aug. 13, 1897, Columbia, Mo. The list below was copied and alphabetized by A. Maxim Coppage.

NAME	BORN	VIRGINIA COUNTY	TO MO.
Adkins, Jno. Richard Englewood, Mo.	30 Jan., 1822	Franklin	1857
Baker, S. R. Stephens, Mo.	3 July, 1837	Hampton	1857
Beasley, Noah Columbia, Mo.	21 Feb., 1829	Rockingham	1857
Booth, R. J. Columbia, Mo.	1 April, 1834	Northumberland	1855
Carruthers, T. H. Columbia, Mo.	22 Aug., 1827	Albemarle	1831
Carter, John W. Columbia, Mo.	8 Nov., 1821	Fairfax	183-
Crumbaugh, Mrs. M. C. Columbia, Mo.	16 March, 1827	Clark	1854
Edwards, John M. Sapp, Mo.	29 Sept., 1831	Culpeper	1842
Fyfer, J. Thomas Columbia, Mo.	5 Feb., 1835	Orange	1856
Hensley, M. P. Columbia, Mo.	17 Oct., 1821	Albemarle	1839
Holmes, C. G. Columbia, Mo.	17 Nov., 1829	King George	1854
Lane, A. V. Columbia, Mo.	25 Nov., 1854	Albemarle	1836
Persinger, James Columbia, Mo.	1824	Alleghany	1849
Price, R. B. Columbia, Mo.	17 Oct., 1852	Charlotte	1850
Settles, D. Woodlandville, Mo.	15 Sept., 1825	Warren	1858
Sewell, John D. Columbia, Mo.	16 April, 1816	Augusta	1838
Spellman, J. A. Hallsville, Mo.	12 Dec., 1816? —46?	Culpeper	1847
Tisdale, Woodson Harrisburg, Mo.	22 Feb., 1806	Louisa	1830
Via, M. L. A. Columbia, Mo.	27 Aug., 1813	Albemarle	1828
West, Mrs. Virginia A.	17 March, 1837		1837

SOME CLAY CO., MO., CEMETERY RECORDS OF VIRGINIANS

Big Shoal Cemetery
P. H. and E. Grubbs of Spotsylvania Co., Va. They had a dau., Elba A. Grubbs, b. 1836, wife of Wm. H. Atkins.

Crollie Cemetery
James Crowley. (Virginia Militia. Rev. War Marker)

Waller Cemetery
Benjamin P. George, of Fauquier Co., Va. (no dates — old)

New Stark Cemetery
Wm. and Elizabeth Bower of Fauquier Co., Va., had two children buried here: Eliza J. Bower, b. 27 March, 1803; d. 23 Oct., 1849, consort of Fountain Waller; Dr. Oscar Bower, b. 9 July, 1805; d. 26 Oct., 1859.

Mary E. Smith, wife of W. A., b. Fauquier Co., Va., 1809; d. 1886. They had a son, Wilfred Smith, b. 27 Jan., 1850; d. 21 March, 1876.

Wilfred Smith, likely the father of W. A., b. 11 June, 1797, Fauquier Co., Va.; d. 30 Jan., 1861.

William J. Stark, b. 16 Dec., 1808, Fauquier Co., Va.; d. 10 Feb., 1892.

Catherine L. Stark, b. 15 Sept., 1833, Fauquier Co., Va.; d. 16 Jan., 1850, dau. of Wm. J. and Emily Stark.

Charles S. Stark, b. ca 1831; killed 19 Dec., 1861, Jackson Co., Mo.

Falia Starke, b. 13 Feb., 1836; d. 6 Feb., 1921, wife of Andrew Westbrook.

Felix Grundy Stark, b. 19 March, 1841; d. 9 Jan., 1863.

Frances W. Stark, b. 4 March, 1839; d. 15 Jan., 1923.

James Thornton Stark, b. 1845; d. 1919.

Josephene A. Starke, b. 31 Aug., 1851; d. 1 Nov., 1922.

Lewis Wm. Stark, b. ca 1850?

Fountain Waller, b. 22 Jan., 1798, Fauquier Co., Va.; d. 27 April, 1885.

Elmer T. Waller, b. 26 Jan., 1812, Fauquier Co., Va.; d. 10 Dec., 1860.

Emily Waller, b. 10 April, 1809; d. 11 Feb., 1891, wife of Wm. J. Stark.

Madeline Waller, b. 15 May, 1832; d. 20 Feb., 1849, dau. of Fountain and Eliza J. Waller.

Oscar Lee Waller, b. 22 Feb., 1866; d. 5 May, 1900.

The following surnames, used as Christian names, were gleaned from Missouri Records by A. Maxim Coppage.

Addison Tinsley	Ausbon Stewart	Blake L. Woodson
Allen W. Brown	Austin Reeder	Gustavus Brown Horner
Allen Raines	Austin Shinn	John Benton McCleod
Allen Thurman		Y. Benton Moss
Allen Womack	John Baker Brame	Burwell Peary?
Anderson S. Harris	Beverly Vaughan	
Archer Bankhead	Berry Spence	Wm. Clay Gibson
Armstead Clark	Bledsoe Holden	Coleman Fudge

Cornelius Payne
Cornelius Reynolds
Cread Yoakum

Dabney Bass
David Dalton Dyer
Dryden Starke
Dudley Kemp

Easton Early
Elliott Bland
Everett Weston

Fields Tucker
Fleming Stone
French Kemper
Fountain Livesay

J. Garland Webb
Garrett W. Moorehead
Gibson Hendricks
Gilaman White
Gilbert Shelton
Gilchrist Porter

Harrison Peters
Harvey Glascock
Hartwell Tucker
Ezra Heath Schooler
Hedgeman Jenkins

Jones Vaughan
Jefferson Glascock
Jefferson Wade
George Jud Rhodes

Leith Hughes
Lewis Corbin
Lewis Lusher
Lewis Neal
Lofton Windsor
Lovell Deer
Lynch Lunstall

Madison Crump
Madison Pugh
Marshall McIlhaney
Wm. Marshall Carlin

Mason Hamilton
Martin Slaughter
Mill C. Kirby
Millender Radford
Thomas Miller Carter
Stephen Miller Jones
Morgan Bailey
Morten V. B. Olivar
Morton Brown

Nelson Fulls?
Nesmond Elridge
Newton S. Noffsinger

Olney Walton

Perry Spencer
Preston W. Bufford
Preston Todd
Preston Becker
Wm. Price Lewright
Polk Corder
Wm. Pope Speed, Jr.

Jno. Quarrells Dickinson
G. Quarrells Foster

Repps B. Hudson
Ritchie Ayres
Roper? Gregory
Rowley Hanks

Shaw Webb
Shelton Dodd
Shumate Kemper
Smith Ball
Spencer Greer
John Steptoe Lewright
Stewart Hall
Swenson Jeffries

Taliaferro Carter
Tilamon Carter
Thornton Roach
Thornton Taylor
Townsend Wright
Travis Murphy

Underwood Beckwith

J. Ward Wood
Andrew Watson Bridges
George Webb Hudson
Wellington Braffen
Whitehead Jeffries
Winchester Cook
Woodson Tisdale

ADDITIONS PART I

Allen, Hugh
    settled, Boone Co., 1828

Ames (family)
    settled in Jefferson Co.

Ball, R. L.
    settled, 1858, Pike Co.

Baunk, G. E.
    settled, 1870, Linn Co.

Baylis (family)
    settled in Ralls Co.

Bedford, Wm. M.
    settled, 1839, Lewis Co.

Bowie. (family)
    settled in Ralls Co.

Carson, J. W.
    settled, 1843, Putnam Co.

Clark (family)
    settled in Lincoln Co.

Cooke, B. H.
    settled, 1857, Chariton Co.

Dodd, Allen
    settled, 1835, Ralls Co.

Dodd, Shelton L.
    settled, 1835, Ralls Co.

Fisher, Rev. David
    settled, 1848, Howard Co.

Given, Adam
    settled, 1863, Randolph Co.

Glascock, George W.
    settled, 1836, Ralls Co.

Goodlet, Mr.
    settled in Henry Co.

Hayden, Joseph D.
    settled, 1838

Henry, W. J.
    settled, 1848, Callaway Co.

Hilleary (family)
    settled in Ralls Co.

Hunter, Wm. G.
    settled, 1838, Franklin Co.

Jennings, D. D. L.
    settled, 1869, Montgomery Co.

Kerby, Wm. C.
    settled, 1867, Randolph Co.

Kirkpatrick, C. W.
    settled, 1868, Carroll Co.

Lay, Elias
    settled, 1832, Randolph Co.

Mansfield, Wm. T.
    settled, 1832, Randolph Co.

Ormes, H. J.
    settled, 1835, Monroe Co.

Owen, E. D.
    settled, 1840, Lincoln Co.

Parr, Nancy
    settled in Monroe Co.

Porter, Wm.
    settled, 1835, Lincoln Co.

Porter, Wm.
    settled in Pike Co.

Porter, Wm. H.
    settled in Saline Co.

Qusenberry, George
    settled in Saline Co.

138

Rector, Vincent
   settled in Ralls Co.

Richards, Phillip
   settled, 1853, Gentry Co.

Shakelford, Wm.
   settled in DeKalb Co.

Staples, W. F.
   settled, 1865, Putnam Co.

Tatum, R. G.
   settled, 1834, Callaway Co.

Wilson, Robert H.
   settled in Saline Co.

Wood, Joseph, Jr.
   settled, 1831, Franklin Co.

Wright, J. L.
   settled, 1864, Randolph Co.

ADDENDA PART V

p. 93. Query 5043(A) was sent in by Mrs. Edith M. Coffey, 40 So. LeSueur St. Mesa, Ark., Jan. 10, 1958.

p. 93. Query 4029(A) was sent in by Mrs. Violetta T. Seaver, Rte. 1, Box 31, Elfrida, Ariz., Jan. 3, 1958.

INDEX

J

Jackson 29, 69, 73, 92, 112
Jacob 113
Jacobs 29, 69
James 29, 114
Jarboe 88
Jarrett 29, 68
Jarvies 83
Jeffers 113
Jeffress 29
Jeffries 29, 65, 69, 136
Jenkins 29, 69, 74, 136
Jenks 29, 70
Jennett 29
Jennings 29, 68, 110, 137
Johnson 29, 30, 63, 65, 69, 71, 76, 80, 104, 105, 106, 124
Johnston 121
Jones 30, 68, 69, 70, 72, 75, 78, 92, 103, 107, 108, 126, 128, 130, 136
Judy 30
Justice 30

K

Kaylor 30
Keach 30, 70
Kearby 73
Keatley 30
Keeble 30, 66
Keen 30, 74
Keeton 30
Keith 31, 100
Kelch 31
Keller 31, 71
Kelly 31
Kelsick 31
Kemp 31, 67, 97, 136
Kemper 31, 65, 77, 136
Ken 32
Kennedy 31
Kerby 137
Kern 31, 70
Kerr 31, 64
Kerrick 31

Keshler 115
Key 111
Keyser 31, 69
Kibbler 31
Kidd 31
Kile 125
Kimberlin 31, 64
Kimbrough 31
Kimler 31
Kincaid 31, 89
Kindig 31, 64, 77
King 31
Kinner 31
Kinsey 107, 120
Kirby 31, 63, 136
Kirkpatrick 31, 71, 137
Kitchen 76, 95, 110
Knight 32
Kollenburn 32
Koontz 32, 71
Kueckellan 32

L

Lacy 32, 123
Laffoon 96
Lair 104
Laird 32, 64
Lamkin 32
Lampkin 32, 69
Landes 32
Landis 74
Lane 32, 63, 66, 71, 74, 109, 123
Langden 32
Langley 32, 64
Larimore 32, 66
Larkin 32
Lasley 68
Latham 32, 76, 77
Lathrop 88
Lauck 32
Lavender 67
Lay 32, 69, 137
Layton 32, 71
Lazenby 32
Leachman 126
Leake 102
Lear 32, 65
Leatherman 32
Leavell 32, 63
Lee 32, 33, 65, 70, 79, 94, 95, 124, 126

Leftwick 33, 64
Legg 33
Leggett 33
Leiter 104
Leland 33, 69
Lenoir 33, 68
Leopard 33
LeRoy 33
Lesley 100
Leslie 120
Letcher 33
Letchworth 80
Lett 118
Lewis 33, 63, 65, 69, 94, 96, 107, 114, 122, 126
Lewright 33, 136
Light 67
Ligon 33, 63
Lillard 33
Lindenberger 33
Lingenfelter 94, 95
Lints 73
Lipscomb 33
Little 33, 72
Livesay 33, 136
Livingston 34, 72
Llyons 34
Lobban 34, 63
Lockheart 75
Logsdon 99
Long 34, 71, 98
Longdon 108
Lough 34, 71
Loughead 67, 72
Love 34, 72, 111
Lovercheck 104
Loverman 34
Loving 34, 68
Lowell 73
Lowndes 34
Loy 85, 86
Lucas 34
Luck 34, 65
Luckett 34
Luckey 112
Luk 76
Lunceford 34
Lunstall 75, 136
Lusher 34, 136
Luttrell 34
Lyell 34, 72
Lynch 103, 104

Witacre 60
Witcher 97
Withers 60, 125
Witten 60
Wolff 60
Wolverton 60
Womack 60, 135
Wommack 60, 68
Wonderly 60
Wood(-s) 60, 63, 68,
    69, 77, 79, 91, 101,
    102, 136, 138
Woodson 61, 112, 115,
    125, 126, 135
Woolridge 61, 70
Woosham 112

Worrell 61
Wright 61, 64, 67, 69,
    76, 106, 136, 138
Wrightman 61
Wrightsman 64
Wulfeck 105, 115, 116,
    123
Wyatt 110, 111
Wyckoff 118
Wynn 72, 76

Y

Yager 61, 68
Yancy 99
Yarnell 83, 85

Yates 61, 133
Yoakum 61, 136
York 94, 95
Young 61, 67, 75, 100
Yowell 61, 68

Z

Ziegler 61

CPSIA information can be obtained
at www.ICGtesting.com
Printed in the USA
FSHW010721081119
63765FS